LEIPOLDT'S CELLAR AND KITCHEN

LEIPOLDT'S CELLAR AND KITCHEN

C LOUIS LEIPOLDT

TRANSLATED BY DR W L LIEBENBERG
BREDIE TRANSLATED BY T S EMSLIE
ADAPTED FOR PUBLICATION BY T S EMSLIE

Bredie was first published in *Die Huisgenoot* in 1933
The other 55 articles were first published in *Die Huisgenoot* between 1942 and 1947

© *Leipoldt's Cellar and Kitchen* T S Emslie 2005
© *My Life with Doc* T S Emslie 2003
© *Introduction* T S Emslie 2005

ISBN 0-620-34665-5

INDEX BY T S EMSLIE AND C A EMSLIE
COVER DESIGNED BY FLAME DESIGN, CAPE TOWN
TYPESET BY FLAME DESIGN, CAPE TOWN
PRINTED AND BOUND BY PAARL PRINT, OOSTERLAND STREET,
PAARL, SOUTH AFRICA

CEDERBERG PUBLISHERS
P O Box 53137 • Kenilworth • 7745

Distributed in South Africa by Book Promotions
P O Box 5 • Plumstead • 7800 • South Africa
Tel: 021-706-0949 • Fax: 021-706-0940
email: orders@bookpro.co.za

For Brenda

Contents

	List of Photographs			ix
	Introduction			xi
	Acknowledgment			xv
	My Life with Doc by Dr Peter Shields			xix
1	Bredie	11	August 1933	1
2	The Governor's Bean	10	April 1942	5
3	Jakkalskos-Soufflé	8	May 1942	8
4	Sherry	29	May 1942	11
5	Potatoes	19	June 1942	16
6	Liqueurs	10	July 1942	19
7	Our Cape Kitchen	7	August 1942	23
8	Veldkool	28	August 1942	26
9	Grog and Bowl	11	September 1942	31
10	A Sucking Pig	16	October 1942	34
11	Curried Meat	6	November 1942	37
12	Braaivleis	27	November 1942	41
13	On Pannas	1	January 1943	44
14	Chicken's Eggs	19	March 1943	47
15	Game I	30	April 1943	50
16	Game II	14	May 1943	53
17	Wild Birds I	18	June 1943	56
18	Wild Birds II	2	July 1943	61
19	Our Brandy	10	September 1943	66
20	Water Hawthorn	24	September 1943	73
21	Crayfish	22	October 1943	78
22	The Genuine Uintjie	29	October 1943	81
23	Biltong	26	November 1943	84
24	Delicious Snail Dishes	7	January 1944	89
25	The Pawpaw	21	January 1944	92
26	Mielies	17	March 1944	95
27	Cooking with Grapes	31	March 1944	99
28	Vegetable Dishes	28	April 1944	102
29	Baking under the Ash	28	July 1944	105
30	Green	15	September 1944	110
31	Herbs in th Kitchen	22	September 1944	113
32	Kambro and Baroe	13	October 1944	120
33	Milk Food	27	October 1944	123

34	Seafood I	15 December 1944	126
35	Seafood II	12 January 1945	131
36	Seafood III	9 February 1945	136
37	Green Peas	16 March 1945	141
38	Dried Peas	16 February 1945	144
39	Tameletjies	25 May 1945	147
40	Sausage	1 June 1945	152
41	Sosaties	13 June 1945	155
42	Brinjals	3 August 1945	158
43	Cold Soup	9 November 1945	161
44	Christmas Drinks	23 November 1945	163
45	Oysters	21 December 1945	168
46	Our Daily Bread	11 January 1946	171
47	Tongue	22 February 1946	175
48	Camp Food I	29 March 1946	180
49	Camp Food II	5 April 1946	183
50	Our White Wines I	24 May 1946	187
51	Our White Wines II	7 June 1946	191
52	Freshwater Fish	27 December 1946	194
53	Red Wine	17 January 1947	197
54	Zebra Meat	24 January 1947	201
55	Brawn	31 January 1947	208
56	Atjar	21 March 1947	210
	Glossary		215
	List of scientific names and their modern equivalents		216
	Index		217

List of Photographs

With the exception of the photographs of Leipoldt (which are held by the University of Cape Town) and the modern photographs (which were taken by the publishers), the photographs listed below form part of the Elliot Collection (and in the case of *Ostriches and Eggs* the Jefferys Collection) at the South African Archives in Cape Town.

Wine cellar, Alphen, Wynberg	*x*
Leipoldt botanising	*xvi-xvii*
Leipoldt reading	*xviii*
Portrait of C Louis Leipoldt	*xxv*
Leipoldt at his typewriter	*xxvi*
Cellar, Drosdty, Tulbagh	*12-13*
Kitchen, Groot Constantia	*22*
Spandaukop, Graaff-Reinet	*28-29*
August Escoffier	*38*
Portrait study	*58-59*
Vegetable stalls, Greenmarket Square, Cape Town	*62-63*
Ship's figure	*72*
Waterblommetjies	*74-75*
Ostriches and eggs	*86-87*
Building	*98*
Picnic lunch, Steenbras Reservoir	*106-107*
Cellar, L'Ormarins, Franschhoek	*114-115*
White House, Strand Street, Cape Town	*118-119*
Portrait study	*128-129*
Woodstock beach	*132-133*
Yzerfontein	*138-139*
Old garden seat, Groote Schuur	*148-149*
Portrait study	*164*
L'ara de Orleans	*172-173*
Travel photograph	*178-179*
Klein Constantia Vin de Constance	*186*
Wine tasting	*190*
Groot Constantia Gouverneurs Shiraz	*198*
Pietersburg road near Pretoria	*202-203*
Zoo, Groote Schuur estate	*206-207*
Luncarty, Newlands, Cape Town	*212-213*

Introduction

Christian Frederik Louis Leipoldt was born on 28 December 1880 and died on 12 April 1947, three weeks after the last article in this book was published in *Die Huisgenoot*. He was an amazingly versatile man, and it is no exaggeration to call him poet, playwright, paediatrician, botanist, journalist, novelist, cook and connoisseur of food and wine. Probably best remembered as the quintessentially Afrikaans poet, Leipoldt is also famous as the pre-eminent authority on traditional Cape cooking. His lifelong passion for food and wine, and for old recipes, prompted him to write about them extensively, and the articles translated and collected here embody a unique *bredie* of culinary and literary knowledge and skill.

Christie (as he was known to his family) was born in Worcester and moved as a young child to Clanwilliam where his father, who had been a Renish missionary, became *dominee* of the local Dutch Reformed Church. He (Christie, not the *dominee*) never attended school and was educated by his father. His expertise in botany was evident when as a youth he accompanied the German botanist Rudolph Schlechter on an expedition into the veld, and conversed with Dr Daniel Hahn, Professor Peter MacOwan and Dr Harry Bolus on trips to Cape Town when he accompanied his father to synod meetings of the Dutch Reformed Church.

In November 1898, some eighteen months after completing his matriculation exams, Leipoldt moved to Cape Town to pursue the journalistic career he had begun as a boy freelancing for Cape Town newspapers from Clanwilliam, a career he continued as a sideline for the rest of his life. In 1902, during the closing stages of the Anglo-Boer War, he relinquished the editorship of a pro-Boer newspaper he had assumed after his predecessor had been arrested, left the Cape Colony and sailed for London. There, at the age of twenty-one, he enrolled as a medical student at Guy's Hospital, and in due course won gold medals for both medicine and surgery. While a medical student at Guy's, he worked to supplement his income in hotels such as the Carlton, the Ritz and the Savoy, and met the famous chef Auguste Escoffier whose skill he greatly admired. After qualifying as a doctor he travelled widely, worked as a medical inspector of schools in London, and in 1914 returned to South Africa where he took up an appointment as the first medical inspector of schools in the Transvaal, but soon found himself seconded as personal physician to the Prime Minister, General Botha, during the South African rebellion and the campaign in German West Africa.

INTRODUCTION

In 1925, after many years as Transvaal 'bushveld doctor', Leipoldt returned to the Cape to practise as a paediatrician and later became *inter alia* editor of the *South African Medical Journal*, medical secretary of the South African Medical Union and lecturer in paediatrics at the University of Cape Town. He lived in Cape Town until the end of his life – for many years at Arbury, the Kenilworth house he shared with his adopted son, Jeff, and Peter Shields, the author of *My Life with Doc* – which appears after this introduction.

Throughout his life, 'in the leisure leased from other avocations' (as he put it in his introduction to *Three Hundred Years of Cape Wine*), Leipoldt enjoyed collecting old manuscript recipes. He discusses this and his interest in the preparation of food as follows in his introduction to *Cape Cookery*:

> 'My interest in cookery dates from the time when, as a little boy in the late eighties of the last century, I assisted, in a very minor and suppressed capacity, at the culinary operations of a very expert Coloured woman cook who bore the reputation of being one of the best in the Cape Colony. Fat to the verge of obesity, she presided over a kitchen whose cleanliness could have served as a model for an operating theatre of a modern hospital, largely because she insisted that punctilious, painstaking ablution was an indispensable preliminary in the preparation of food. Her inculcation of these elementary principles, often accompanied by a good-natured but nevertheless painful prodding of my juvenile person with the large wooden spoon that was her sceptre, helped me – in later days when I learned to better my taste and broaden my experience – to realise how any infringement of them inevitably impairs the excellence of all cookery.
>
> 'The Ayah's art was the result of many years of instruction and experience in the traditional methods of Malay cookery, whose outstanding characteristics are the free, almost heroic, use of spices and aromatic flavourings, the prolonged steady, but slow, application of moist heat to all meat dishes, and the skilful blending of many diverse constituents into a combination that still holds the essential goodness of each. Her dishes, that were eaten by Governors, Prime Ministers and Very Important Persons, were made from old recipes that were firmly enshrined in her memory, for she never referred to written or printed directives. Nearly every one of these recipes is to be found in cookery books that were then already well known – without, however, the little modifications that her own ingenuity and experience had enabled her to add for their improvement. All of them had already been written down, in manuscripts for domestic use for those who had to rely on such aids when preparing food.

INTRODUCTION

'When I returned from Europe in 1914, it was a labour of love to collect such cookery manuscripts, and to compare what they contained with the printed collections of directives that date from the year 1483. That entailed the acquisition of representative cookbooks, and although I had, at the time, no intention of emulating Viel or any other great collector of books on food and drink, I found the task of comparing and collating so entrancing, the search for recipes in manuscript so exciting and the pride of possessing interesting rarities so uplifting, that what had begun as a passing fancy remained as a serious and not altogether unproductive study.'

Probably the finest and without doubt the most entertaining fruit of this highly productive study is the series of articles published under the rubric *Kelder en Kombuis* in *Die Huisgenoot* between 1942 and 1947. In 1963 these articles were collected and published by Tafelberg Publishers in a book entitled *Polfyntjies vir die Proe*. In 2003 they were translated into English by Dr W L Liebenberg, adapted for publication and published by Stonewall Books as part of *Leipoldt's Food & Wine* – a trilogy comprising Leipoldt's *Cape Cookery*, *Culinary Treasures* and *Three Hundred Years of Cape Wine*.

The book you are now reading, *Leipoldt's Cellar and Kitchen*, is the middle book from the trilogy with adjustments to improve the text and to incorporate the suggestions of some critics (for example, the term *waterblommetjies* is used instead of water hawthorn). It also includes a translation of *Bredie* which has not until now been available in English.

All the articles that appeared in his column *Kelder en Kombuis* were written under the pseudonym K A R Bonadie, and this anonymity gave Leipoldt the imaginative scope to invent the Bonadie family he refers to so much. It is as if the author, who never married, longed for a family of his own and created the Bonadies as a vicarious and sublimated way of satisfying this yearning. (This suggestion is not altogether fanciful, as he did adopt a son, Jeff, who bore the surname Leipoldt, and Peter Shields was brought up by him although not formally adopted.) No doubt Leipoldt attributed some of the qualities of his own and other families to the Bonadies, but it nevertheless seems that the creation of the extended Bonadie family may in part have been a literary way of compensating for the inner loneliness he expressed so exquisitely in his poetry.

Whatever the explanation, and of course none is required, the reader meets a host of Bonadies in the pages of *Leipoldt's Cellar and Kitchen*. There is *Grootoom* Gieljam, whose destruction of his vineyard after the temperance missionaries persuaded him of the evils of alcohol and whose opposition to the use of wine in cooking were taken as proof of him having rounded the bend. It was *Grootoom* Gieljam who taught the narrator as a boy to catch and cook small crayfish from the rocks at Kalk Bay, and this too was taken as a sign of strangeness by the family – the Bonadies were not keen on crayfish.

There is the wine farmer *Oom* Danie, who was appalled that his forefathers had brought snails to South Africa as food, but who now enjoys them when *Tant* Hessie makes a snail dish from time to time.

Oom Mias states that meat, bread and coffee have never given him rheumatism; *Tant* Kolba's recipe for a leg of game comes from the late Mrs Raats, who in turn got it from her great-grandmother; and *Tannie* Lisbet says *harlie* and *hullie* instead of *hulle*.

Oom Karools was in France during the First World War and there acquired the habit of sprinkling cheese over his soup, while *Tant* Alie regards anything less than real sosaties as 'just some of that French rubbish you get in their restaurants'.

There are many unnamed *tannies* and *ou-tannies*: one makes the best biltong ('like a cut ruby, red and transparent') covering it with cheesecloth and hanging it in the chimney for nearly three months; another bakes bread from genuine farm flour ground in the old mule mill; a third makes real *boerewors* and regards anything else as *sommer gemors*; one has vegetarian leanings and thereby sets a bad example to the rest of the family; and another dismisses all the fuss about vitamins because the Holy Scripture makes no reference to them.

These *ooms* and *tannies* are not necessarily all relatives of the narrator, but most of them are. Many qualities shared by the Bonadie family are mentioned: they are liberal and therefore eat everything that is tasty; they do not like their game to announce itself from afar; they are brandy drinkers, taught from childhood to regard a good brandy the crowning achievement of the wine farmer; they are farm people but have lost their touch for camping out on the veld; they know that God created grapes for wine to gladden the hearts of men, and that wine is one of the healthiest of drinks; and they are impatient, especially with people who are full of themselves – that is to say, who do not agree with them.

Neef Frans wrote his doctorate on lizard tongues; *Kleinjan* as a first-year medical student was genuinely afraid to try his first oyster; and *Oom* Danie considered that there was no meat on earth that could hold its own against zebra.

INTRODUCTION

The articles are suffused with a yearning for life on the farm and for the old ways of doing things. In Leipoldt's last article, on *atjar*, K A R Bonadie says:

> 'There are those who are able to speak without emotion about the dying off and disappearance of old habits, old friends, old fashions and old things, and who would not shed a tear about the loss of something our forefathers loved and cherished. They are, as the Latin poet said bluntly, "unfeeling stones that do not notice the slow erosion of wind and rain". It is they who today satisfy themselves with So and So's Pickled This and That, Tom Dick and Harry's Sauce, Potdamn's Pickle, Ouma's little Wake-me-up, and heaven knows what else is scraped out of bottles and tins and served up with our best dishes.
>
> 'We Bonades are different. We like the old stuff. We are loyal to what our forefathers cherished.'

Leipoldt has preserved for all time these wonderful insights into old Afrikaans lifestyle and culture. As publishers we have been liberal in our use of photographs, mostly from the South African Archives in Cape Town, in order to reinforce the nostalgic flavour of these culinary treasures.

I hope we have succeeded. For we too like the old stuff; and we are loyal to what Leipoldt cherished.

T S Emslie
October 2005

Acknowledgment

The contributions of the following persons are acknowledged: Barbara Knox-Shaw for her botanical and culinary expertise contained in notes to the text; and my co-editors of *Leipoldt's Food & Wine*, Paul Murray and Anne Emslie, whose editorial influence lingers in this publication.

TSE

My Life with Doc

I hope that these memories of my years as part of Dr C Louis Leipoldt's household will give the reader an insight into the domestic side of the author and thereby enrich his or her reading of these articles.

I was twelve years of age when, in 1930, I went to live with Leipoldt at his house, Arbury, in the Cape Town suburb of Kenilworth. 'Doc', as we called him, had an adopted son, Jeff, a few years younger than me, and the three of us lived together until Jeff and I went off to fight as volunteers in World War II.

Although I have now lived for the past twenty-five years in England, where I was born, my impression is that most South Africans think of Leipoldt as an Afrikaans poet, but do not know enough to appreciate the many other sides of this versatile man.

Doc was very liberal for his time. He was also great fun and was very, very mischievous. You never quite knew whether he was pulling your leg – it was always a problem to know whether or not to take him seriously. For instance, I remember him telling us that in China it was considered a delicacy to take a live baby mouse by the tail, dip it in honey, put it in your mouth, and let it scamper down your throat!

Doc claimed to be a Buddhist. I think he needed to break free of the dictates of his strict Protestant upbringing, remembering that his father had been the *dominee* of the Dutch Reformed Church in Clanwilliam and that he never went to school – he was taught by his father and could recite long extracts from the Bible. We didn't go to church. Doc wasn't against organised religion – he just wasn't interested in it.

Doc played a lot of tennis. I remember that Mr Justice van Zyl often came to tennis on Sundays (we had a court at Arbury) and that his daughter was a very good tennis player. Doc did no running on court, but was nevertheless an effective and dangerous player: he would stand there and place his lobs with great skill.

He was a brilliant billiards player; and played a great deal of bridge, often with Mrs Bolus – I think the Boluses were like family to him. He must have been a very good bridge player as he had a formidable memory.

Doc had no dress-sense whatsoever. I remember going swimming with him at St James pool, and his swimwear was so ghastly that Jeff and I didn't want to be seen near him. He probably didn't care. One Saturday evening he ventured forth in a dinner jacket with his bowtie so unbelievably skew that I instinctively went up to him to straighten it. He stopped me, saying: 'Don't. They won't recognise me if you do that.'

For many years we didn't have a wireless at Arbury – Doc wouldn't allow it. But in 1937 he suddenly went out and bought a very large one. He would sit and listen to Adolf Hitler's speeches, getting very angry. Of course he could understand German, whereas the rest of us couldn't.

We spoke mainly English at home, and Doc actually did a lot of his writing in English. He wrote several poems in English that were published under the pseudonym Pheidippides. I would say that about half of Doc's friends who visited the house were English-speaking, and the other half Afrikaans.

We used to go for wonderful trips in the countryside, and one always met lots of interesting people in his company. I remember visiting General Smuts on his farm at Irene, outside Pretoria, and thinking that his wife, *Ouma* Smuts, was the maid, so unpretentious was she. We often visited General Smuts.

Doc loved Clanwilliam and the Cederberg, and went there fairly often. They were his spiritual home. He knew a teriffic number of people in that part of the world, and wherever he went he would call on friends.

Doc would always sing while he drove. He would tease me about the Irish Republican song, the one about hanging men and women for wearing the green, and he would often sing this song while driving. He wasn't really musical, but he loved church music and would go to church to listen to musical performances.

After the war Doc didn't drive much, and he gave me his car when I was demobilised and returned to Cape Town. Occasionally he would borrow it to go off botanising, and it was always filthy when he returned it.

Doc used to tell wonderful ghost stories, especially when we were out camping. Of course he would tell them at night, just before we went to bed. They were always made up on the spot. I particularly remember one about people being poisoned by mushrooms, and about the horrible deaths they died. (Needless to say, Doc used to collect mushrooms himself when the opportunity arose.)

Doc did not cook on an everyday basis. He employed a cook for this purpose. One cook he employed just before the war was a German woman, and I remember that we gave her quite a hard time. I didn't then give much thought to the food we ate; and while I can say that we always ate extremely well, I cannot say that it was particularly exotic.

Doc himself cooked when he gave a dinner party, which he did fairly often. There were always interesting people at his dinner parties, and Jeff and I were always included.

Doc loved arguing. He would have made a great lawyer. He was also a great talker, continually asking questions – usually pulling your leg. He would suddenly decide to give you a hard time, and then the temporary verbal assault would begin. He loved to present you with an alternative view of whatever point you were making, even if you were merely stating a fact.

There were rules in the house, but Jeff and I were never afraid of Doc. He instituted a sort of 'prefect' system with older boys, usually medical students, looking after us, as he was often away lecturing at the University of Cape Town Medical School in the evenings. He instituted a 'black book' system, something I think he had picked up at Rugby School in England. Five black marks meant a hiding – but Doc wasn't really a disciplinarian and the hiding never materialised. Where he was strict was on one's attitudes to people. If Jeff or I commented disparagingly on other people, he would always say: 'Don't be such a snob.'

Doc had worked as a medical inspector of schools in England and he held a high opinion of English public schools. He approved of them. He would say to Jeff and me that we really ought to be at school at Rugby in England.

He did get fed up with us at times, for instance if one of us trod on one of his best flowers. Then he would storm off in anger, but generally he was very even tempered.

Doc would set Jeff and I 'exams' approximately once a month. He didn't test what we knew, but set us tasks to find out and discover things before the next 'exam'. In retrospect I think this was very worthwhile.

I think Doc was reasonably comfortably off, but not wealthy. He left cash of about £20 000 in his estate, and Jeff and I each inherited some £10 000. (I was the executor of his literary estate, and in this capacity I assigned the copyrights owned by his estate to the University of Cape Town when I left South Africa in 1978.)

Doc always had wine with his meals, and Jeff and I were also always given wine. Doc used to make us describe it, something I wasn't much good at. He considered wine to be a good thing, and we all enjoyed it. My recollection is that Doc's preference was for red wine. He was never snobbish about wine, or about anything else for that matter. I never saw him 'tight'. He seldom had more than two glasses of wine.

Doc would have loved to see the current state of development of South African wine, which was still very ordinary in the 1940s, and he would no doubt be pleased to know that in the twenty-first century I remain very fond of wine.

Doc used to come home with his medical bag stuffed full of books, having stopped off at the library on his way. He was a very fast reader and would borrow about five books at a time, often reading all five in one night. Sometimes he would toss one at me, saying as it flew through the air: 'Here, this might interest you.'

He had many books. One wall of his study was lined with them. These he bequeathed to the South African Library.

Many people seem to think that Doc was, or might have been, homosexual. I must say that I cannot see that it matters; but if he was, we never saw anything of it at all. Not a hint. Of course one didn't discuss such things in those days, at any rate not in the way people do nowadays, but quite frankly the possibility never crossed our minds, and I am absolutely certain that there was nothing like that at all in our household. There is no question of it being otherwise.

It is true that he didn't have much to do with women, except women friends of long standing. And he didn't have women in the house, except our German cook. I remember him kicking up a fuss when her daughter came to stay, but I imagine that that had more to do with us – he was afraid one of us might get her into trouble.

Doc had a Hugo Naude portrait of a French woman hanging on his wall at Arbury. He found it stuffed behind a couch at Naude's house, said to Naude: 'Don't you want this?' and Naude asked him whether he would like it. It now hangs on my wall, and I love it.

On the subject of the Anglo-Boer War, my impression is that towards the end of the war Doc had blotted his copybook, so to speak, in the eyes of the British. He was reporting on the war from the Boer side, and he had annoyed the military authorities. I think it was important for him to leave Cape Town when he did, or he would have landed in trouble.

Oom Gert Vertel and other poems dealing with the war were, I think, based on real incidents.

I imagine that living in England must have changed Doc's attitude to the English whom, until then, during the war, he had had every reason for regarding as the enemy.

A lot of things Doc said were taken up the wrong way, for example the controversy over his statement that it would be better for schoolchildren to be given wine than milk. At that time milk was dished out to schoolchildren in mugs, and it was often contaminated. This was the context of his remarks about wine being better for schoolchildren than milk.

I was at Medical School, after my return from the war, when they called me out of a lecture with the news that Doc had had a heart attack. I went straight to see him, and visited him every day until his death about five days later. I used to take him books. I think he sensed that the end was nigh for he said to me: 'I see the little goblins. They've come to get me.' (He always used to joke about goblins or little something-or-others.)

'Oh, nonsense,' I replied, but he died during the night.

I greatly enjoyed living in Doc's home, and I learned an immense amount from him. Thinking back, I was exceedingly fortunately – I had lost my own father, also a doctor, who died in 1925, and whom I adored; but Doc stepped in and provided me with a good, wholesome, easy childhood.

And yes, I loved him. He was like a big bear, with a somewhat gruff voice. I always think of him as a big bear.

Doc was happiest, I think, when he was out on the veld botanising.

Dr Peter Shields
Berkhamsted
August 2003

1
Bredie

I have long since given up the task of trying to identify the precise etymology of our Afrikaans word *bredie*. Years ago Dr van Oordt, with whom I spent a delightful September afternoon wandering across the Cape flats, told me that it comes from the Portugese word *bredos*, and that it was in turn received by the Portugese from Goa. I had no idea whether this was so, but when he went on to tell me about the Greek word for *bredie* – more about that in a moment – I was so overwhelmed that I threw in the towel and abandoned my inquiry altogether.

My curiosity did however return, and I consulted my linguistically learned friends on the subject. They referred me to Lichtenstein, who states that the word *bredie* was used by the old Cape farmers to signify certain varieties of spinach, especially *rumex*. Our wild spinach, a cousin of the Algerian kind, is *misbredie*; the *rumex* is *Rumex acetosella*, an imported type of sorrel also known as *perdesuring*[1] or *hondesuring*[2] – never used by us as a vegetable as far as I know.

Professor Bosman tells me that the word *bredie* probably comes from Malagasy – one of the few Malagasy words we have.

Early travel writers refer to *bredies* as vegetable mixtures prepared with red pepper and salt – which can be classed as imitation French *purées*. But such *bredies* are nothing like the *bredies* we enjoy today. Our modern *bredie* recipes refer to vegetables, stewed or *smoored*[3] in animal fat and meat juices, with meat added; and I see no connection between this and the Portugese name for a variety of spinach.

Linguists are sometimes highly imaginative in their pronouncements. I know of one who maintains that the word for the Indian anaesthetic *hasheesh* comes not from the Arabic word generally accepted as the root thereof, but from a western word that means something altogether different. It can be interesting, even instructive, to inquire into the origins of words, but there is seldom certainty in the matter and one often seems to achieve more by the exercise of a little imagination.

Whatever the lexicographers – the *ooms*[4] who assemble dictionaries – may say about the provenance of the word *bredie*, in practice, in the hurly burly of

---

1 Literally 'horse sorrel'.
2 Literally 'dog sorrel'.
3 Braised.
4 Uncles

everyday life, we know what it means: a mixture, a *deurmekaar*,[5] which in cookery has a generally positive connotation, although in other fields it often implies something a little bit off.

'Now that's a *bredie* for you,' was a favourite expression of one of our old-time *parlementslede*[6] – in those days we never used the word *volksraad*[7] – when I used to sit high in the gallery of what is now the large parliamentary dining room, noting down everything that was said and, if it was in Afrikaans, translating it. I remember how the speaker, Dr Barry, before he became Sir William, once expressed doubt as to whether the above expression was 'parliamentary'. Even in those days it had a connotation – an innuendo ever so slightly defamatory, somewhat bespattered with mire, mildly unclean, a touch misleading – and was thus 'suspect' when used in parliamentary combat with other honourable members. We convinced Sir William that the literal meaning was: 'What a hash!' – with the exclamation mark – and thus it stands translated in reports of old debates on the *Brandsiekte*[8] Act.

I remember hearing General Botha say, 'Now you're really in the *bredie*,' when he had a good hand of cards, and to me this sounded much better than our rather feeble translation of the customary English expression.

But this is also not the kind of *bredie* that concerns us. Our concern is with the work of art prepared by the good cook – or ruined by the poor cook – perhaps one of the oldest of all prepared dishes. The first description of our culinary *bredie* is found in *Hong So*, the oldest cookbook in existence, a Chinese book of recipes that pre-dates our western calendar. It is described as a mixture of turnips, radishes, ginger, carrots and bacon that is slowly *smoored*. The modern equivalent Chinese dish is chop suey, which is however prepared without the turnips and with the addition of celery and onion-stew.

In Greek cookbooks we come across it again under a name that is probably the longest in any language. Unfortunately we do not have the original recipe – only a reference to the dish and its impressively long name, in *Ecclesiazusae*, 1160, by Aristophanes. I have to consult my notes in order to write it down as my memory is unequal to the task, and I seriously doubt whether any of my readers will succeed in remembering it. Here it is:

---

5 Mix-up.
6 Members of Parliament.
7 Parliament.
8 Scab in sheep.

Lopadotemachoselachogaleokranioleipsanodrimupotrimmatosilphioparao melitokatakechumenokichlepikossuphophattoperisteralektruonoptegkepha lokigklopeleiolagoosiraiobaphetraganopterugon.

It may well be the longest word in any language, comprising 78 syllables and 169 letters. You can find it, if you wish to check the veracity of what I say, in Liddell and Scott's *Greek Dictionary* (1863 edition), where it is described as 'a dish made from several kinds of fish, meat and chicken'. We say simply – and more succinctly – *bredie*.

The English hash, which is how we often translate our *bredie*, is no *bredie* at all, as it contains no vegetables. It is a meat dish, and the word comes from the old French *hashis*, from which the modern French word *hacher*, 'to carve, or slice thinly', is derived. *Hashis* is however no longer used as a term of French cookery.

The oldest cookbooks describe a dish, almost exactly like our potato and bean *bredie*, called *salmagondis* (in modern American cooking *salmagundy*, which can also be a sweet dish). They say the word is a combination of the Latin *sal* (salt) and *conditus* (pickle), but I doubt whether this is so. I judge from the perspective of the kitchen because the original *salmagondis* was not a pickle but a true vegetable *bredie*, slowly *smoored*.

In Spain we come across *bredie* under the name of *olla*, usually a dry bean *bredie* with meat and onions; in Turkey it appears as a rice *bredie*, and in Eastern Europe, ostensibly under Eastern influence, as a flour *bredie*, more or less like the Hungarian *tarhonya* or the Italian *risotto*.

We can immerse ourselves in speculation of all kinds trying to discover the origin of our vegetable *bredie*, but what is its true ancestor? Was it a well-known dish on the European continent? If so, which? In the old cookbooks I have consulted I have not found any recipe which, if strictly followed, produces anything like what I would call a *bredie* in our Afrikaans sense of the word. The earliest recipe that can rank as *voortrekker*[9] to our long list of *bredies* is only two hundred years old.

In my view it is among the *ollas* prepared under different names on board ship that we must search for the ancestor of our *bredies*. Jacquin, in his well known

---

9 The *voortrekkers* were the first people to *trek* away from the influence of the Dutch East India Company at Cape Town.

book on Cape sorrel, states that the first *seevaders*[10] to sail around the Cape landed here to fetch sorrel from a *kloof* in one of the mountains, to be prepared as a *purée* with meat and bacon, and used as a preventative against scurvy. There was even a *Skeurbuikskloof*[11] somewhere in the Peninsula, even though nobody can identify it today.

A Dutch cookbook published in 1720 gives a recipe for *skeepsmansmoes*[12] which is not dissimilar to our cabbage *bredie*. There are several recipes for such vegetable dishes in *Aaltjie*,[13] and I once enjoyed a delicious green bean *bredie* in a Rotterdam eating house that proudly catered for its predominantly maritime patrons. In Vera Cruz, that attractive harbour city in the Gulf of Mexico, you will find outstanding *skeepsbredies*[14] that accord fully with our tomato, *waterblommetjie*[15] and pumpkin *bredies*.

We should probably take our cue from Jacquin and make greater use of veld sorrel when we prepare our *bredies*. Our national diet is not yet what is should be – it has not yet fully adjusted to our circumstances and way of life. This is why we encounter so much illness from inadequate food, especially in the cities where tinned food is popular – not that our food is insufficient, but rather that we ruin the food we do have by preparing it badly.

Today we know how important it is to prepare food properly. We know about the vitamins of Fischer and the catechins of Blum, and we are able to discern better than the scientists with all their cleverness that there is an extra something in vegetables, meat and flour. We do not yet know what that extra something is, but we know that it influences the health of the eater – and that it can easily be spoiled by the inadequate preparation of food.

It would be a good thing if the art of cookery were introduced as a subject at school – not for girls only as at present, but as a compulsory course for every pupil above the eighth grade. A hundred years ago boys had some knowledge of the culinary art; today cooking is left almost entirely to their sisters, and the imperfections of their knowledge are manifest.

11 August 1933

---

10 Literally 'sea-fathers'.
11 Literally 'Scurvy Kloof'.
12 Literally, 'shipman's mixture'.
13 *Aaltjie, of de Zuinige Keukenmeid*, a cookery book (literally, 'Tiny Eel, or the Stingy Kitchen Maid').
14 Literally, 'ship-bredies'.
15 Water hathorn, *aponogeton oxylis*. See chapter 19.

2
The Governor's Bean

It would be hard to find something more genuinely Afrikaans in a vegetable garden than the good old *goewerneursboontjie*,[1] or *hereboontjie*[2] as it is also called. This is not something you are likely to find discussed in any overseas cookbook. Take for instance the *Larousse Gastronomique*, that comprehensive manual for the modern chef. There is no mention whatsoever of our admirable *goewerneursboontjie*, which is even overlooked in Afrikaans cookbooks, although here and there you might come across a casual reference to 'dry beans'.

Yet what could be finer than an old-fashioned *goewerneursboontjie* of the large variety? When green, they are magnificent; but it is a shame to pick them before they have reached maturity, and they taste much better when ripened in the sun. They are at their best when the pods have just opened, the two halves curling up to expose the treasure they have guarded with such care. And how splendid are the colours they display – subtle hues of red, black-brown, white and yellow. They lie there like fragments of the finest Amàndola marble. It is true that we now rarely see the *goewerneursboontjie* in all its old-fashioned glory, and it seems as if the species has become smaller, more wrinkled and less colourful. There are even some pale-yellow, dirty-white descendants to be found – inferior-tasting South American types that are far less pleasing aesthetically.

So try and obtain the good, old-fashioned variety if you can, preferably from a farm somewhere in the south-western part of the Cape. Go for those that have grown in river soil and held their ground against the ravages of the southeaster. And please do not treat them like ordinary dry beans. These are aristocrats, entitled to their privileges, and they have their likes and dislikes. So keep them well dried and properly cleaned in an airtight jar, out of reach, where there is no chance of the jar being – as children might mutter in youthful, mock astonishment – mysteriously smashed by some inexplicable mishap. And do not for a moment think that this is too much to ask of an already overworked housewife. It is well worth the effort, for it preserves the flavour. As Ayah Mina – that wonderful old soul who taught me respect for the *goewerneursboontjie* – always used to say, 'The taste, *Kleinbaas*,[3] the taste is what makes it worth its weight in gold.'

---

1 Lima bean, literally 'governor's bean'.
2 Gentleman's bean.
3 Literally, 'little master'.

I do not entirely agree. The *goewerneursboontjie* is not only the tastiest, but possibly also the most nourishing of all our beans. Its nutritional value – those who speak of 'calorie value' are simply being foolish, for we do not choose our food according to how much 'firewood' it provides – is far more than that of meat or fish or fruit, and it contains just about everything one needs to live, including all the new-fangled vitamins so fashionable these days. Not everything, of course – you cannot survive on governor's beans alone.

And so? Since the cookbooks are unfortunately silent on how to prepare and cook them, allow me to offer a few recipes of my own. But be warned – long-suffering and patience are required when dealing with *goewerneursboontjies*.

To cook them, remove them from the airtight jar – a cupful is enough to start with. Examine them, and discard any that are not pristinely pure, perfect and pleasing to the eye. Wash them in cold water to get rid of any lingering grains, then place them in a clean saucepan and cover them with tap or fountain water. Let them soak awhile, but definitely not too long. Even when it comes to the lesser dry bean types, I am always horrified when I read the instruction in a cookbook to 'soak them overnight in cold water'. Phantoms of Carême and La Chapelle![4] That is no way to treat a governor's bean. Too long a soaking will stimulate growth, resuscitating its dormant lust for life and activating that most mysterious of chemical metabolisms that can ruin the taste in an instant. So soak them for an hour and a half at most, no longer.

Drain off the water and submerge them again, this time in lukewarm water with a pinch of salt. But in heaven's name, no bicarbonate of soda.

Nothing, alas, can preserve the magnificent colour of the beans. When cooked, they lose their colour and turn brown – light brown when cooked slowly and thoroughly, as they should be, or a darker brown when cooked too fast. Keep the lid on the saucepan, but give it an occasional shake, and add a bit of warm water from time to time so that the beans remain submerged. When they are soft, take the saucepan from the fireplace, drain the water in a colander, and shake the beans dry.

For connoisseurs who prefer a simple, pure vegetable taste, they are now

---

[4] A Carême, author of a five volume work on French cooking (1835), perfected the art of *haute cuisine*. Vincent La Chapelle, author of *The Modern Cook* (1733), was *Chef de Cuisine* to the Prince of Orange and Naussau.

cooked and ready for the table. They are especially good when cold, for it is then that they have the genuine *goewerneursboontjie* taste – something between that of a chestnut and a dried medlar. You can serve them with a sour sauce, or as a salad with a simple mixture of vinegar and pepper, a touch of mustard and a dash of oil.

But what about something a bit more sophisticated, something more refined? Some of us are not content with sheer simplicity – we prefer the lily gilded, a whiff of perfume with the fragrant mignonette.

For the benefit of these connoisseurs, put the beans back in the saucepan with a pinch of pepper, ginger and mace. Add a cup of meat or chicken soup, and cook slowly with the lid on. In another saucepan braise a sliced onion (with a suspicion of garlic, if desired), and when it is light brown, mix in a few tablespoonfuls of tomato sauce. Dilute with a few spoonfuls of the soup in which the beans are cooking, then add the mixture to the beans, stirring carefully to keep them intact. Cook for a few minutes longer, and serve with a sprinkling of parsley.

Another method. Put the beans in the saucepan with a large tablespoonful of butter or soft, preferably chicken, fat. Add pepper, mace and herbs; and braise slowly, taking care not to break the beans. Serve with grated nutmeg or a sprinkling of parsley.

And what should one drink with it? It is a colourful dish, and aesthetics demand a wine of colour – so serve a red table wine, one that is not sweet.

10 April 1942

3
Jakkalskos-Soufflè

One of my friends from the Congo is a food connoisseur, a gourmet of the highest – or possibly the lowest – order. He is so fastidious a perfectionist that old Griet, who can just about make an excellent soup, and whom I have taught to sprinkle fennel leaves over a leg of lamb (when she remembers), nearly choked when I announced: 'The gentleman who speaks with a hot potato in his mouth is coming for dinner tonight'.

My friend had asked me to serve him something truly indigenous. I replied that there was no such thing as an authentically Afrikaans dish, and that all we have are some traditional methods of preparing food.

'But give me a little while,' I told him. 'I'll let you know as soon as I have something good I can guarantee you've never tasted before.'

This was a promise I simply had to fulfil. What on earth could I offer him that was so Afrikaans he would be unable to find it in *Larousse*, that wonderfully exhaustive encyclopaedia of food?

Should I give him *waterblommetjies?*[1] Alas, it was not the right time of year. Or *klipkous?*[2] But that could be had in Australia or Vera Cruz, that Cape Town-like city in the Gulf of Mexico. Or smoked ostrich egg in a parcel of puff pastry? That was a possibility, and he would definitely not find it under *Oeufs* in *Larousse*. But wait, there was something he would not find anywhere else on earth - *jakkalskos*.[3]

The know-all botanists call it the seed or 'fruit' of a parasitical plant, *Hydnora africana*, first described by Thunberg. That famous traveller mentions that the Hottentots ate it, but seems to have had no idea that it could be cultivated. It is found in sandy soil, in the shade of a *melkbos*,[4] on whose roots it thrives as a parasite. The seed – if we are to believe *Oubaas* Marloth, who investigated the matter thoroughly and has a rather idealised colour picture of it in his expensive book – is carried down to the roots by ants. There it sprouts and, after a few weeks, the flower emerges from the sand. It is a somewhat strange flower with an unpleasant smell, but

---

1 Water hawthorn, *Apogoneton distachyos*.
2 *Perlemoen*, or abalone.
3 Literally 'jackal food'.
4 A shrubby euphorbia, probably *Euphorbia mauritanica*, which Marloth describes as the main host (R Marloth, *Flora of South Africa*, I, 178).

fortunately we do not have to worry about that – it is only the fruit we are interested in.

It is actually a kind of subterranean bulb, although – according to the botanists – it is not really a bulb at all, but a rounded fruit somewhat like a guava. It has a thin, mahogany-coloured skin, and juicy, custard-like flesh containing dozens of small seeds. Dr Marloth tells us that porcupines, baboons and jackals dig it up and feed on it. He could safely have added that, from time immemorial, two-legged connoisseurs have been doing much the same.

When I was young I often used to see the *jakkalskos* fruit at the old fish and vegetable market in Cape Town. In those days it was a celebrated and rare treat. The chef at the White House in Strand Street would sometimes serve it as a dessert. She would prepare it as follows.

Cut open the fruit with a silver or wooden spoon. ('Whatever you do, *Basie*, please don't use steel; somehow it makes a difference to the taste, and then *Basie* might just as well eat tapioca pudding.') Scrape out the soft inside and press it through a sieve to remove the small, hard, bitter seeds. Beat it up with a touch of cream, a glass of jerepigo (nowadays I would use a good sherry) and a pinch of fine sugar. Sprinkle with cinnamon, and serve with a biscuit in a cream glass.

Last year I managed to get hold of a few nice large specimens. One was already too old to use, but two were still fresh and juicy. I attempted, in the manner of Carême, a trial run, and invited my connoisseur friend over as the guinea-pig.

'This is a really strange kind of soufflé,' he said. He is a cautious man, and prides himself on not being easily led up the garden path when it comes to food. 'But I would never add cinnamon to medlars,' he added, in the tone of the master showing a youngster precisely how the ablative was correctly used by the Romans.

'This is, of course, not medlar soufflé,' I said. 'But tell me, how do you like it?'

'Interesting, but good,' he answered. 'With guavas I always add some maraschino. In this case it would definitely have been an improvement.'

'Wrong again,' I said. 'This is no guava, although you could possibly call it a younger brother – a subterranean younger brother at that!'

My dish was quite simple. The juicy inside of the *jakkalskos*, relieved of its burden of bitter pips, was beaten up with the white of three eggs, a little sugar, a tablespoonful of cream, and a glass of sherry. This was poured into a soufflé dish well greased with butter. As befits a soufflé, it was put into a glowing oven a few minutes before being served, with a grating of cinnamon on top, and taken to table as soon as it had risen nicely – the precise, exact, apostle-truth moment to serve a soufflé can only be learned by experience, often bitter experience. A soufflé, if it is truly a soufflé and not a bastardised flour pudding, should be served piping hot, soft as a cloud, and crispy-hard on the outside.

The taste of *jakkalskos* soufflé is, well, impossible to describe, much as you cannot describe the taste of pineapple soufflé. Just try it yourself if you ever get hold of some *jakkalskos*. And have a glass of muscadel with it! Then you will truly be able to say: 'Now I've really eaten something indigenous to our own South Africa!'

8 May 1942

4
Sherry

It is customary – justifiably, in my view – to have something to drink before dinner. Our forefathers have done so from time immemorial. A *pimpeltjie* of wine before the meal was the expression in the old days, when that seaman's term still had currency. Today, nobody knows what a *pimpeltjie* is. But when I was young, the old ayahs in the cool shade of the vegetable market that used to be one of the sights of Cape Town used to employ that term for what we would now call a *pierinkievol*;[1] they also spoke of a *pimpeltjie* when referring to a 'small bunch' of something. But originally a *pimpeltjie* was a measure of wine, a small glass taken before the meal.

From a health point of view, there is something to be said for having a sip of wine before the main meal of the day. It is not just that alcohol stimulates the stomach to produce its digestive juices, but probably also the way in which the amino acids and oils in the wine enable you, twenty minutes later, to appreciate good food better.

The question, then, is not whether to drink, but what to drink. Definitely not those heavy mixtures of fortified wines, liqueurs, gins, Canadian grain-spirits, English beer-brandies, or even Russian vodkas, and absolutely not the one hundred and three variations of the American cocktail. They spoil your sense of taste and ruin your appetite. The only possible exception – but I would question even that – is the mixture consisting of one-third lime juice and two-thirds first-class Bols.

No, the very best drink before supper is a small glass of genuine sherry. It contains everything you need for the preparatory stimulation of the stomach lining, and too little alcohol to have a damaging effect on the appetite. Sherry – that is the best pre-prandial drink!

But what exactly is a sherry? I would be the last to defend, or even justify, the ridiculous fashion of giving the family names of established European wines to our Cape varieties. I shudder when I hear of a Cape hock or a South African burgundy. But with sherry it is different. Originally, in the distant past, it was a wine made exclusively in and around Xerez de la Frontera, in the south of Spain, by pressing red and white grapes with a wheelbarrowful of gypsum, and making from that a very light wine that could survive transportation, exposure to air and climatic change. It was then a very cheap wine, and not at all fashionable. The English soldiers in Wellington's army adopted it as their

---

1 Saucerful.

daily drink, and took a taste for it back to England (where it had, however, already been known since the time of Shakespeare), with the result that it became fashionable, especially in the western part of the country. English winelords then bought up vineyards in the south of Spain and spent a lot of money improving the wine.

Experts established that sherry was the only wine to undergo a double fermentation, but with the passage of time all sorts of superstitions arose about it. One of these was that it becomes much softer and better when sent on a journey around the world, heaven alone knows why. This legend of the overwhelmingly delicious quality of sherry that has circumnavigated the globe was undermined by one of the Walters. He bound a keg of sherry to one of his 'travelling' printing presses, letting it turn and shake about for eighteen months, and found that there was no noticeable difference between it and one that had been spared all the motion. Nevertheless, the fashion of sending shipments on a world trip gave us here in South Africa (or rather our forefathers, for we do not get it any more) the opportunity of drinking first-class sherries. The sherry of 1882 was especially famous – after the harvest of 1870 it was perhaps the best wine on the market – and the *raya* or second-class version thereof could cost up to £200 a barrel. For one or other reason a shipment was sold here, and some of it was still to be found at the old Poole's Hotel and, strangely enough, also at a well-known old boarding-house in Three Anchor Bay.

Today sherry is a 'made' wine, in the sense that it is not a pure harvest wine. It also differs in the way it is produced. When the grapes have been pressed and the first fermentation has taken place, the must is 'ignited' with a special germ, the so-called sherry '*flor*', that induces a second fermentation. This causes just about all the alcohol to disappear from the wine, leaving it with more amino acids and oil-rich substances, and all this is due to a highly complicated chemical process about which the *cognoscenti* can tell us very little. It is, in fact, because this second fermentation is so complex and mysterious that no one can tell in advance what the outcome will be. It may be an almost clear, quite bitter, very dry wine; it may be darker, richer, oilier; or it may be highly aromatic but very bitter. All three must first be blended and prepared for the market. This is done by adding wine-spirit or a sweet wine (when the *oloroso* or *amoroso* type is preferred), and especially by adding other sherries that have stood in barrels for years. The best sherries are blended by using the *solera* method. This simply involves, at the risk of undermining the mystique associated with making a good sherry, a shelf of sherry barrels arranged according to age. A good modern sherry is a blended wine in which the different older sherries are properly mixed. Assume, thus, that the sherry farmer started with a barrel of wine from 1920 and kept a supply of that and each subsequent year's produce up to 1940. The sherry of 1941 would then contain some of each year's wine, and it would thus obviously make no sense to speak of the sherry as a vintage wine. The sherry of a particular year could still dominate, though, in spite of careful blending by the *solera* expert.

Sherry is a wine that can be exposed to the air without going flat. Indeed, it is preferable to uncork a bottle of sherry a few hours before drinking. It should be enjoyed without warming or cooling – normal room temperature is sufficient to allow the oily taste to come fully into its own. The unfalsified *fino* – almost colourless, aromatic, bone-dry, and bitter without any trace of brackishness – you will not find for sale. Only the KWV has it, for those who are able to coax it from them. The article for sale is the somewhat stronger, fortified, sweetened wine, of which every winemaker has its own brand. I dare not name my own favourites here, and it is really not necessary to do so, for everyone should simply follow his own taste, or rely on a reputable wine merchant to make a recommendation.

The excellence of sherry is due to the quality of its various components, the most important of which are the oils, fatty acids and amino acids, and the least important of which is the alcohol content. It is a wine that should be sipped slowly and emphatically, preferably on its own. As a table wine I recommend it just before the meal, possibly with the soup (unless the taste of the soup is too floury – so not with a *purée*), and possibly even with a fish like *katonkel*[2] or *halfkoord*.[3] It really does not go with anything sugary, and it is far too proud of its own flavour to keep the inferior company of fruit and walnuts – its own nuttiness and its own fruity oils are sufficient, thank you very much. Therefore enjoy it as a *pimpeltjie* before the meal – preferably not the sweet variety – or as a drink on its own, for which the *oleroso*, darker, or semi-sweet varieties are best.

Try it at about eleven in the morning, especially on a beautiful sunny day when the *vygies*[4] are blossoming and the sheaves of wheat are being brought in from the lands.

29 May 1942

---

2 Barracuda.

3 Yellowtail

4 Figs, literally; a term used for all the plants in the Mesembryanthemum family.

5
Potatoes

It is indeed strange that we should classify potatoes as *groente*.[1] A potato contains neither vegetable juice nor chlorophyll. It is a subterranean food supply for a vegetable plant whose leaves, flowers, seeds and fruit we do not use at all. Other vegetable plants whose bulbous food supplies we also use – such as beetroot, various types of carrot, and turnips – have leaves that can be eaten. Beetroot leaves make an excellent stew, for instance, and carrot and turnip leaves can quite profitably be added to vegetable *purées*.

But with potatoes it is different. It is thought that the potato comes from South America, whence it migrated to North America about a thousand years ago. Scholars have argued about the identity of its original ancestor, but – in spite of considerable botanical research – the answer remains elusive. The general hypothesis is that the original plant had very small potatoes – about as large as the subterranean knolls of the species of *Kleinia* found in the *Springbokvlakte*[2] – and that by selective breeding it developed into today's larger potato. However that may be, it is safe to assume that the potato is one of the most important foodstuffs in the world today.

As such it must feature in any culinary reckoning, as indeed it always has. When La Chapelle wrote his authoritative *Le Cuisinier moderne en cinq volumes* in the early eighteenth century, the culinary art was already acquainted with no less than three hundred recipes for the preparation of a potato. In the somewhat ostentatious dedication to his book, 'A Son Altesse Serenissime Guillaume-Charles,[3] Henry Fris' – I challenge any matriculation student in this country to tell me who His Illustrious Highness was – La Chapelle commits himself to pure simplicity and pledges not to be a chef for the rich only. Nevertheless, some of his recipes are so extravagant that no modern housewife would follow them without adaptation. In one of his recipes for potatoes, for instance, he prescribes *inter alia* three litres of cream, half a litre of butter, and the beaten yolks of three dozen eggs. Ayah Toontjies would have had a fit at the mere thought of having to beat all those eggs.

Like his Italian counterparts, La Chapelle was well aware of the fact that potatoes are not as innocent as they seem. Like onions, potatoes are in fact poisonous.

---

1 Vegetables, literally 'greens'.
2 Leipoldt is probably referring to *Kleinia stipuliformis*, which has knobbly stolons, from the area north of Pretoria.
3 This translation of Vincent La Chapelle's *The Modern Cook* (London, 1733) was dedicated to Prince William of Orange, whose *Chef de Cuisine* La Chappelle was.

Do not be alarmed at this chemical truth, for we consume many things that contain poison. Egg yolk, for instance, contains a particularly strong poison. And ghoo beans contain prussic acid, probably the strongest poison we know. Potatoes contain solanine – which, even in its weakest form, can cause painful stomach cramps. And indeed potatoes sometimes do cause precisely that.

In my youth the most prized cookbook in this country was *Aaltjie, of de Zuinige Keukenmeid*.[4] The first edition of this book mentions nothing about potatoes being poisonous, but subsequently an editor must have felt constrained to include a word of warning, for the third edition warns against potatoes that are 'not ripe' and that 'may be the cause of sudden discomfort'. The story is then told of a family that ate unripe potatoes and suffered such bad food poisoning that they were ill for days. Also mentioned is a case where potatoes occasioned death.

It is well known that poisonous solanine is found in the stalk and roots of the potato, especially in young potatoes that have not yet matured. As the potato matures its poison content becomes less, but solanine is produced once more when it starts sprouting. The answer is therefore not to use potatoes that are too young or that have sprouted, and – to be completely safe – to remove carefully the eyes of every potato. Boiling water dissolves the solanine, so when potatoes are well boiled even the young ones become harmless. But raw potatoes and young potatoes that are not properly baked or boiled can still, to this day, occasion 'sudden discomfort'. Be warned, then, and select full-grown, adult potatoes – those that, as it were, have matriculated or have the vote, but excluding those of marriageable age, for it seems – from the latest statistics, at least – that marriageable age is often accompanied by a poisonous precociousness.

There are numerous methods of preparing delicious potatoes, as is evidenced by the veritable 'commando' of recipes in *Larousse*[5] – which, by the way, is not at all comprehensive, for I know quite a few that are not included. Take, for instance, potatoes à la Ayah Toontjies.

'Take six medium potatoes of the mealy variety, *Basie*,[6] and cook until they are very soft. Remove any dust and sand, and scrape out the eyes. Put them in an

---

4 Literally, 'Tiny Eel, or the Stingy Kitchen Maid'.

5 *Larousse gastronomique*, first published in Paris, 1938.

6 Literally, 'little master'.

iron pot, with a cup of water and a little salt, and let them boil with the lid on – until the skins burst, my *Basie*. Take them out and peel them with a pocket-knife, my *Basie*. Then place them in an earthenware pot, with a pinch of ginger, a sprig of plucked fennel and a large dollop of butter, and put it in the oven. Shake the pot occasionally, but let them absorb the butter thoroughly, my Basie, without getting burnt. Sprinkle with grated nutmeg and send off to table with a baked chicken.'

In Vera Cruz I saw an old ayah do exactly the same, with only one difference – she sprinkled grated cinnamon instead of nutmeg and used a pinch of saffron instead of fennel. Both dishes are first-class, provided you use those mealy potatoes that are not so easy to find these days.

Ayah Toontjies's second recipe is also not to be found in *Larousse*.

'Boil the potatoes, as before, in their skins before peeling them. Boil six young turnips in the same way. Grease your earthenware pot well with fat or butter, and cover the bottom with a layer of diced potato. Sprinkle with grated cheese mixed with a little salt and pepper' – Ayah Toontjies was sometimes bold enough to add chillies, but this is a matter of taste, or perhaps more properly of inflicting pain! 'Cover with a layer of diced turnip; sprinkle once more with grated cheese; then another layer of potatoes. Cover with a bobotie custard (a cup of milk beaten with two egg yolks, a few spoons of cream, and a pinch of saffron or turmeric for colour) and place in the oven.' A delicious dish when properly cooked.

Not easy enough? Too extravagant? All right then, here is the simplest and perhaps – after you've tried all four hundred or more recipes – the very best way of preparing Parmentier's fashion-vegetable for the table.

'Take large, mealy potatoes. Clean well and cut out the eyes. Place in the oven, which needs to be quite warm (use a piece of paper to test the temperature). Let them bake until the skins start bursting open. Remove from the oven, and wrap each potato in a handsome little napkin. Serve with molten butter and a mixture of three parts of fine salt to one part of white pepper.'

Baked potatoes like these taste best outdoors on a cold winter's evening. But the potatoes really must be mealy, otherwise it is just a calcified ambrosia.

19 June 1942

6
Liqueurs

My old friend, Jaap Snoep,[1] is very particular about liqueurs. The other day he brought me an old bottle covered in cobwebs. 'It's a Van der Hum, sixty years old. My late *tannie*[2] kept it all this time. It must be really excellent.'

We opened the bottle. This was not easy as the cork was rotten and had to be extracted carefully, bit by bit. The liqueur was turbid, and although it still tasted somewhat like the old Cape liqueur, the resemblance was not great. To be frank, the old *tannie*'s sixty-year-old liqueur was rather a disappointment.

That was to be expected. As in the case of brandy, no liqueur is improved by lying corked in a bottle for ages. The mysterious change that the wine-spirits and other ingredients of an older, quality brandy – from which a good liqueur should be made – undergo with time is a chemical change that is largely due to the air to which they are exposed. In a well-corked, lacquered bottle, the only air that has contact with the liqueur is the small amount locked between the bottom of the cork and the surface of the liquid in the neck of the bottle. It can therefore, when the bottle is kept upright, influence only a very small surface of the liqueur. Even when the bottle is kept on its side and the small amount of air has greater exposure to the liqueur, it is hardly enough to effect any change in the quality. It would, of course, be completely different if the liqueur were stored in a barrel, but then there would not be a drop left after sixty years – it would have evaporated completely.

A good liqueur should, however, not lose its quality when stored with care. The deterioration of the old *tannie*'s liqueur was simply due to the bad cork and, although I did not dare tell this to Jaap, the fact that it was not a first-class liqueur in the first place. I have in my time enjoyed a Noyau, or almond liqueur, that was more than two hundred years old, and it was still as pure and aromatic as if it were just a few years old.

Liqueurs are the alcoholic extracts of spices, with or without the addition of syrup. The alcohol content is, and should always be, quite high, otherwise there would be a danger of further fermentation, with inevitable deterioration in the taste. The main component of any good liqueur is therefore a first-class brandy; and the better the brandy, the better the liqueur will be. Do not think that you can ever make a fine liqueur from an inferior brandy.

---

[1] Literally, 'Stingy Jack'.

[2] Aunt.

There are many liqueurs on the market, and it should be clear from the above definition that it would be impossible to limit the variety of spice extracts. The most important and popular types are world-famous. Among them are the yellow and green Chartreuse, perhaps the most famous, originally made by monks in Chartreux Abbey from honey, hyssop, cinnamon, saffron and herbs distilled with brandy and then mixed with a sugar syrup; Curaçao, bitter-lemon liqueur, cherry liqueur, Danzig liqueur, Maraschino, Mastika and a variety of other liqueurs that contain relatively little sugar compared to the sweet Chartreuse; Van der Hum, and all the fruit liqueurs. Liqueurs that are not sweet, for example kummel, are nearly all distilled liqueurs with a high alcohol content, and are therefore hard tack. On the other hand, the *crêmes* of sweet liqueurs are mostly extremely sweet, with a high sugar content and less alcohol. Some, like *crême de cacao*, contain only enough alcohol to prevent fermentation, and are thus nothing more than fortified sweet wines.

Our Afrikaans Van der Hum belongs to the *crêmes*. It is not our own invention, since a similar liqueur is made in the West Indies, and probably also in China. I have been unable to establish exactly how old it is. Nor have I been able to find any mention of it in print prior to 1850. This is a subject worthy of further inquiry, for this liqueur of ours is a product of which we can be justly proud; and I strongly recommend that research on the origins of Van der Hum be conducted as a labour of love by some student in search of a thesis topic. It is not mentioned in *Larousse*, but Baron Vaerst evidently knew it – a quotation from him is the oldest I have found. The earliest printed recipe I have been able to get hold of is that of Mrs Cloete in the first edition of *Hilda*[3] in 1891. I do, however, have a written recipe from the Schwabe family that was probably written in 1836, and is more or less the same as that of Mrs Cloete.

'Dissolve three pounds of black sugar-stick in six bottles of good Armagnac Brandy, and leave to stand for two days; mix a hundred Ceylon cloves with half a pound of ground thin cinnamon and the ground dried peels of five *naartjies*.[4] Add one ground nutmeg and a shred of mace. Pour the brandy over the mixture and stir well; leave to stand in a cool place in the cellar, covered with a wet napkin. Stir well daily. After two months, filter it two or three times through a cloth until it is nicely clear. Decant into bottles, cork well, and seal or cover the cork with beeswax.'

---

3   *Hilda's 'Where is it?' of Recipes* by Hildagonda Duckitt.

4   Tangerines.

Variations of this recipe can be found in later cookbooks. Some suggest the addition of allspice or cardamon, others the use of a small piece of *bitterskil*;[5] one also mentions a few bitter almonds. I have tried them all, and still prefer the old Cloete-Schwabe recipe. It produces a first-class oily liqueur in which the taste of cloves mingles with that of *naartjie* peel. Our best South African brandy is just as good – perhaps even better – than the French Armagnac or Cognac, and it is still possible to find some good brown or black sugar-stick, which is best dissolved by first grinding it.

Van der Hum is, of course, not our only liqueur. When I was very young I knew a Kukumakranka liqueur, made from sugar-stick, brandy, honey, cinnamon, orange peel and a few ground kukumakranka[6] seeds – a strange drink with a very odd flavour. There is also sugarbush syrup liqueur, made from sugarbush syrup,[7] brandy, anyswortel,[8] cloves and nutmeg – a shiny-yellow liquid with a fairly pungent taste. I still know *tannies* who make a loquat liqueur every year, as well as one who makes a very good liqueur from *kafferpruime*.[9]

10 July 1942

---

5 Literally, 'bitter peel'.
6 *Gethyllis* spp.
7 The nectar of *Protea repens*, the *suikerbos*.
8 Aniseed root *Annesorhiza* sp.
9 Literally, 'Kaffir plums', the fruit of *Harpephyllum caffrum*.

7
Our Cape Kitchen

In the good old days, when Cape Town still showed signs of being a real mother city, nurturing western civilisation, it was possible – in an old-fashioned way – to learn something of real Afrikaans cookery. A nation's culinary art cannot be judged by what is served in hotels and restaurants – to make an accurate appraisal, the connoisseur must have special friends with excellent cooks. The best traditional food is invariably found in private homes, not in public eateries.

This is no less true of Cape Town than of anywhere else. Fifty years ago, the food in our hotels and fashionable cafés – such as that of Kamp – was mostly prepared and served in accordance with European standards. There were, of course, important exceptions, one being the famous White House in Strand Street – which had a good collection of game in its backyard. (I especially remember a young camel that, alas, did not survive very long.) The White House was well known for its excellent table. Even at eight o'clock in the morning, you could get *sosaties* with the customary fried bananas and no less than six different *sambals*.[1] Luncheon was something special, and from time to time the menu would contain delicacies such as turnip and tomato *bredie*, curried crayfish soup, saffron *bobotie* with almonds and raisins, and stewed *veldkool*.[2] Among the sweets was one that was prized by *plattelanders*[3] and Capetonians alike – thin, juicy, fragrant pancakes with a delicious topping made from eggs, cream and Van der Hum. Another hotel where the food was good and the cellar really impressive was the old Royal in Plein Street. Later, the Queens in Sea Point was also well known for its excellent table, but it did not specialise in genuine Afrikaans food.

Traditional Afrikaans dishes were found in private homes and in smaller boarding-houses. There you could enjoy first-class traditional fare, properly prepared over the moderated heat of a wood fire – we would not have considered scorching our food with a hot wire! The best known of the Afrikaans boarding-houses was probably that of old Miss Wahl in Queen Victoria Street, the popular home-from-home of many *platteland* Members of Parliament. The hostess was herself an excellent cook, who had the gift of being able to prepare simple yet exceptionally delicious dishes. Some of the house recipes, such as her crayfish salad, crayfish *frikkadel*,[4] bean soup and

---

1 Condiments.
2 Literally, 'veld cabbage', *Trachyandra* sp.
3 Countryside dwellers.
4 Meatball.

milk tart, were as traditional as you could get. One of the finest things available there was the coffee, served with plain cake and one or other fine preserve.

The question remains whether we have a culinary art that can validly be described as genuinely and indigenously Afrikaans. In favour of this proposition is the fact that we do have certain food types – such as *klipkous*[5] and *waterblommetjies*[6] – that are unique, and we have at least one method of preparing food that is not to be found in *Larousse* – the preparation of porcupine skin. On the other hand, there is hardly any so-called 'Afrikaans dish' the preparation and contents of which were not known to our forefathers in Europe. *Bobotie*, for example, is described in an old cookbook published in 1609, years before the establishment of a European settlement at the Cape. Our *bredies* are nothing more than the meat and vegetable mixtures that were fashionable in the South of France, Spain and Italy during the Middle Ages. They would not, of course, have used mace, nutmeg, pepper and other spices – such additives were far too scarce then to have been used in the common kitchen. It was only after the Dutch East India Company started importing spices on a large scale – in one year over 100 000 tons were imported from India – that the ordinary cook was able to get hold of them to add flavour to his dishes.

What we call traditional Afrikaans cooking can be compared to that found in the area south of the Ardour River in France. It is the part of France that was probably the longest under English influence. It is an area where, like here, the oxen are used for working the fields and transporting goods, where beef is generally less tender and plump than in other districts, and where goat's meat, mutton and pork are preferred. There you will find the closest relative to our *boerewors* – sausage made of a mixture of goat's meat and pork, flavoured with spices and improved by the addition of sweet wine such as that from Jurançon. It contains the same little squares of pork fat that are so characteristic of good *boerewors*, enabling it to be properly *braaied*[7] over an open fire without depriving it of its juiciness. There you will also find the bean and fat soup so well known here, the grilled *pannas*[8] that are hardly known here any more but always used to be made when a pig was slaughtered, and also the stewed offal, with or without a turmeric or tomato sauce.

---

5 Ear-shell.
6 Water hawthorn, *Aponogeton distachyo*.
7 Grilled.
8 Scrapple. See p 40.

There also you will encounter the habit of dishing up, in all its grisly splendour, an ox's head, complete with horns and skin, roasted in the oven – something completely unfashionable here but still found in the Transvaal. The last time I enjoyed it, and it was a real delicacy, I was in the company of General Botha, who expressly declared that the cheek of an ox-head roasted in this manner was the tastiest meat human teeth could ever chew.

Our contemporary schools for domestic science have thus far not managed to produce excellent cooks. Why, I really do not know – possibly because our culinary art, like all our other arts, is still based on the English model. We are good imitators, but we seldom create anything original, of our own imagining – we are seldom roused by inspiration springing from an inner desire to create something of our own, willing to risk failure in the attempt. Our Afrikaans culinary art is about as feeble as our *volkspele*,⁹ and these too are imitations of what we have inherited from Europe. Yet we have enough material to enable us to develop our own methods of preparing unique, characteristically Afrikaans food. We have seeds, leaves, herbs, roots and bark capable of imparting a very different flavour and taste compared to those found in conventional cookbook recipes. I do not know, and really do not care, whether these innovations would actually be improvements. I plead only that we should try them.

The art of cooking is, in essence, the art of making food tastier and more nourishing, and additives are both useful and necessary to this end. A dish without salt is not only tasteless, but also less nourishing than one that has been properly salted. Salt is a spice that needs to be used as carefully, but also just as boldly, as ginger, fennel, or cinnamon. I know a type of sage that improves the taste of a potato *bredie* twenty-fold when added to it, and a geranium leaf – a type that grows somewhere in the Eastern districts – that considerably enriches the flavour of a chop.

If we were to take our cooking more seriously, we would utilise our indigenous treasures from veld and *kloof*. But without experimentation, there will be no progress.

7 August 1942

---

9 Folk dances.

8
Veldkool

Now is the season for *veldkool*.¹ Just after the winter rains, when the world is green and the veld is sown with sorrel, it is time to harvest this delicious veld food that most people living in the cities have yet to discover. Once they find out how delicious *veldkool* is, it will quite possibly become cultivated in our gardens, as there is no reason why it cannot be 'tamed'. I have cultivated the smaller type in my own garden for years with hardly any effort, for it sows itself and provides enough each year for a few cookings. The larger, possibly more tasty, type is, however, less easy to cultivate. I tried sowing it, but without success. Then I tried transplanting it, similarly without success. But perhaps a more knowledgeable gardener will be able to establish even the giant *veldkool*, that grows almost to the height of a man in the Karoo soil, in the vegetable garden.

Veldkool is, oddly enough, a type of lily. It belongs, so the botanists assure me, to the same family as our aloes and chincherinchees. The particular subcategory that *veldkool* belongs to is the *genus Anthericum*, most of the members of which are found in South Africa.² Most of them are edible, but some have a nauseatingly bitter taste, although I do not know of any that are significantly poisonous. The two varieties that are best known in the platteland are the little, small-leaved *veldkool* and the large, slime-leaved *veldkool*. Both are commonly called *Hotnotskool*, or wild cauliflower. In some districts the small-leaved variety is called *slaaikool*, and the broad-leaved one *steelkool* because it forms branches. The first is found in sandy soil, and its flower buds – the only part of the *veldkool* that is eaten – do not stand high above the ground. Sometimes it even becomes a creeper. The second variety is found in clay soil. It is particularly abundant in Karoo soil or in shale on the slopes of hillsides, although it is also found on plains where the soil comes mostly from sandstone. It has a much broader leaf than the smaller kind and is never a creeper, but has upstanding flower stems with four to twelve buds on each branch. Sometimes, when the veld is beautiful after the rains, it is easy to pick a whole batch for the pot in a few minutes. Only the flower buds should be picked – when the blossoms have opened they are no longer as juicy, and the fibre of the stems is tougher.

---

1 Leipoldt describes two species of *Trachyandra*, the low-growing *T. ciliata* ('slaaikool', salad cabbage) and the much-branching *T. muricata* ('steelkool', or stalk cabbage), which prefers clay, though he may also be thinking of the broad-leaved *T. falcata* which grows in sand. The 'giant veldkool' may be the (poisonous) *Drimia capensis*, which is superficially like a *Trachyandra*.

2 When the lily family was reorganised, the Trachyandras were taken away from the Anthericums and placed in the Asphodel family.

No research has been done into the vitamin content or any other nutrition provided by *veldkool*. But the experience of generations has been that it is an excellent vegetable, comparable to chicory, spinach and chervil as far as its nutritional value is concerned. Like normal cabbage, it contains a reasonably large percentage of aluminium, which happens to be a slow-working poison that our bodies cannot use. But the fact that garden cabbage contains this metal has never stopped us from eating it, and there is no reason at all for avoiding *veldkool* simply because it contains a bit of aluminium.

I am not very impressed by the way vitamins are worshipped nowadays, but I would say that *veldkool* provides in abundance all the necessary vitamins that could be expected of it. Even if it contained none of these new idols, or lacked A to L, or whatever letter the known line-up of vitamins has reached, I would still put in a word for it.

For *veldkool* is truly one of the finest and most delicious vegetables to be found in sunny South Africa. Taste is, of course, not debatable. Jan prefers marrows to asparagus; Magriet has an aversion to scorzonera.[3] But I have never come across anyone who said no to a dish of deliciously prepared *veldkool*. And when I do meet someone like that, I shall know for sure that there is something wrong with him.

To prepare *veldkool* properly for the table, the freshly picked flower buds need to be soaked for a quarter of an hour in a bowl of salt water to get rid of sand and dust, and also any little bugs hiding in the petals. Then place them – the flower buds, not the bugs – in an iron or earthenware pot. Never use an aluminium saucepan, for that would spoil the taste. This is not a warning I need give the knowledgeable cook – she will know that it is a sin and a mockery of everything that is good to cook vegetables in aluminium equipment. But for the unschooled, this is a tip worth noting, especially nowadays when we are endlessly cajoled into acquiring such equipment for the kitchen. Cook the buds, very slowly, in a little water; add, according to taste, some mutton, preferably from the rib side, with a morsel of fat. Take care with the fat, for *veldkool* must never be fatty; the fat, meat and veldkool should complement each other, and more or less melt together into a delicious mixture. Stew slowly over a moderately weak fire. Some cooks then press it through a strainer and add cream, butter and even egg yolks. My own view is that the only thing that really goes nicely with a well-braised *veldkool*,

---

3 A dandelion-like plant, with a black edible root.

after it has been properly salted and peppered according to taste, is a bunch of yellow sorrel leaves, finely chopped and added when the *veldkool* is nicely soft. Garden sorrel can also be used, but its taste is a little too wild and spoils the fine flavour and peculiar plumpness of the *kool*. Many other recipes could, of course, be used to prepare *veldkool*. It could be served as a *purée*, as a tasty soup, as a soufflé baked in the oven, as a pie, or as an open vegetable tart. I have also had it with a Mornay or cheese sauce, but prefer it in a simpler guise, without any additions that detract from its inherent delicacy. The one exception I would make to this is when it is served on occasion as the base for a sole prepared in the Florentine manner. The orthodox rule is to serve the sole on a layer of spinach. Try it on a bed of nicely cooked *veldkool*, and see how wonderfully this enhances the taste.

One of the good things about *veldkool* is that it will never spoil the taste of even the most delicate wine. You can safely have a first-class Riesling, even – if you still have one in your cellar – a tasty Rhine or Mosel Auslese with it. I would not go so far as to say that *veldkool* would complement or improve the flavour of such a light wine – no vegetable, as far as I know, does that. But many vegetables do not go so well with good light wines, whereas *veldkool* definitely does.

28 August 1942

9
Grog and Bowl

Nowhere will you find greater ignorance as to the meaning of words than in cookery. This is understandable. Every technical subject has its own language, its peculiar expressions, sometimes limited to a small coterie of connoisseurs – a kind of *argot* or kitchen language into which only the few have been initiated. One can therefore readily assume that some of the words currently in use originally had totally different meanings which have been lost and which learned scholars, in spite of all their sniffing around, have not been able to discern.

Such a word is 'grog'. Its etymology is that a British admiral, Vernon by name, had the habit, in 1709 or thereabouts, of always appearing on the officers' deck in a waistcoat of *gros grain*, a term that metamorphosed in the English language into *grogram* – or, as we would say, *skurwegoed*[1] – so that his sailors gave him the nickname of Grogram. It was this same naval chief who tried to protect his people from scurvy by giving them a daily portion of rum or sugar brandy, and according to linguists the name 'grog' for a mixture of brandy and other liquids grew out of this habit.

I find this explanation almost as farcical as that which tries to make us believe that the English 'sirloin' is derived from the story of King James I being so taken with it when he ate it for the first time that he bestowed a knighthood on the piece of meat. The truth is that linguists are as ignorant of the origin of the word 'grog' as they are unable to give an acceptable explanation for the etymology of the word *pons*.[2]

They are more authoritative when it comes to the word 'bowl', for its derivation makes sense – a drink that is mixed in a bowl, or in something that is round or bowl-shaped. We can readily agree with that, even though it tells us little about the type of drink that it is.

In practice – the cook's practice, that is – the two words 'grog' and 'bowl' are very different, because 'bowl' usually – though not always – implies a chilled or cold drink, whereas 'grog' mostly refers to a warm one. Grog and punch are more or less the same thing, with the simple difference that a punch is usually a much larger quantity of liquid whereas grog refers to a single drink. There are other differences as well, but I see no need to distract the reader with such technicalities.

---

1 Coarse stuff.
2 Punch.

In a nutshell, a 'grog' is something mixed in a glass, cup or small mug, and meant for one or two people; 'punch' is the same kind of drink prepared for more than one person; and 'bowl' is a cold punch that usually consists of a mixture of white or red wine with fruit, herbs and flower petals, with or without sugar. There are exceptions to this rule – many of them. But if there were not an exception to every rule, our lives would be extremely dull and unpalatable.

Grog is typically a warm drink, suitable for cold winter evenings with the wind howling outside and rain dripping from the roof. It is under such conditions that it is sought after, and its wonderful aroma fully appreciated. But there are also many kinds of grog and cold punch. All have as their main constituent alcohol, or wine-spirit, in the form of a good – though not necessarily first-class – brandy to which warm water (or tea, or any other kind of decoction or infusion of herbs or fruit, or whatever) is added, after which it is sugared to taste and flavoured with spice. It is in the skilful addition of herbs and spices that the real talent of a good grog-maker resides. Here, locally, we have an embarrassment of choice: *naartjie* peel, aniseed leaf, *boegoe*,[3] *kukumakranka*,[4] and even sheep-bush[5] add flavour that you would not get if you were limited to East Indian spices like cinnamon, nutmeg, mace and tamarind. Then we also have lemon leaves, bay leaves and geranium leaves, all of which were used by the old people in warm grogs and punches.

Without the addition of wine-spirit or brandy, a grog is not really a grog but a *tisaan*, or warm tea (with or without sugar) – an infusion of herbs in boiled water. We still find this in the form of sage tea and elder tea – perhaps the only remainders of the many *tisaans* the Huguenots brought with them. With the addition of milk and cream, a grog becomes a cream or milk punch; when eggs are added, we have an *advokaat* or egg punch; and with a meat extract we have meat grog. These are, however, not proper grogs, but really just different kinds of soup with a rather high nutritional value.

A bowl, on the other hand, is a cool drink, preferably chilled until nearly frozen, and it is best enjoyed on a warm summer's day. Its nutritional value is usually low, because the alcohol content is low, and the sugar content should also be low. The following recipe, from the old handwriting of Mrs Schwabe, will serve as an example.

---

3 *Agathosma* spp.
4 *Gethyllis* spp.
5 *Tripteris* spp.

'Take three flasks of light white wine, and pour into a bowl over two cups of white sugar, a teaspoon of chopped lime peel, a snippet of thyme, a ground peach pip, and a blade of mace. Leave overnight in a cold place. Mix, a few hours before serving, with the same amount of cold fountain water, strain through a cloth, and pour the infusion into a glass or earthenware bowl in which a handful of jasmine flowers, two dozen clean strawberries and half-a-dozen mulberries have been mixed. Stir together well and allow to cool thoroughly. Serve with a punch spoon in large glasses; and add to each glass a pinch of ground cinnamon.'

Today I would add a few blocks of ice from the fridge, and omit the mulberries and perhaps also the peach pip – a piece of bay leaf would do better. The mace can also be omitted.

Every cook can try her own variations on these bowls. You could, for example, replace the strawberries with pieces of pealed pineapple for a pineapple bowl. For a peach bowl, use snippets of cooked, bottled peaches – canned peaches also make excellent bowls. All sorts of flowers can also be added, as long as they do not have too strong or sharp a smell – they mostly serve to give the drink colour and to make it attractive, but can also influence and greatly enhance its taste when used skilfully.

In English cooking the bowl is replaced by the 'wine-cups', of which the 'claret-cup' (light red wine with lemon peel, a piece of cucumber peel and some sugar, with soda water added), 'champagne-cup' (champagne with whatever additions are preferred), 'hock-cup' (Rhine or Mosel wine diluted with ice-water, cucumber peel, lemon peel and a few blossoms added according to taste) and 'fruit-cup' (any fruit juice diluted with soda water and whatever else). These bowls mostly contain soda water and therefore have to be prepared just before serving, otherwise they would lose the sparkling taste preferred by so many guests. The addition of a glass of brandy improves just about any 'cup' of this kind, except perhaps the champagne variety, which already has enough wine-spirit in it to make anyone who is not careful tipsy.

11 September 1942

10
A Sucking Pig

'Paradox – an apparent contradiction.'

This is how the dictionary defines something the sensible cook would simply call a misnomer. A *speenvarkie*[1] is not a pig that has been weaned – it is a pig that still suckles, that can in time be weaned – something that, if you were an expert cook, you would never consider doing. Such disregard for time would leave you with a *gespeende varkie*, a weaned pig, instead of a *speenvarkie*, a sucking pig.

The expert cook knows that there is an enormous difference between the two, both from a purely gastronomical point of view and from that of the butcher. The not-yet-weaned piglet is in a class of its own. It has something no older member of the pig family can ever have. Something … no, much more, since it is, as the oldest cookbook on the subject puts it, 'unique amongst the meats, a jewel without equal'. Such a crown jewel and kitchen pearl, indeed, that history tells of a time when only gentlemen of noble lineage had any lawful right to enjoy it. It is for precisely this reason that cooks and cookery books are so full of stories, some pathetic, some silly, some simply banal, about the honour and respect accorded the sucking pig by our forefathers.

There was, for instance, the kindly earl who would deftly remove his hat whenever he met a group of sucking pigs. Brillat-Savarin, the food connoisseur, tied bows and tassels to his sucking pigs, just as the goodly king of Cockaigne did to his subjects, to show how highly he regarded the little creatures. And the learned monk of I-know-not-what abbey used a sucking pig to rescue himself from the hands of a heathen hero. Literature is well acquainted with the sucking pig. One of the very best pieces of English prose is the tale – sucked from the Prophet's fingers, but no matter – of how it came about that mankind prepared and savoured such a culinary gem.

I stand back for no man when it comes to my genuine, unfeigned, passionate, sincere and complete appreciation of the sucking pig, although I would not go so far as to acknowledge the little creature's excellent qualities by emulating the famous Earl of Cuissy. When I see it wandering around – the sucking pig, that is, not the earl – I am less than fascinated. It is only when I see it slaughtered and ready for the kitchen that I begin to wax lyrical as if it were Jacques Perk's rainbow.

And it is thus that I now approach it.

---

[1] Literally, a weaning pig.

First, as to its appearance. If it is a real not-yet-weaned sucking pig, then it will be tiny, no more than a few weeks old. The sow's milk is still inside it and no other food has passed its lips. No sucking pig of ten to fourteen pounds for me, and not for you either if you want to eat a real sucking pig. A small one, about eighteen inches long from the tip of its nose to the curl of its tail, virginal, innocent, pure.

See to it that it has been properly scraped. No hair should remain, especially not on the head, nor in and around the ears. Wash well inside and out, and dry thoroughly. The question whether to coat that beautiful white skin with breadcrumbs is something the expert cook would never ever even consider – the mere thought would be heresy! Drip, drip, drip – this alone will do to obtain that delicious, brittle crackling that should be the covering of the dish.

And what about the filling? Well, dear reader, let me plead with you and beg you not to gild the lily, not to sprinkle Eau de Cologne over aromatic morning glory. Take care, therefore. Be extremely careful with the sage, rosemary, mace, and all the other spices. They are very useful when preparing the already weaned pig, but when it comes to the sucking pig they are superfluous. Its own little liver, fried in olive oil, then ground with bread crumbs and soaked in milk, pepper, salt and a few coriander seeds – there you have a filling worth more than even that suggested by Carême (who added cream and a pinch of saffron). Sow together well and coat the seam with lemon juice. Rub the skin well with a lemon and place the lemon (or if you wish a bay leaf) in its little mouth.

Place the little creature in a saucepan, deep enough to protect it from getting too much heat in any one place, add soft fat or butter, sprinkle with fine salt and a touch of pepper, and place the saucepan in an oven that should be quite warm – not quite as warm as that meant for Sadrag and his friends, but still warm enough to immediately, or at least within a few minutes, thicken the juices of the virginal skin. Turn the little creature regularly and keep pouring molten fat or butter over it. Do not be impatient – be thorough and make sure that not a millimetre of skin remains without dripping, and that the heat of the oven on the surface of the piglet is even. This is the only way to get the lovely golden-brown and ten times more delicious brittle crackling that should be as crisp and tender as a wafer. As soon as it is done, you can cover the saucepan with a lid and lower the heat. The little creature can be left to braise in the dripping, just long enough to cook its own meat properly. But again I advise caution. The precise moment for moving the little jewel to a cooler environment is something the expert cook will have learnt only through bitter experience.

Suppose the moment has arrived. Take the piglet out of the saucepan and place it on a napkin in a shallow dish – this makes it easier to carve at table. Garnish by placing a small lemon in its mouth, a sprig of parsley around its tail, and keep it warm until it is taken to the table.

What about the sauce? If it is a proper sucking pig, the dripping left in the pan will not make much of a sauce. It can, however, be used as the basis for a sauce. Mix a spoonful of buckwheat meal with a few spoonfuls of good sherry or red wine and stir; add salt and pepper and, when more or less thick, half a cup of cream, sour or sweet according to taste. There you have your sauce, but as far as I am concerned, the Bonades always prefer to have the sucking pig without sauce, with good rice (cooked until a bit mushy), stewed sweet potato, guava jelly and mealy potatoes. More would be mere wantonness.

And to drink with it? On this the experts differ as widely as the public does on politics. My oldest cookbook, that of Scappi – he calls himself *Cuoco secreto di Papa Pio V* and his book was printed in Venice in 1579 – says 'definitely a tough red wine'. La Chapelle prefers a white wine that is 'not too sweet'. Between these two extremes every man can choose for himself. I have experimented on my own and can only say, with my hand on my waistcoat, that a white wine with 'body', flavour and a slightly strong aftertaste is just the thing for bringing out the full value of the little jewel. But it is a matter of taste. I know of many connoisseurs who have their sucking pig with communion wine, and I respect their taste. The Bonades are not fanatical dogmatists.

16 October 1942

11
Curried Meat

The old Ayah who gave me my first cooking lessons, in my early youth – and I must admit that, in all honesty, the old soul taught me more than *Mâitre* Escoffier, for whom I had the honour of washing dishes and filling a sucking lamb with chestnuts – always said: 'My *Basie*, raisin rice and *pienangvleis*[1] – now that is something that *Basie* will never learn to make properly. Only we Blacks can do so, not Dutchmen!'

In those days – as I have said, it was in my tender youth – I still had the cheek to suggest to the old soul that a woman could never really be a first-class cook. Father Abraham knew it. Remember the story of how he caught three men, there under the oaks at Mamre, when it was so hot. He told Sarah: 'Go and make the *roosterkoek*',[2] but he himself was busy in the kitchen with the tender veal, the curds and whey, and the sweet milk. That he could not, of course, leave to his wife, even though she was Sarah. Because Abraham, I imagine, was a sensible man, one who knew something about cooking. Veal with curds and whey – I bet the three men had a delicious meal.

Now that I am older I feel I must apologise to Ayah Hanna. I know that I cannot make curried meat as it should be made. The 'yellow raisin rice' – that is no miracle, although often enough one ends up with some kind of bungled Italian mushy rice. But curried meat – the real, genuine, unadulterated, traditional, unequalled thing – that requires far too much patience for my liking. I therefore appreciate it all the more when I happen to get some to eat. Even when made by a woman! I know a few who can prepare it excellently, even though not in Ayah Hanna's more or less ritual way.

I can still see the old soul in my imagination – she is long dead and buried, and the harvest festival at the time of her funeral was, as the family wrote to me (I was then too far away to contribute my own gardenia) the topic of conversation in the location for a whole month – there in the Bonade kitchen, busy preparing her curried meat. First, the meat itself. Good, fresh lamb or mutton – the ribcage, cut into neat, short pieces, carefully dried, with ground pepper, a bit of ginger powder, salt, and – do not forget – buckwheat meal rubbed into it. Buckwheat meal – where does one find it today? Who still grinds it? And yet, it is the very best flour for meat dishes.

Then everything gets braised in soft fat with some very finely chopped onion.

---

1 Curried meat.
2 Grill-cake.

Before the onion can brown – it should just start getting the colour of an almost ripe loquat before you pull it aside – put the lid on the pot, and allow the meat to stew very slowly.

Take a copper mortar, dusted with buckwheat meal, and place in it a diced red chilli, a diced green chilli, two tablespoonfuls of coriander seed, a snippet of green ginger, a pinch of coarse cinnamon (the thick kind, that is not really cinnamon but cassia, although it is always sold as cinnamon sticks and also taken for it by those who know no better), a young orange leaf, a scraping of lemon peel, a clove of garlic, two large spoons of molten butter, a few cloves, six peppercorns, a piece of fennel stalk and, last but not least, a spoonful of turmeric. Now use the pestle, and pound and rub and grind what is in the mortar. Why? This is something I asked Ayah Hanna, and I must say that she did not answer me in the manner of the cheeky Temanite: 'Would a wise man with a windy knowledge give offence by filling his stomach with the east wind?' Politely and humbly, as it behoved a descendant of slaves to address the child of a Bonade, she said: 'My *Basie*, it is to get the soul out of it and into the meat'. And she added drily: 'If it is not fine, it might break the old master's teeth.'

Then make it into a cold, thick sauce. Dilute it now with something that requires equal patience – tamarind soaked in water, with the pips taken out, and then two cups of sour milk. I was told how to make that in an appropriately thorough manner, but never got the hang of it. I simply use any old curds and whey that have a bit of sourness, which would perhaps explain why my Dutchman's curried meat is never first-class.

Now stir it in and around the stewed meat, and let it braise – but definitely not cook. 'Bubble cooking' would spoil the sauce. And braising it too long makes it watery. Some people – but not the Bonades – mix a few spoonfuls of tomato sauce with it. Others, who lack genuine turmeric, use curry powder, but the sauce is itself a homemade curry sauce and requires nothing else.

Nothing else? Well, not quite. Taste it. See if it has enough salt, and if not, add some. The salty taste should definitely not be overpowering, especially in the case of good meat.

There are those who make curried meat from cooked or roasted cold meat. There are also those who have mustard with milk tart! It is not for them that I am writing. May tinned food be their nourishment until the end of time!

There is no doubt that curried meat from the pot is well worth the effort. What to serve with it? The usual yellow rice with raisins, of course. But what else? *Sambals*, made of quinces, onions, cucumbers. Chutneys. Stewed prunes. It is a matter of taste. I prefer my curried meat, which I eat with a spoon, with rice, cooked dry, and a portion of *sambal* or chutney – nothing else. To each creature his own craving!

And to drink? No fragrant first-class wine, of course. That would be unfair, not only to the curried meat, but also to the wine. *Oom* Daantjie van den Heever, who really loved curried meat, used to tell me that communion wine was the best, but again I shall merely say that it is a matter of taste – every man should decide for himself.

Do not assume that *penang*[3] meat is just a common curry. It is an exalted, crowned, imperial curry. Even though it is named after a part of the globe that could hardly be regarded as paradise, it is what our heathen forefathers imagined the gods would eat. For there is reason enough to believe that the 'ambrosia'[4] the old poets spoke of was nothing other than some kind of ginger-chilli-turmeric curried meat.

6 November 1942

---

3 Curried.
4 Food of the Greek and Roman gods.

12
Braaivleis

One of the most expensive cookery books you will find is a small one by a certain John Smith, printed in the year 1642, in which he describes the culinary art of the American Indians. It is a rarity that the Bonades are not wealthy enough to afford. The last one up for sale was bought for £900 and now forms part of an American library. But my grandfather, who was very keen on cookery, made use of the opportunity when he got hold of the book for perusal to excerpt a few pieces, among which was one on *braaivleis*.[1]

Most cooks in our country think of *braaivleis* as *gebraaide vleis*.[2] This is not entirely correct. Burnt meat is meat that has been exposed to a degree of heat that assails the outside of the meat so intensely that the juices in the outer layer of meat immediately coagulate and stiffen. When the heat is continued, the outer layer burns – a failure we often come across in hotels when we order chops and to our disappointment find that we are chewing pieces of burnt fibre.

Braaivleis, on the other hand, is meat prepared in such a way that the first shock of heat is just enough to bring about that coagulation of the meat juices in the outer crust, after which it is slowly and evenly *braaied*[3] – in other words, subjected to a more or less even heat that is high enough to cook the inside of the meat until tender without charcoaling the outer crust. *Braaing* meat well is an art that requires diligent attention from the cook. It is easy to ruin the meat when, for instance, the heat is too dry and too sharp. For that reason it is just about impossible to make good *braaivleis* with 'the wire', since an electrical appliance cannot really *braai*. The American Indians knew well that *braaivleis* requires moist heat. They enfolded meat in leaves and roasted it in a hole in the ground. Even today this form of *braai* is used in America. On the large plantation farms in the southern states, in Virginia and South Carolina, a whole sheep or even a whole ox is roasted in this way. The hole is lined with flat stones and a large fire is stoked in it, and when it has burnt out, the meat is placed on the stones and covered with green leaves. On top of that another fire is made. A good cook can make a very tasty *braaivleis* with such a 'barbecue' – one that has all the characteristics of a piece of meat roasted in front of the fire or on a spit, and much juicier than spit- or pot-roast.

We prefer the pot *braaivleis* – meat that is roasted in an iron pot. (Never use an aluminium pot!) This is perhaps the easiest way, but I doubt whether it is

---

1 Barbecued meat.
2 Burnt meat.
3 Roasted.

the best, although the other way – *braaing* in front of the fire – can hardly be done in a modern kitchen. Our forefathers had their kitchens made for it. On a large, open fireplace, with the help of a wood or charcoal fire, you can *braai* a leg of mutton very nicely. All you need do, to make a success of it, is to turn the meat so that the heat roasts the surface evenly, and baste it well with fat or any juice that will prevent the charring of the fibres. When doing it in a flat pot, it is also necessary to baste the meat well, but then the meat (especially when covered with a lid) is exposed to less heat. This comes close to simply baking the meat, and the art of it is precisely to prevent that from happening, so that the meat will not bake but roast instead. When *braaing*, a chemical reaction takes place that affects the taste and tenderness of the meat. Too much heat will char the fibres, and even the smallest bit of charring will spoil the taste. On the other hand, too little heat will leave you with meat fibres that are cooked, that lack the *braai* taste completely and that are tough.

We usually tend to overdo *braaing*. That is to say, we tend to leave the meat over the heat too long with the result that, although there is no question of charring, it is too well done. White meat – chicken or veal that has been bled to death – is difficult to *braai* properly. For both of them the first shock of heat needs to be enormous, without charring the outside crust, but hot enough to form an even '*braai*-coating' on the outside, in and under which the rest of the meat can then *braai* slowly and thoroughly. Both types require careful basting, preferably with their own fat or sauce. Beef, which in our country does not have much fat, needs to be basted even more, while mutton, which contains more fat, can be *braaied* easily in an iron pot. It is a matter of taste whether the cook will *braai* right through or stop *braaing* when three-quarters of the meat is done. Some prefer their *braaied* beef with the inside still raw – connoisseurs maintain that this is the only way of getting the best out of the beef. But that is certainly not the case with game, mutton or lamb. They have to be *braaied* through and through, without charring of course.

Grill or pan *braaing* are variations that are suitable for smaller portions of meat. They are, however, methods of *braaing* that, for various reasons, tend to make the meat quite tough, and the cook therefore needs to know how to counteract this tendency. One way of doing so is to marinate the meat beforehand by soaking it in vinegar, wine or a mixture of vinegar and oil for a few hours. Another is to separate the meat fibres from one another by pounding them with a stick or wooden mallet. Even a piece of hard old meat can be *braaied* in this way to produce a tender piece of *braaivleis*. A piece of beef, the 'cut' or 'steak', one and a half inches thick, can never be *braaied* tenderly on a grid or pan if not prepared in this way. The art lies in the cook scorching the piece of meat properly on both sides, without charring it, so that the inside can *braai* as much as you wish without acquiring the toughness of the outer crust.

Braaivleis goes with any vegetable – cooked, or raw as a simple salad. Many connoisseurs prefer something sweet with it and serve stewed prunes or peaches. Sharp sauces, such as horseradish, mustard or chutney, go well with *braaied* brown meat, but seldom with the white meats.

With regard to wines, the general consensus is that red wines go better with *braaivleis*, but naturally you would have to take into account what side dishes are served. No Bonade would think of insulting a good cabernet by swilling it down with a horseradish sauce, or with a cucumber salad doused in vinegar. A well-*braaied* beef 'cut' with potatoes and beans is a perfect accompaniment for the wholehearted appreciation of a dry red wine, and the connoisseur will enjoy the best imported red wines with it. A fruity white wine could also be served with *braaivleis* without affronting the taste of either.

27 November 1942

13
On Pannas

The other day an English friend asked me to translate the Afrikaans word *paljas*. When I tried to explain that it was just about impossible to express its meaning in English, he poked fun at my knowledge of language.

'Well,' I said, 'the Bonades are by no means language *indunas*.[1] But you should know that there are words in every language that are not easy to define, and are not even found in dictionaries.'

'Oh well,' was his reply, 'that's just another of your wild statements. I could give you the meaning of any English word instantly.'

'Very well,' I said, 'if you'd like to bet on it, give me the meaning of the word scrapple.'

'Oh dear ... but there isn't such a word in English. Where does it come from?'

'There is, and it's a very good old English word. You'll find it in old as well as modern English cookbooks, although you might not find it in the *Oxford Dictionary*. Mr Fowler may think he knows it all, but he doesn't.'

'I don't believe that,' my friend said, quite upset, for he regards Fowler as the greatest authority on the English language.

'Look here,' I said, and I showed him Mr Grover's recipe. 'There it is in black and white: "Make scrapple on the same day that you butcher", which we could translate into Afrikaans quite correctly as: "*Maak jou pannas op dieselfde dag waarop jy slag*".'

This language-game with my English friend inspired me to try and find out whether we still make *pannas* today. To my astonishment I found that most women in our country are totally unfamiliar with the dish. The word is nowhere to be found in ordinary cookbooks. Mrs Dijkman makes no mention of it, and the encyclopaedic *Larousse* only lists *panache*, which it happens to define incorrectly. The correct meaning of *panache* you will find in *La Chapelle's* fourth book, although the recipe does not coincide with that in old Westphalian cookbooks. Leipoldt's *Kos vir die Kenner* (which has no index, with the result that my patience was sorely tried by the time I found it

---

1 In context, authorities or experts.

on page 253) describes it, but says nothing about the name, and his recipe is also not exactly the same as that in the Bonade archive.

I consulted *Tannie* Lisbet on the matter.

She is one of the older generation that still says *harlie* and *hullie* instead of *hulle*, and is as stubborn as a scorpion when offered a 'cocktail'. But her memory is still strong.

'Mother always told us,' she said, when I mentioned my problem, 'that it comes from Germany. It should actually be *pannhas* because it is made and baked in a pan. I cannot remember whether the recipe is to be found in *Aaltjie*.'

No, it is not in *Aaltjie*. That 'stingy kitchen maid' seems to have known as little about it as Mrs Dijkman and *Hilda* and *Larousse*. Nor is it to be found in the famous *Volmaakte Keukenmeid*,[2] published with permission in Amsterdam in 1755 – I possess a rare signed edition, with the warning, in Dutch, that 'the publisher recognises as genuine only those copies that have been personally signed by the printer, Steven van Esveldt' – although it does describe at length how to make *beulingen*,[3] for which *Tannie* prefers the French word *andoetjes*. Only in the cookery books published after 1800 do I find mention of *pan-asse*, *bloed-panes* and *Westphaliese Pannhas*. The English spelling varies as much – for example, 'Skrapil', 'Scruppel', 'Dutch skrappel' and Mr Grover's 'scrapple'.

Short and sweet, *pannas*[4] is a first-class dish, and the time has come to restore it to a place of honour, especially as it is so easy to prepare and tastes so good. Our recipe is taken from old Mrs Schwabe's personal *Notes*, and seems to be a translation of a much older recipe found in a German cookbook dated round about 1750. The Schwabes, who were well known in Worcester – the *oubaas* started doing woodwork there sixty years ago, and came from the city of Ulm – mostly practised the art of German cooking. Here is the recipe, without any claim to copyright.

'Braise pieces of liver, heart, brain, lung and other intestines of a pig in lard until well done. Grind well, and add a cup of blood, a few spoons of vinegar, salt, pepper, and coriander seeds. Cook in an iron pot any bones of the pig

---

2 'Perfect Kitchen Maid'.
3 Sausage.
4 Scrapple.

taken from the meat scraps with a bay leaf, a pinch of ginger, a few slices of onion, some rosemary, and a portion of grated lemon peel. After cooking it for one and a half hours, strain the soup through a cloth and place back in the saucepan. Add the ground heart, etc, and allow to boil slowly. After it has boiled up a few times, stir in enough wheat flour to make a stiff porridge. Stir well with a wooden spoon, to keep it from burning, and take care that no lumps are formed. Pour the porridge into a shallow tart pan and let it stand until nice and stiff. The layer of fat covering it will preserve it. To serve, cut in slices and roast in lard, with or without bacon.'

I can assure you that, as old Mrs Schwabe would have said, it '*schmeckt sehr schoen*',[5] especially at eight o'clock with fried eggs and a piece of sour dough bread.

1 January 1943

---

5 Tastes very good.

14
Chicken's Eggs

There are hundreds of cookbooks devoted to eggs, and literally thousands of 'egg recipes'. In practice this super-abundant wealth of knowledge about the art of making eggs boils down to the fact that the egg is a foodstuff that not only lends itself to being prepared in all sorts of ways, but is also difficult to spoil – even when the cook is ignorant or careless.

In itself the egg is a microcosm – a small little world, as *Oom* Mias would have said – of an appropriate, well-balanced diet. Today one hears and reads much about malnourishment, about 'indispensable food ingredients' like vitamins and homeopathic particles of some or other metal, such as copper or silicon, without which, the experts tell us, it would be impossible to exist, not to mention the 'well-balanced diet'. Not long ago the know-it-all experts informed us that wheat, meat and coffee constituted a highly dangerous and unsuitable diet. *Oom* Mias, who has had a very amicable relationship with all three for seventy years and more, was underwhelmed when I informed him of this. His answer reminded me of the French grandfather who, when told that coffee is a slow-working poison, answered promptly: 'Very slow, I've been drinking it for eighty years.'

'*Ag nee man*, Koos,' *Oom* Mias said, 'I can honestly say that meat and bread and coffee have never given me rheumatism.'

In a chicken's egg you will find meat as well as bread, and perhaps even – on this third point no Bonade can speak with authority, since our family does not dabble in any complicated chemical science – one or more of the ingredients of coffee. Which is to say that the egg contains all the necessary nourishment the human body could want. It contains fat, meat (the egg white, which is rich in protein) metal salts, carbohydrates, and complex acids of which science still knows very little.

It is also very handy, as it can be enjoyed without further preparation, and is an easily digestible food, every grain of which is used by the body. This is not something we can honestly say of all foods. Of every pound of meat we eat, our body probably uses only about a third – on the rest we waste energy that could be better used for something else.

The beaten raw egg – with or without something to make it more appetising – is a first-class food. It is often used in cooking, especially when making sauces. As soon as the egg is heated above a certain temperature, certain important changes take place. One is the coagulation of the egg white, which makes it hard and white. The whites of some eggs – penguin eggs, for instance, and plovers' eggs – coagulate without becoming cloudy or white. Their nutritional value is no less for this, as they contain the same protein as chicken's eggs. Through heat the egg yolk, the yellow, also coagulates, although to a lesser extent – or rather in a less noticeable way, as the oil and fatty acids in the yolk influence and slow down the coagulation process. Every good housewife knows this and takes care, when stirring egg yolks into soup, not to let the soup boil lest it curdle.

How heat is applied to the egg is another point to be taken into account, as can be seen in the case of hard- and soft-boiled eggs. Complete coagulation of the egg white and yolk, as in a hard-boiled egg, requires no more from our digestive system than a partly coagulated egg – a soft-boiled egg, with the white not quite hard. Indeed, an egg that has been boiled for half an hour is more digestible than a soft-boiled egg. The yolk is even used for feeding babies that cannot tolerate milk or *meelbol*,[1] and is very good for use in dishes for the sick and convalescing. The thirty-or-more-year-old eggs that the Chinese are so fond of are always boiled for an hour and a half. Then they are shelled, cut into thin slices and served with a sour sauce. They taste a bit like turnips gone soft, and what makes them delicious is the sauce with which they are served. Hard-boiled eggs can be kept for months, on condition that they do not come into contact with anything dirty, and all you need do to prepare them for serving is to boil them again for five or six minutes.

It is hardly surprising that among the hundreds of recipes, many ways of preparing eggs are to be found; and, curiously enough, some of those found in old cookbooks, and used by our forefathers here and in Europe, are now just about unknown by us. Take, for instance, poached eggs with a black, sour butter sauce, or with a wine sauce – referred to in culinary art as *a la Armenonville*. There are also countless 'coloured eggs' – yellow, green, red, and even rainbow. The prettiest are 'cardinal eggs', in which ground crayfish eggs are mixed with beaten eggs, boiled in little pots, and decorated with more crayfish eggs to achieve a beautiful cardinal red colour. A more amusing than tasty egg dish is the so-called 'dragon' or 'giant' egg that imitates the normal chicken egg on a grand scale. Its preparation is somewhat tedious. The separated yolks of two dozen eggs are beaten and hard-boiled in a round mould, after which a layer of egg white is carefully hard-boiled in a separate mould. The large yolk is carefully placed upon it, then the mould is filled up

---

5 Baked flour for infants.

with the rest of the egg white and the whole lot hard-boiled. If the cook manages to do it all without any cracks appearing, you will have a large egg that looks rather like a pretty white pudding. It is cut and served with a portion of béchamel or hollandaise sauce. As for the taste – I don't consider it worth the effort. It is a great deal of trouble for minimal reward.

Every egg dish, if not herbed and spiced too much, will retain its egg taste, which goes well with any light wine. It is therefore not difficult to choose what to drink, and you can safely offer your guests a semi-sweet white or red wine with any egg dish.

19 March 1943

15
Game I

To have game at its very best, to enjoy it as it should be enjoyed, you have to eat it around the campfire after a tiring but pleasant day in the veld, during which, if you like killing animals, you have taken part in bringing down a buck or, if you do not enjoy hunting, you have walked with the hunters to enjoy the wild. There, surrounded by convivial fellow-campers, you will encounter the old-fashioned 'hunter's pot' if the cook knows what is expected of him. This is game – preferably buck with partridge, pheasant or peacock – stewed without adding any water, and braised slowly for hours above a wood fire that is never sharp enough to eliminate the juiciness. When game is exposed to too much heat too rapidly, the result is 'frayed meat' – the way our old *tannies* were fond of serving hare – but that, too, makes an excellent dish.

Unfortunately we seldom get the opportunity of enjoying game under such conditions. We have to make do with the leg of game we get from friends who hunt or from the butcher. It is mostly *blesbok* or *springbok*, seldom smaller game such as *grysbok*, *duiker* or *steenbok*. As winged game belongs to a different category and requires a different treatment, I will for now restrict myself to buck.

The game we usually get is more often than not meat that has lost its stiffness and has already started decaying. This means that in the meat fibres chemical changes that reduce the toughness of the muscles have started taking place. The fatter the meat, the quicker the process of decay. But game is usually not fat. On the contrary, you need to anoint it well, preferably with lard or hard suet. This needs to be done immediately, as soon as the leg of game is prepared. In our home we are also in the habit of marinading game. This not only makes it tender but also prevents the further decay that follows when the meat is simply hung. It is a matter of individual taste how far one allows the process of decay to continue. We Bonades, for instance, do not like it when our game can be smelt outside the kitchen while being roasted. Others like their game to announce itself from afar. One of the oldest cookbooks advises one to bury the leg of game and only use it when it starts showing signs of new 'life' – but so disgusting a preparation is surely not compatible with any civilised sense of taste.

The leg of game therefore needs to be larded. This is no child's play. It has to be done skilfully so that, when the leg is carved, every slice will contain two or three pieces of fat. Use only good, hard lard, without skin of course, and preferably fat that has not been salted. Then comes the marinading. We Bonades use a marinade comprised of three-quarters dry wine and one-quarter vinegar – some of our neighbours use vinegar only, others again only wine.

Tant Hester always used to add a touch of saltpetre, but I do not consider this necessary. Before putting the leg in the marinade, it needs to be rubbed with salt, pepper, a pinch of powdered dry ginger, and a small piece – a very small piece – of garlic. Then place it in the lye, to which a bay or lemon leaf can be added. Let it soak for at least twenty-four hours. If it has been well larded, this will be sufficient. The lye then penetrates through the larding holes and the meat is thoroughly soaked. If you leave it to soak longer, it becomes too soft; and too much acidity spoils the wild taste of the game.

Remove from the marinade, and dry well. Sprinkle with fine buckwheat meal – rub it in so that a thin layer is formed over the outside. Place in a pan or iron pot over a rapid fire with nothing but its own fat, and allow to brown on both sides. As soon as the outside has been browned, add a few tablespoons of fat to the pot or pan, with half a cup of red wine and salt and pepper to taste. Move the pot or pan to a cooler side of the stove, and allow the contents to braise slowly. Shake it often, so that the sauce covers the meat, and keep the lid well on. How long it should stew like this depends on the weight. Three hours would be enough for a normal leg of blesbok, but it is preferable to let it steam longer rather than shorter. Half-roasted game is never good to eat, and always tough. Test whether it is done by poking a piece of wire or a *sosatie*[1] stick into it every now and then. This is where your knowledge of cooking will show. A capable cook will know, by observing whether the poked stick is too dry or too moist, exactly when the game is done.

When it is ready, remove the leg, place it on a dish, and keep it warm in a cool oven until it is served. Take the sauce and use it, according to taste, to make a simple 'own sauce' – a sauce consisting of nothing more than the juices of the meat, along with the fat and what remains of the wine – thickening it somewhat with fine flour or maizena and, of course, with the addition of further salt and spices to taste. Or make of it a more refined sauce, such as our forefathers liked. Beat up a few spoons of plum jam with a teaspoonful of good brandy, stir it into the sauce, and thicken it with fine flour. Or beat currant jelly into the sauce and add a cup of sour cream. All sorts of variations can be tried – it is, once again, simply a matter of taste. Some people prefer to have their game with nothing but its own juices; others prefer it with a portion of jelly, stewed prunes or sweet chutney. For game served in this way our Afrikaans taste demands a reasonably *pap*[2] cooked rice, stewed sweet

---

1 Kebab.
2 Soggy.

potato and a simple salad. Dry cooked rice definitely will not suffice, but game goes well with vegetables such as cauliflower and carrots.

What to drink? There is only one kind of wine that really goes with game and that is a dry red wine, preferably one of the more robust, honest kinds, like a cabernet or a shiraz. There are various excellent wines of this kind on the market, and most wine farmers make their own that are possibly even better than those you can buy over the counter. A touch of 'bitterness' in the wine, such as a dash of pontac[3] would give, is recommended – it will strengthen the 'wild' taste of the game. This is especially good when the game is served with a cream sauce.

30 April 1943

---

3 A wine made at the Cape from the early days of settlement.

16
Game II

'That's not really true,' *Tant* Koba told me when she heard I had written about *braaing* a leg of game, 'you can't really say that a *braaied* leg is the best kind of game.'

'Sorry, but that is not what I said, *Tante*. I made it perfectly clear at the outset that the best way of preparing game is to make "hunter's meat" of it.'

'That is not something I would know anything about,' said the old dame, whom no torture in the world would ever force to admit that men can cook better than women, and who therefore has but a vague notion of what we are capable of when out hunting in the veld with an iron pot and a hardwood fire. 'But the old recipe I got from the late Mrs Raats, that she got from her great-grandmother – wait, I'll see if I can get it for you ...'

Now that recipe is not one that I would rate very highly. It goes as follows: 'Take three pounds of venison and cut it in pieces; some sausages; a pound of the minced meat of a hare with some fat ...' *Tant* Koba declared it a *hutspot*.[1] I call it a mess!

Our own old Bonadian way of preparing a real 'frayed' dish – as was the custom at harvest festivals, or when participants in a funeral procession had to come from faraway farms and naturally had to be given something to eat – seems to me more appropriate for the palate of a true connoisseur. I must concede, in all honesty, that it is a difficult dish to prepare. It is about as difficult as making a first-class fish stew – called *bouillabaisse* by the French, which one used to be able to have at the White House in Strand Street – which requires many different kinds of fish. And for a genuine frayed game stew you need at least three kinds of game.

I can still remember when I was young – *ja-nee*,[2] as the Latin poet said, a day or a memory that is forever 'white-chalked'. On a remote farm somewhere, with large oaks and a magnificent poplar grove that for us children was a universe filled with countless possibilities, the *baas*[3] was fed up with the bush doves that were forever causing problems, swarms of them, as large as the grasshoppers spoken of in Exodus chapter ten. I doubt that I will ever see so many bush doves together again. *Outa* Augustus made a hiding-place on the

---

1 Literally, 'hotchpotch'. A mixed stew.
2 Literally, 'yes-no'.
3 Master.

lands from *kraalbossies*, leading from it a small furrow in which he sprinkled chaff and bran with the odd bit of rye. He then took up position in the shelter with a long *voorlaaier*,[4] and when hundreds of bush doves had descended on both sides of the furrow, head to head, to have a good feed, he let loose. We got more than two hundred bush doves from just that one shoot, and the next afternoon we had a frayed stew the like of which I have never tasted since. But I must admit, conditions were different then. Where could you now, for love or money, get hold of three or four types of game in the Lowveld without going and hunting them yourself?

But let us say you do have the opportunity. Then proceed as follows – it will pay off, and your guests will mark the meal with white chalk for as long as they have memory and good taste.

Place a few pounds of the meat of any buck, preferably the soft strip off the back, in an iron pot; add a few doves, a Coqui francolin, a pheasant, and any other kind of game – winged or earthbound – you can get hold of. If you can find some warthog, so much the better; if not, take a piece of lard, not too salty, cut it into little dice, and add it to the mixture. If you are using large game, with marrow in the bones, chop the bones open and there will be no reason to add any other fat. If you do not have game marrow, add a large lump of hard fat or butter.

Allow the mixture to steam slowly over the fire, and stir often so that it does not stick to the pot. No water is needed – the juice of the meat will be sufficient. Whether or not you add onions, spices, or even potatoes is a matter of personal preference. I do not consider it appropriate, but this is a matter of taste. The same goes for whether or not, later – when it is done and nicely 'frayed' – you should add wine, vinegar or cream. Wine gives it a darker complexion, and we Bonades like our frayed stew to be light. Vinegar does not really do for the taste what the old transport riders maintained it did – I think their stews were always made of half-dry meat and were therefore not very tasty. As to cream, especially if it is sour, opinions are divided. I admit that it gives a strange and, to my taste, very pleasant tang to the game, but it seems to me rather like the gilding of the lily that the old playwright warned against.

There is one addition that I came across for the first time at a Dingaan's Day[5] festival in the Waterberg and that I can recommend passionately, with my

---

4 Muzzle-loader.

5 South African public holiday on 16 December, now known as the Day of Reconcilliation.

hand on my heart (or rather, my stomach) – dumplings of minced ham, small as marbles, cooked in the stew. A real treat!

And to go with it? Whatever you like. A good slice of toast, fresh from the oven, coated with farm butter – try it, no matter how plebeian it may sound. Soggy rice, a baked potato or a sweet potato, stewed dry beans, salad, and any kind of vegetable. This is not important – just as no side dish means much when you eat a really good fish stew. Game stew, prepared in our old-fashioned 'frayed' manner, requires no more than a deep plate and the appetite of a connoisseur.

The most important matter, over which the cook should exercise great care, is that every piece of game must be fresh – the smallest hint of decay will render it unsuitable for a good stew. Then, the meat should be stewed slowly and patiently, without water, and should be properly shaken so as not to stick to the pot. Thirdly, the lid of the pot should be lifted as seldom as possible – the stew needs to cook in its own steam. The longer it stews, the better it will eventually be. The mistake made by those who know no better is to let it heat up too quickly, with the result that the softer meats undergo that remarkable chemical process that gives the whole stew a burnt taste. This might add to the taste of a chop, but it ruins a good stew.

Tant Koba agrees that it doesn't really matter what you drink with such a stew. If it is a first-class stew, you need not bother much about what to drink before you have taken a second or even a third helping. Thereafter, a glass of sweet wine will go down well. I would not recommend a first-class red wine as this would be fair neither to the stew nor to the wine. When two champions compete, it is difficult not to take sides.

14 May 1943

17
Wild Birds I

We have so many different varieties of winged game that there is a veritable commando of recipes in cookbooks dealing with their preparation. In one of my oldest volumes, written by hand in 1835, I found the following.

Partridge in Red Wine. One medium-to-large partridge; one bottle of red wine; two large onions; one tablespoonful of buckwheat; one peeled lemon; salt; pepper; a lump of butter.

Place the butter and the onion, thinly sliced, into a saucepan and heat until it is lightly browned. Cut the partridge into nice, even pieces; add to the onions; sprinkle with flour, salt and spices; steam slowly; add the wine. Put the lid on the saucepan and stew slowly; shake the saucepan well. When the partridge is nicely soft, remove and serve on a bed of cooked rice; sprinkle with parsley.

This is a variation of one of the oldest recipes for winged game, but perhaps not the best. The cook who wishes to prepare fowl, especially wild fowl, properly must go to work in a precise and meticulous manner.

First of all, with regard to the birds themselves, the vast majority of them have dark flesh. In certain cases – such as pheasant, peacock and young partridges – a small part of the breast is more or less white, but even then not quite the white of a turkey or a farm chicken. The best kinds always have black or brown flesh. From a purely aesthetic point of view, therefore, they are not suitable for serving up cooked, but they are well suited for use as *braai* or stewing meat. I have actually eaten 'green doves', plump after having fed on wild figs and marulas[1] for a few months, cooked and served with a white sauce *nogal*.[2] They tasted excellent, but the orthodox cook – trained in the school of Carême and La Chapelle, who maintained that the eye needs to be nourished as well as the mouth – would not have regarded them as a first-class dish. And I have to admit that this is not the best way to prepare 'green doves' – possibly one of the most delicious of all our wild birds.

Water birds like wild duck, African coot, heron, wild geese, etc, all have black flesh that is oily. They have a tough, somewhat thick skin that is difficult to rid completely not only of the large feathers but also of the fluff. In most cases it is therefore preferable to skin the bird before placing it in the pot. An even better idea is to get rid of the oil, or lachrymal, gland carefully as soon as it

---

1 The fruit of the marula tree, *Sclerocarya caffra*.

2 Moreover.

has died. It is necessary to rid any bird of its intestines as soon as possible, and in so doing to take care that the gallbladder does not burst, as the tiniest drop of gall will spoil the taste of the meat. There is one exception to this rule, which is when you are dealing with tiny birds such as *mossies*[3] or *rooibekkies*.[4] These are baked or *braaied* hard as crumbs and served on toast without removing their insides. Some connoisseurs are of the opinion that our quails should be prepared in the same way, but I prefer my quails properly gutted, even when served on toast.

How long should one hang wild birds before *braaing* them? This is a matter of taste. There is no inherent reason why the extra bit of flavour due to decay in the meat should be preferable to the natural 'wild' taste of the game itself. The high priests of the culinary art – I am thinking here of the venerated Brillat-Savarin – say categorically that a pheasant tastes best when prepared as soon as possible after being shot. This accords with what science teaches – that decay brings only one advantage, namely that it makes the meat fibres tender and thereby counters the stiffness that comes with death and causes the fibres to be tough. In many cases, for example bustards and peacocks, the taste of decay definitely spoils the pleasant natural taste of the bird's meat.

The tastiest meat of any bird is the breast of the flamingo, a delicacy unmatched by any other meat. It is, by the way, not true that a flamingo's meat, as the old Cape travellers used to say, is just as rosy as its feathers. It is black-brown meat with short fibres, exceptionally soft, and requires little fat. The flamingo is, of course, no longer available as food – it has become 'royal game' like elephant or white rhinoceros. But it is still one of the most delicious birds you will find. I know of only one other that can compete – the breast of a juicy, fat, grey lourie that has been living on *moepels*[5] for a month.

Because a bird's meat is rather 'thin', it should always be well larded – something most cooks tend to forget. Placing a few strips of bacon across the breast of the bird is insufficient. It pays to insert thin pieces of bacon into the breast meat with the help of a large canvas needle, especially when *braaing* it on the grill or in the pan.

The filling is another thing the cook needs to consider carefully. The best filling

---

3 Cape sparrows.
4 Waxbills.
5 Fruit of the red milkwood, *Mimusops* sp.

is obtained by using the liver and pluck[6] of the bird, finely ground, thoroughly mixed with spices and breadcrumbs, and soaked in milk. The spices must be chosen with care. Some wild birds have a very delicate taste, for instance Coqui francolin, speckled rock pigeon and sand grouse, which should not be overwhelmed with sage, thyme or garlic. A good cook will know how to use even saffron and chillies in such a way that they add to the flavour of the game without drowning it. But be warned about the fat. Whatever kind of fat you use – hard or soft fat, butter or oil – it must be first-class and not the least bit rancid, as this will spoil the taste and possibly make the meat tougher.

When preparing wild birds, especially wild water birds, one should make much more use of wine and vegetables. One of the oldest and best partridge recipes is that in which the game is braised with cabbage, and served on a layer of it. I have tried it with *veldkool*, with *waterblommetjies*, and with the young pod leaves of some thorn trees in the bushveld. I have even tried it with the flower buds of an aloe, and it worked very well, but unfortunately that particular aloe is not always obtainable. You can also stew birds with root vegetables – carrots, turnips and artichokes – as well as with fruit. A Cape *dikkop*[7] stewed with oranges and served with snippets of orange peel baked in oil will make your mouth water. In Natal I once had some bush partridge[8] served on a layer of stewed pawpaw. It was delicious.

The addition of wine, even just a few spoonfuls, when the bird is roasting or stewing in the pan, always improves it. It is also good to add a tiny bit of wine to the sauce, especially when it is thickened with flour. As for the birds themselves, the larger kinds taste better roasted than stewed. The smaller ones, on the other hand, usually taste better when stewed slowly.

Something the cook should remember is that an excellent soup can be made from the leftovers of any kind of wild bird the day after the guests have eaten it. The bones and skin, especially of water birds, will still contain enough to provide you with a strong soup that can be served either as a simple *consommé* – a clear soup made with egg white – or as a thick soup with vegetables.

18 June 1943

---

6 Heart, liver and lungs.
7 The Spotted Dikkop.
8 Either the Crested or the Natal Francolin.

18
Wild Birds II

It would be difficult to say which of our wild birds has the best qualities from a culinary point of view. Years ago at the old Darling Street vegetable market, which some of us remember well, wild birds used to be for sale. This was in fact the only place where you could find wild birds. I remember how, as a child, I used to see cranes, *dikkops*, herons, flamingos (at that stage not yet 'royal game') and peacocks there, as well as some not so 'genuinely noble' game such as red-winged starlings, cormorants and albatrosses. Today there is really only one place in Cape Town where wild birds can be bought, and that is at the fish market in Dock Street, but there you will only find sea birds – and they really do not taste good. The old Darling Street sellers used to tell me that, apart from the flamingo, which is without doubt the best, they rated the guinea fowl most highly. I do not regard it as such, although I will admit that the taste of guinea fowl depends on the time it was shot and the farm it comes from. We still do not fully appreciate how much bird-meat is influenced by the food the bird eats. In America they understand this well. There a duck is rated up to three shillings per pound higher when it has been fed on celery, and a Muscovy duck that has been fed on turnips and cucumbers is even dearer. You also find the opposite. In the Rustenburg district I once shot a little swarm that was literally inedible – the taste was disgusting, indeed nauseating – and it turned out that the birds had fed on elderberries. I similarly found sand grouse (Namaqua sand grouse, although they are found throughout South Africa) that were inedible because of some or other food they had eaten.

It is of course simply a matter of taste which wild bird you prefer. Unfortunately we do not have much to choose from. Most of us have to make do with partridge, pheasant, bustard, guinea fowl or perhaps wild duck. Of these, one might take the guinea fowl and the wild duck as representing the two main groups – those with white meat and those with dark meat.

A guinea fowl, tame or wild, is usually quite plump, but not plump enough to be prepared without larding. Its skin, like that of the partridge, is not tough, and it therefore does not need to be skinned. But it is necessary to scald it to get rid of the fluff. The cook then needs to rub it well, inside and out, with butter or fat. Whether a little spice – even garlic – should be added to the butter or fat is something every person must decide for himself. I always use a bit of crushed *naartjie* peel mixed with grated nutmeg – it adds an extra touch of delicious flavour without overpowering the taste of the guinea fowl. Lard the breast, and as far as possible also the thighs, with very thin strips of bacon, without the rind, of course. Fill with a mixture of crushed liver,

heart and lung, a few ground walnuts, a piece of lemon peel, breadcrumbs soaked in milk, and salt and pepper to taste. *Tant* Alida always used to add onions as well, but I believe this to be a mistake. An even bigger mistake is to follow the very English custom of stuffing it with sage. Remember, a guinea fowl, tame or wild, is a white-meat bird, delicate tasting and very tender. Therefore treat it with the greatest care. Baste it diligently, first with fat until nice and golden brown, then with its own sauce, to which you may add a few tablespoonfuls of good jerepigo. When it is nicely done, add salt and pepper and serve as warm as possible with good potatoes, soggy rice and cauliflower. Stewed prunes are also a good accompaniment, as is any kind of red wine, or even a good bottle of white. It goes with anything.

Our wild duck is something completely different. It is, in the first place, a tough animal, with little 'short meat' and a hard, tough skin, which happens to be one of its best qualities. In the case of a moorhen or coot, I would recommend that you skin it – just as Apollyon did to Marsyas, but of course in a less cruel fashion. (The one *oubaas* skinned the other alive, but that is not necessary when it comes to wild duck.) Give the duck a good once-over, as it were, with a magnifying glass, to make sure that no little feathers remain; extract whatever you can find, and scald with a burning stick all the remaining fluff, especially round the neck and between the wings. Remove the oil glands; make sure that the crop is nice and clean; and cut off the neck as close to the body as you can. Carefully remove the innards and take care not to break the intestines and the gallbladder. Wash and dry well, inside and out. Grease inside with butter, with or without a touch of spice. *Tant* Alida always used turmeric and I concur, although I cannot really say why – it is just the sort of habit you acquire with experience without really being able to give any reason for it. As regards the filling, this is something the cook needs to consider carefully. A duck filling needs to be tasty and should also add flavour without taking away any of the juiciness and definitely without making the meat watery. A firm '*braai* filling', as you would use for a hare or a sucking pig, is therefore not desirable. Neither is a watery, porridge-like filling such as a pineapple-peach-guava mixture. It is true that the so-called 'Creole duck' gets a pineapple filling, but it is not our wild duck that is used for this purpose – usually a Muscovy or other, smaller kind of duck which has more 'short meat' than our yellow-billed or shelduck. The preferable filling is again one that uses the duck's own innards, assisted (duck liver being a delicacy that should be eaten with the roasted duck) by what we can borrow from the innocent little farm chicken. Mix together well some minced bacon, chicken liver, a piece of duck liver, the duck heart, a piece of duck lung, a strip of red chilli, a cooked potato, a ground raw sour apple, a small onion, a piece of leek, a sprig of parsley, salt, coriander and pepper; dampen with red wine; stuff the duck with it; sow up and grease the seam well with butter. Smear the outside of the duck with fine breadcrumbs – preferably from bread made with buckwheat flour – and place in the saucepan above a thin layer of bacon. Put it in the oven and let it brown quickly; then pull it away and baste it well with fat and wine, allowing it to roast very slowly. Some prefer the duck meat to be rare, still dripping blood when cut, whereas others like it 'well done like porridge'. Again it is a matter of taste, and I myself consider the right choice to lie somewhere in between. What the cook needs to bear in mind is that the skin needs to be completely edible. It is one of the most delicious parts of the bird if well prepared. The duck's liver is cooked together with it and served up as an accompaniment, each guest receiving some. It is as delicious as Muscovy duck liver if properly cooked and not scorched until it is hard and tough.

The best dish to serve with wild duck – for that matter with any roasted black-meat bird – is a good green salad, preferably made with vinegar and oil, and not with mayonnaise. This is all you need – it goes best with the duck, and root or pod vegetables are too luxurious for a simple roast duck. With a salad like that you would of course drink a 'rough' wine – a first-class white with a delicate bouquet would not go with it. Therefore serve the guests a good farm wine – a sauvignon or a jerepigo, even a shiraz if it is not too tart. If there is no salad, or at any rate if the salad is not made with vinegar, a finer burgundy is preferable.

2 July 1943

19
Our Brandy

There are few things about which there is more misunderstanding, prejudice and ignorance than our brandy – and yet it is really such a simple matter. I admit that brandy, viewed from a purely chemical perspective, is extremely complex – about as complex as bread or *mieliemeal* if you start unravelling them chemically. But no one really looks at what we eat or drink through the eyes of a biochemist. Life is far too short for such an exhaustive approach.

Our forefathers did not know brandy. They were only acquainted with alcohol in the form of fermented liquor such as the different types of beer, wine, fermented milk and other similar drinks in which the carbohydrates are converted to alcohol and carbon dioxide as a result of the work of bacteria. It was only about twelve hundred years ago when the Arabs accidentally discovered that you could distil something from these fermented drinks that is completely different in its effect on the human system, that humankind came to know brandy. It was such a novelty, with such wonderful characteristics, that they named it 'life water', a name that still exists in French. The scientific name for wine spirits is but a translation, or rather an imitation, of the words 'spirit in itself' – which expression was not intended to refer to anything learned but was simply considered an appropriate name for the end result of distilled wine.

Brandy is therefore the wine spirit that is derived from fermented wine when distilled. It is, however, not pure wine spirit, for we regard wine spirit – alcohol – as the particular chemical substance derived from any kind of fermented liquor when distilled. Thus from fermented rice you get arrack; from fermented grain vodka, gin and schnapps; from fermented peaches peach-blits, and so forth. The basis of it all is wine spirit – ethyl alcohol. But brandy is something more and much better than mere alcohol. It is wine spirit in which a whole range of chemical substances that are susceptible to conversion and change have been dissolved – which makes the whole better or worse, according to one's skill in making good or bad brandy. No chemist knows exactly what brandy consists of, what the eventual conversion processes are going to achieve, or how the different combinations of amino and fatty acids are going to react with each other. Research on this topic is as difficult as that dealing with the making of wine, although in the case of brandy it is less a matter of the strange influences of bacteria that make studying the taste and quality of wines so difficult.

For the layman it is not necessary to study the chemistry of brandy. I would also advise him not to try as it will only give him a headache. He should however know something about brandy as a drink, which is straightforward enough.

First, allow me to dispel a few myths. Brandy is a poison – that is completely true. A poison is something that kills live cell fibres. Boiling water is therefore also a poison; so are vinegar, chillies and potato peels. We absorb these poisons into our bodies on a daily basis when we eat, and when we drink coffee and tea. In some of our vegetables there are poisons that are much, much stronger than that in wine spirit. We can therefore readily admit that brandy is a poison. Anyone who dares drink pure wine spirit will very quickly discover what a deadly poison it is.

The practical reality, of course, is that our body is a complex laboratory that daily extracts from what it consumes that which is suitable and useful for it, and converts and renders harmless everything that is poisonous. As long as we do not overwhelm it with a particular poison – like suddenly administering a lump of prussic acid it cannot possibly cope with in an instant – it converts the poisons we eat on a daily basis into useful fuel and bricks for building tissue. Wine spirit is one of the poisons it is capable of dealing with very well indeed. It does this so easily that we can readily state that wine spirit is one of the best food fuels you can find. Thus the body can process, in much less time, a quantity of wine spirit having the same fuel value as an equivalent amount of meat, which therefore requires it to do less work. So while it is true that brandy is a poison, it is also a food and a fuel supply that is easy to process.

No brandy, however, consists of pure wine spirit. It contains many other substances and some of them – those we call amino acids – have a nutritional value we have not been able to quantify. A lot of research will be required before we will know with any certainty why one food poison agrees with us better than another. We are still at the beginning of such investigations and the more we come to know about this, the more we will be forced to adjust our traditional views on food and nutrition.

One truth that research has proven beyond doubt is that the moderate use of a food that we find delicious is, in the long term, not damaging to the body, whereas the immoderate use of even the simplest food can impede the growth and development of our body tissues.

For us Bonades this is a great consolation. We are brandy drinkers – not heavy drinkers – and we have been taught from childhood to regard a good brandy as the best and most perfect product of the vine, and therefore as the crowning achievement of the wine farmer. When I was young old *Oom* Theofilus Schreiner once visited our district with Mrs Stuart, his niece. They recruited the whole confirmation class – with the exception of the brothers Bonade, who were too headstrong for that – and founded a 'Band of Hope'. They showed terrible pictures of what would happen to your stomach and intestines if you drank brandy. Our magistrate even protested against a picture of the liver of an official that ... Need I say more? I now know that science has adjusted its view of the liver and the intestines considerably, and that the current general opinion is that a moderate user of brandy has just as much chance of living long and remaining healthy as someone who drinks no brandy at all. I remain mum about which of the two will enjoy his life more. This is a matter that everyone should decide for himself.

Nor is it my wish to go on about abolition and the abuse of strong drink. I will restrict myself to brandy as a table drink. Now that I can console myself with the truth that brandy is no worse a poison than coffee or *mosbolletjies*,[1] I can deal with it as a delicacy.

One of the reasons we are still so against brandy – especially those who prefer to partake of alcohol in the form of imported whisky – is that there is still some prejudice against the so-called '*dop* brandy'.

There are two kinds of brandy to be found on the market. The one is pure wine brandy, made from distilling wine only, and the other is brandy made from distilling wine mixed with skins and sediment. The trade names for them are French. The French call the first *eau de vie du vin*, or 'water of life of the vine', and the second *eau de vie du marc*, or 'water of life of the skin'. The second has considerably more ingredients than the first, but that does not mean it is stronger. The 'strength' of a brandy is its wine spirit quality, and that depends on the way it is distilled – a technical subject I shall refrain from going into here. Connoisseurs regard a good '*dop* brandy' as more delicious and healthier than a good 'wine brandy', but it is simply a matter of taste if both are good. According to the law, we are now no longer able to buy '*dop* brandy' – at least not that which is made here. We are therefore concerned, when talking of South African brandies, solely with wine brandy.

I make bold to say that our best wine brandy can compete with the very best

---

1 Must buns

foreign types – even the famous cognacs from the Charente region in France – and do not have to stand back for them at all. The KWV has during the last twenty-five years done much to improve all our local brandies, and the best ones on the market are all blended with KWV brandy. Naturally each firm has its own 'type' of brandy, blended and made according to its own recipe. But in every type the main role is played by a good, ripe, completely natural wine brandy that may not be less than five years old.

A lot of nonsense is spoken about 'old brandy'. Some – I trust not too many of my learned readers – still believe that there exists something like a Napoleon brandy, that is to say a brandy made before the year 1815. Now there are indeed brandies to be found that are that old, just as there are wines that are older still. But while some wines – not many – can remain in a bottle for fifty years or more and be improved by age, this is not the case with brandy. Once brandy is bottled and protected against the air, it remains unchanged. It neither improves nor deteriorates, assuming that it is well corked. There is perhaps one exception to this rule – a bad brandy becomes even worse with time in a bottle. Good brandy ripens in the vat, where the wood can breathe and the many ingredients can slowly but surely undergo chemical change. It is the vat that gives the brandy its colour, although it is normal in the trade to enhance the colour with additives allowed by law. It is not only the colour that is influenced by the wood of the vat but also the taste of the brandy and its nature as a liquid, and the longer the brandy remains in the vat, the better it becomes, although it is difficult to say at what point it could be regarded as overripe. It is not practical to keep brandy in the vat too long, for it evaporates, and a small vat of brandy will dry up after ten years. It is therefore clear that no brandy can stay in a vat for a hundred years. It is equally clear that brandy from 1815 that has been kept in a bottle will today be no better than it was then, and we have brandy today that is considerably better than that of earlier times.

The truth is that very old brandy is just about undrinkable, because it is so saturated with ethereal salt and volatile acids that it will burn your mouth and lips. A small quantity of such a very old brandy is used to blend a good younger one – it gives the younger liquid more body and a pleasant bouquet, aftertaste and oiliness. Such additives should however be used with the utmost care, for the 'blending' of brandy is a matter for the connoisseur and it is therefore done exclusively by experts attached to the large firms.

For the normal afficionado a good wine brandy of about ten to twelve years is just as good and tasty as a much more expensive one blended with an age-old liquid, be it imported or local. We now have many such good brandies on the market, and you can get them from any wine merchant. Try the different kinds. Pour a few drops of each in a dry wine glass – it is by no means necessary to use a large 'brandy glass' – and sample each first with your nose and tongue. (If you have false teeth with a metal plate, remove them before tasting; teeth with gold or metal fillings also do not help when it comes to judging brandy.) Warm the glass between your hands to cause the volatile acids to evaporate. Do not pay too much attention to the colour – unless it is too dark, the colour will in most cases have been enhanced by adding burnt sugar or something like that, which will not influence the taste very much. Too light a colour may make you suspect that the brandy has not matured for long enough in oaken vats, but your tongue and palate will be a better guide than your eye. Now taste the warmed liquid; 'feel' it on your tongue, and let it warm some more – so that the back of the palate can taste the flavour. Try to judge the extent to which the taste is even, oily and without 'bite' but still has a pleasant tingle. Then swallow and savour the aftertaste. Take a small sip of water and try another sample in the same way; and decide according to your own taste which brandy you prefer.

Now squirt a few drops of soda water in one of the glasses and try again. See which of the different samples passes the mixture test. A first-class type will immediately impart its good qualities to the mixture; its flavour will, as it were, be germinated by the carbon hydroxide; its tingling taste will be strengthened to a certain extent. On the other hand, you will, if you have a sensitive palate, immediately spot the lesser kind – that which still has some volatile acids that a good brandy should have given up to the wood of the vat. A subtle change in the aftertaste indicates the presence of the secondary wine spirit – a touch of 'bitterness' might then even be noticed. Now compare your observations during the mixture test with those made when tasting the pure liquid, and make your choice.

The brandy you like most is the one that will best agree with you. Do not be impressed by labels or advertisements – make your choice according to your own taste. And then treat your choice with love and understanding. Enjoy it in moderation, preferably after a good lunch or supper, with or after coffee if you like it in its naked purity. Otherwise, again in moderation, with clean spring water, or, if you prefer, soda water. And on a cold winter evening, when the wind is howling outside and you are sure that your lambs are safely protected in the *kraal*, with warm water, a piece of cinnamon, a lump of sugar and a flake of lemon peel, as a warm drink.

10 September 1943

20
Waterblommetjies

Now is the time for *wateruintjies*,[1] and my dear readers should understand clearly that one of the blessings that European civilisation brought to this country was to teach the 'uncivilised' how to make best use of their natural resources. My late *Tannie* Trifosa – there was no such name in our family, but *Oupa* called the twins Trifosa and Trifena because he happened to be reading the sixth chapter of Romans the day they were born (*Tannie* Trifena succumbed before the day she was to be baptised) – *Tannie* Trifosa used to tell me that the best *waterblommetjie* harvest is in spring. Her great-grandmother told her that in the old days of the Dutch East India Company, people from the Hantam came to dig up the real hawthorn. But we no longer do that today – we only eat the upper part, the flowers. What she told me is true: Thunberg,[2] who was apparently some sort of *smous*[3] around here, tells us that people also did that in his time, and that the hawthorn was the bulb and not the flower. But when we tried to dig it up, we only found potter's clay and a dead water skunk!

We will therefore restrict ourselves to the hawthorn flowers and stalks – even from those you can make a wonderful stew. It is a pity that they are so scarce nowadays. Previously it used to be possible to find a *klonkie*,[4] on the Parade or on any street corner, with half-a-dozen bunches of *waterblommetjies* for threepence each. Now you have to pay – can you believe it? – up to two shillings a bunch, and be thankful that you managed to get it at all. The week before last I saw the *vlei* full of flowers – the smell was reminiscent of a funeral – but was there a *klonkie* to be found to wade in and pick them? Not a single one! I had to roll up my own trousers and, of course, the first thing I stood on was a jerepigo bottle. I am still limping, but we managed to return home with three or four bunches for the pot.

The Bonade recipe has fructified into half a dozen, and there will probably be further variations if the stuff becomes more widely used. It is really a shame that so much of our first-class veld food is so little known. We sell, just imagine, spinach – that has as little taste as curried cucumber – for sixpence a bunch, and cauliflower for I know not how many shillings a head, and we

---

1 Water hawthorn, *Aponogeton distachyos*, commonly known in South Africa as *waterblommetjies*.
2 Carl Peter Thunberg (1743-1828), a famous Swedish botanist who stayed at the Cape from 1772-1775. He made three journeys to the interior, and collected 3 000 plants, of which 1 000 were new to botany.
3 Hawker.
4 Coloured boy.

treat with contempt *waterblommetjies*, which are far more delicious and abundant for the picking. And in the veld there are many other delicious kinds of food that we neglect simply because we know nothing about them any more.

When we start moaning and groaning on the subject of politics, or whatever else, there is no end to it ... but with all this fuss about the shortage of paper my space is limited – so I shall stifle my thoughts on the subject of the domestic training of the younger generation and return to *waterblommetjies*.

The secret of a good *waterblommetjie bredie* (as with every green vegetable *bredie*) is the marriage of the green – in this case, the white – vegetable with fat. The basis of every stew should be a few pieces of fat mutton rib, well braised either in its own fat or with the aid of a bit of caul. *Tant* Tifrosa once showed me how she used ox-marrow for her stew, but that seems to me a bit extravagant, especially in a time of war when we cannot even get hold of enough good marrow bones for soup. I am also not convinced that marrow fat improves the taste of a green stew. I think the particularly good taste that *Tant* Tifrosa's stew had – and I grant that no one could make a better stew than she – was due to the sprig of rosemary she always added. We need to use herbs more. I recently searched in vain for a leaf of basil ... but wait, my space is limited.

Braise the meat well, and braise it properly – do not roast it! And do so slowly and carefully, for as the *Stingy Kitchen Maid* says: 'The stuff tends to burn very easily and therefore needs to be handled with care'. And once it has burnt you can forget about your stew. With vegetables it is different; when they have been 'lightly burnt', just take them from the fire immediately and place the top part in another pot – that way you can still save them.

In the meantime, wash the *waterblommetjies* – taking only the flowers and flower petals and the youngest, softest stalks – in salt water; dry; and place on the fire in an iron pot with enough water to cover them. Allow them to boil. The water will extract the brown, bitter juice from the stalks, and as soon as it is reddish brown, the pot should be removed. Drain through a colander and throw out the red water – *Tannie* Trifosa always used it for her zinnias, and was genuinely convinced that it improved their colour. The things that superstitions can make people believe! Now add the *waterblommetjies* to the braised meat, and also add a lump of fat. Some say butter, but I cannot see why – fat and butter do not mix very well. Add too, according to taste, a bay or lemon leaf, or a bit of whatever herb you choose. I have already mentioned that my old *tannie* was very keen on rosemary, and it is worth trying. Place the lid on and braise well for twenty minutes. Shake often, and take care not to let it burn.

Now take two or three handfuls of sorrel leaves – the yellow sorrel that grows in the vineyard is best.[5] If you use garden sorrel, cut the thick stalks away first and cut up the leaves well. Add boiling water, then dry well. When using the wild sorrel that is much softer, you do not have to carve up the leaves first. Just bruise them when getting rid of the water. Then add them to the stew and braise again. Stir well, so that the vegetables braise nicely in the fat and become oiled through and through. Take care that the heat of the fire does not become too strong, for then the stew will lose its green colour. To finish, the spice: add salt to taste, a piece of green ginger, a sliver of green chilli, and a thimbleful of fine white pepper. Dish up and serve with soggy rice.

I know that there are people who add cream. This is a matter of taste, but I prefer my *waterblommetjie* bredie without it. A *waterblommetjie purée*, like spinach without meat or fat – that is something to which you can add as much cream as you wish. But *waterblommetjie* and meat *bredie* should rely on its own flavour and richness, which it can do very well.

What to drink with it? One of our good white wines, well chilled and not too dry. A Riesling, if that is available, or else a Sauvignon. Both go well with the delicate *waterblommetjie* taste that also pervades the meat.

24 September 1943

---

5 *Oxalis pes-caprae*, which is quite unrelated to culinary sorrel.

21
Crayfish

According to what the old folk tell me, a taste for crayfish was not common in past times – at least not amongst white people. The Boer people never liked it much, and in my great-grandmother's recipe book, in which there are many recipes for fish dishes, crayfish gets no mention whatsoever. I regard it as one of the few bad traits of my otherwise well-nigh perfect family that there are, even today, Bonades who turn up their noses when crayfish is spoken of.

Sometimes, when quietly contemplating the nuances of human nature – in which pastime I sometimes indulge while attending to some or other delicacy on the fire – it occurs to me that one of the reasons why *Grootoom* Gieljam used to be regarded by the family as smelling a bit off was probably his love for this outstanding crustacean. I remember how he once took me to Kalk Bay, where he initiated me, from the rocks, in the art of catching small crayfish. They are no longer to be found around there, and even if they were you would not dare fish them out with a basket – one of the new laws, among the hundred thousand others in existence, is a prohibition on molesting small crayfish.

And yet, where will you ever find anything more delicious than these tasty, juicy little creatures? When I speak of crayfish, I refer not to that red, hard-boiled 'factory' substance that is sometimes delivered or comes from cold storage at an exorbitant price, and that people in hotels, in clubs and – yes, believe me – in private homes use to make 'crayfish salad'. I refer to the small crayfish that really are worth eating, or the larger ones, preferably female, that are almost as good.

Try to find one of them. Get hold of it while still alive, struggling, and able to pinch your fingers with relish; one that is still – well not quite black, but that strange green-blue, blackish body colour with various hues of gold, depending on how the light catches it. And please do not throw it into boiling water. If you are extremely sensitive and a member of the Society for the Protection of Animals, you may kill the little creature first by slipping a knife into its head. Miss Duckitt advised that for crabs, but while admitting that there was a measure of cruelty in immersing crayfish in boiling water, she readily agreed that it was the most common method. Her own cook, she tells us, always cut through the neck of the crayfish with a knife, and those who consider this a more merciful method could do likewise.

I place my crayfish, small or large, in a pot with a cup of sea water, a few strips of seaweed, a few slices of lemon, two or three Pittosporum leaves, a quartered onion with a piece of onion leaf, and a sliver of mace. Then I put on the lid and place the pot on the fire. Within ten minutes my crayfish is done. When eaten very hot with a sour sauce, it tastes delicious, like soft-cooked beetroot, like something you cannot imagine if you have only tasted the type of crayfish that is bought wholesale and cooked *en masse*. But it tastes even better if you let it soak for a few hours in the soup in which it was boiled until it is cold through and through.

You can make a number of delicious dishes from crayfish cooked in this way. I shall touch on only a few. One of them is made according to an old recipe of Mrs Schwabe from Worcester. In her day they used to get the crayfish from Kleinmond or Gordon's Bay, and then it was still fashionable to sell only the very best 'maiden crayfish'. Her recipe is similar to that found in the recipe book of Miss Elizabeth Raper, written in 1756, which appeared in print for the first time in 1924 when the Nonesuch Press reprinted it in a deluxe edition, of which there is probably a copy in our State Library. The two recipes differ slightly, and that of Mrs Schwabe is to my mind more acceptable.

Crayfish in its shell. Take all the flesh out of the shell, tail and legs, especially the fatty meat just beneath the shell; crush it fine in a mortar along with an equal weight of ox-marrow or caul (the marrow is better) and stir in some salt, pepper, breadcrumbs, two egg yolks, a cup of whipped cream, a pinch of chilli, and a tablespoonful of lemon juice. Fill the empty shells with it and place them in the oven until baked.

It is delicious, but today I would replace the breadcrumbs with rusk-crumbs because our government bread is completely unsuitable for any culinary work of art. I would also place a few lumps of butter on top when I take the shells out of the oven. I have also, on occasion, added a pinch of saffron to the mixture, which gives a beautiful colour to the dish. For variation you could add any garden herb, and I always find that a piece of *naartjie* peel goes well with any crayfish dish.

A second recipe is one I inherited by word of mouth from *Grootoom* Gieljam. He always used to prepare his little crayfish on the beach after boiling them in seawater.

Egg Crayfish. Take out the flesh and cut it into small shreds, the smaller the better; braise with a bit of onion, chutney, thyme, pepper and a crushed chilli in butter or fat until it starts getting nice and brown; add a few beaten eggs and stir briskly until it is all quite thick.

We always used to enjoy this simple dish on the Kalk Bay rocks, and not a morsel would remain for the *klonkies* who were watching eagerly. In my kitchen I always used to adjust it – I would hardly say improve it – in various ways. I would add a glass of brandy, which makes the eggs a trifle watery but improves the taste. Or a few oysters, two or three anchovies, and a few spoonfuls of ground almond. You could also play different tunes with spices, but beware of garlic.

A third recipe comes from one of the oldest handwritten manuscripts known to me, and I rather think that this is the way the Chinese cooks served it in the olden days when they had little 'eating houses' on the spot where our Broadcasting Corporation office stands today.[1] They were then the most knowledgeable cooks in the country, and we are indebted to them for many of our Afrikaans cooking methods.

Pineapple Crayfish. Crush the meat, especially that of the claws, and mix with cream, ginger, mace, a teaspoonful of honey, a pinch of ground red chilli, a tablespoon of Chinese (soy) sauce, and a pinch of salt. Cut out the inside of a pineapple so that the peel forms a hollow container. Cut part of the inside of the fruit into small strips, add the crayfish mixture and stir together. Fill the pineapple with it, place in a pot with a little water, put the lid on tight, and allow to steam for twenty minutes. Take the mixture out of the peel, cover with a sour sauce, and serve.

This is perhaps a bit complicated, but the dish is well worth the trouble. When made in the right way it looks a bit like crumpled *mielie* bread but, as for the taste, that is ... well, quite unique. The pineapple flavour is particularly good. I sometimes replace the soy sauce with a glass of good brandy.

22 October 1943

---

1 That was in 1943. Today the African Life Centre is to be found there.

22
The Genuine Uintjie

Writing elsewhere on the subject of *waterblommetjies*,[1] I made the point that it is not really correct to regard them as *uintjies*,[2] and that the name really only applies to the bulb and not the foliage and flowers that we now use for our *waterblommetjies bredies*. An *uintjie* – really nothing but a little onion – is, as far as I know, always a bulb, and also always that strange kind of bulb that is surrounded by tissue and can be shelled. Such genuine *uintjies* have been known for ages. The old travellers who traversed the Cape a hundred years ago,[3] from Thunberg on, mentioned it. They said that the indigenous people used such bulbs for food, and they said it without any hint of surprise. This is itself unsurprising – after all, our forebears in the old European motherlands also ate *uintjies*. In the famous *Herbaal* of *Baas* Gerhardt,[4] the merits of different kinds of *uintjies* were discussed – some were suitable for inner or outer use as medicines, others again for peasant food. Without exception, they are all foreign to us here in South Africa. Our own kinds of *uintjie* were, of course, unknown to *Baas* Gerhardt.

After asking around a bit, I discovered that there is a difference of opinion among our own *uintjie* connoisseurs as to the genuine article. The name *uintjie* is generally given to an iris or *vlablom*,[5] so well known as a food that the learned botanists gave it the name *Moraea edulis*, or edible *vlablom*. There are many kinds of *Moraea* in our country, and some of the bulbs are poisonous, like those of the related family *Homeria* that we call the tulip. Then again there are edible tulips, although I would not advise anyone to make a tulip stew without a thorough knowledge of them. In his list of Afrikaans flower names, Dr Muir gives the name *uintjie* to our *waterblommetjie* and *Moraea edulis* only. Dr Fourcade, who has a thorough knowledge of the flora in the Humansdorp to Knysna area, also knows of only the two types of uintjie. In the southwestern districts (real *uintjie* country!) other kinds of *uintjie* are to be found. *Bobbejaanuintjies* are the bulbs of a *Babiana* type, which grows between the stones of the Olifants River and the Kamies Mountains and is rather difficult to dig up, although baboons manage it quite easily. *Hotnotsuintjies* are the bulbs of a type of sorrel, *Oxalis lupinifolia*: the beautiful picture of this type of flower in the quarterly magazine of the Pretoria herbarium was a painting of

---

1 See chapter 19.
2 An edible bulb, literally 'a little onion'.
3 The mid-nineteenth century. Leipoldt is being a little vague here. Thunberg was in the Cape from 1772-1775.
4 Gerard's *Herball*, 1597.
5 Literally, 'custard flower'.

uintjies sent from Springbok to an *uintjie* eater there, a few bulbs of which just happened to land in his garden by mistake. Another delicious kind is the bulb of *Cyanella capensis*, *bokuintjies* or *klei-uintjies*. Then there are also the little bulbs of the different *Moraea* types: in the Sandveld, for example, there is the large yellow *uintjie*, the purple *uintjie* and the *witblom-uintjie*, as well as the *slymblom-uintjie* and the *kaneel-uintjie*. They are all part of the *Moraea* family, and once you have seen the flower you will not easily confuse it with the simpler tulip flower.

We may quite possibly have many other edible bulbs. According to *Baas* Gerhardt, the bulbs of our chincherinchees are edible, and also those of *ferweeltjies*.[6] In comparison with the real, genuine *uintjies*, *Moraea edulis*, they are, however, all quite inferior.

When I was young there used to be an abundance of *uintjies*. An *outa* who was a shepherd used to bring bunches of them to the village. For a few *oulap*,[7] you could buy a bunch of anything from fifty to a hundred little bulbs that must have taken three to four hours to dig up as the *uintjie* embeds itself deep in the ground and it is usually in the hard Karoo clay that it finds its shelter. In sandy soil it is, of course, easier to dig it out, but connoisseurs will tell you that clay *uintjies* taste much better than sand *uintjies*.

A bunch like that provides plenty of food. Cut off the stalks and cook the bulbs with just enough water, preferably lukewarm, to cover them, and do not cook for too long. Fifteen to twenty minutes will suffice. Take them out, allow them to cool, and you can then eat them with relish as they are easily shelled. They taste like young potatoes or chestnuts; some kinds are less sweet than others, and the *Bobbejaanuintjie*, usually the largest, is mealier and therefore perhaps more suitable for further preparation. But cold cooked *uintjies*, eaten just like that, are already a delicacy.

You could, however, experiment a bit. Crush them in a mortar with a touch of nutmeg, mix with cream and a beaten egg, and place in the oven – which should be just as warm as that in which you would roast a guinea-fowl. If all goes well you will have a delicious soufflé on your hands.

Alternatively, stir the crushed *uintjies* with a touch of sugar, a pinch of ginger

---

6 *Sparaxis*.

7 Pennies.

and two or three eggs; and cook slowly in a earthenware pot. You will then have a delicious pudding that can be served with *moskonfyt*[8] as syrup, or with a wine sauce. If you would like a first-class soup, add a few cups of milk to a scraping of lemon peel, salt, a pinch of white pepper, and ground *uintjies*. Bring it to the boil once only and pour into the soup tureen, in which you have already whipped up an egg with a teaspoonful of cream and a little brandy. You could wish for nothing better. If you would like a thicker soup, add more ground *uintjies*; if you would like it thinner, more milk. My old *tannie* always used to sprinkle chopped parsley over it, but I do not fancy that, although it does make the white soup look pretty. *Uintjies* 'blend' well with all kinds of spice, because their own taste is not too strong. But you still have to be careful, as it is easy to spoil the *uintjie* taste by an excessive use of herbs or the use of herbs that are too strong.

The *tannie* whom I have already mentioned had vegetarian leanings in her latter days, and was thereby a very bad example to the family. We Bonades have always been liberal people: we eat everything that is tasty and cannot be bothered about what Dr Hay, or whoever, has to say. Anyway, my old *tannie* sometimes used *uintjie purée* to make 'artificial chops', just as some people now make them from lentils and beans. I consider it heretical to do such a thing, but each to his own taste. What this does show, however, is that with the *uintjie* as a foundation you can get up to all sorts of dietetical tricks.

If only we could get our *uintjies* onto the market. What would a Carême not have been able to do with them? My own experiments are curtailed year in and year out for lack of sufficient material. But I have been fortunate enough to succeed in making a delicious *uintjie* ice cream. And next year I shall try to use *uintjies* instead of chestnuts for that crown jewel of the culinary art, a Francatelli pudding.

29 October 1943

---

8 Grape syrup.

23
Biltong

When the long-awaited *Great Afrikaans Dictionary* appears, we will probably obtain certainty about the derivation of the word 'biltong'. I am familiar with what the lexicographers say about it, but their explanations do not entirely satisfy me. I would encourage them to do a little more research, to try and find out whether there was not some bastardisation long, long ago.

The Bonades' own library, which is reasonably well stocked, contains nothing at all helpful concerning the derivation of the word. My old *tannie*, relying on her recollection of what her great-grandmother told her, was convinced that it meant nothing other than what it should mean. 'It goes without saying, Karel,' she would always say, 'that it looks like a tongue and is cut from that part of the ox that it would not be decent for me to mention.'[1] She was a prudish old dame, who never managed to convince me. For I have never seen biltong that looks like a tongue, and biltong made from the buttock is not what I would call first-class. It is fillet that makes the best biltong, although I must admit that the large muscle often recommended for biltong (for example by Mrs Dijkman, and in our earliest cookbook, printed in Natal)[2] does make quite good biltong.

In Switzerland I came across genuine biltong. There they call it *bindenfleisch*, and it is under this name that it is known by *Larousse*. In Mexico I found biltong under the name of *carne secca*, which means 'dried meat'. Later, in South America, I came across it under the name of *tasajo*. It is found everywhere in the world for, after all, it is nothing more than dried meat.

There are as many recipes for such dried meat as there are for onion soup, some simple, like that of Dumas[3] (who always carves his onions with a razor), and some highly complicated, like that of Scappi,[4] who adds garlic, *duiwelsdrek*,[5] thyme, and who knows what other herbs and spices.

But just as in the case of onion soup, the taste of the biltong depends upon the quality of its main ingredient, the meat. It does not matter whether it is game or the meat of a tame animal, whether you make your biltong from a sable or from an ox – if your meat is not first-class, your biltong will be no good.

---

1 The Dutch word *bil* refers to a buttock.
2 See *Leipoldt's Food & Wine*, Stonewall Books, 2003, pp22, 27.
3 Alexandre Dumas (the Elder), author of *Grand dictionnaire de cuisine* (1873).
4 Bartolomeo Scappi, author of *Cuoco Secreto di Papa Pio Quinto* (1570).
5 *Asafoetida*.

This is all too evident in the awful dried-out ostrich biltong we sometimes have to make do with here in the south, and that tourists take to be the genuine version of our South African delicacy. I do not believe in trying to eliminate all evils in our society, or even in trying to curb them, with strict laws, but deep down I consider that nothing is as objectionable as when my fellow citizens palm off such 'biltong' on ignorant foreigners. I know that in trade, as in law, the principle holds: 'let the buyer beware'. But we have some fine assets – our wines, our brandies, our penguin eggs, our biltong – and it is in our own interests to make sure that these products have a good name.

Therefore, quality meat is the first prerequisite. A tip for the hunter – do not be satisfied with just cutting away what you cannot use at table, and drying it out on a string next to your tent. Choose some of the best meat. Preferably a muscle without sinew – the thick muscle-meat found alongside the spine, known as the *haasvleis*.[6] Cut off all the fat – there is enough fat in the tissue – and game biltong should never have outside fat. Rub it well with a mixture of salt, coriander seed, pepper, nutmeg, a touch of saltpetre and some vinegar to moisten it. Hang it up to be wind-dried. Rub it once again, and hang it up again until properly dry. Then you will have a first-class biltong that will be easy to grate, shave or cut into thin slices, that will keep for years and never lose its flavour if you keep it away from moist air. I know that this is not the usual way of doing it. The typical hunter leaves it to his workers to make the biltong. They cut what they get, muscle and sinew and whatever else comes with it, do not always salt it evenly, never use spices, and the biltong is seldom cut with skill. I grant that even biltong made in this way can taste good, but in comparison with that which is made with more care ... well, there really is no comparison.

Beef biltong is something completely different. It should not be grated, for well-made beef biltong is too moist to be scraped or grated. The proper way is to cut it into thin slices, which are then eaten with butter on nice fresh brown bread. Making this kind of biltong requires patience and knowledge. It also requires a good, preferably young, fat ox, with muscle tissue that is not yet tough. The biltong maker should choose his meat as soon as the ox is slaughtered. My oldest Cape recipe, that of Mrs Schwabe, says: 'Take the round muscle that leads to the bottom part of the leg, and choose one that is about as thick as your forearm'. I do not know exactly what she is referring to. There are different round (ie buttock) muscles and I myself would, as I have

---

6 Fillet.

said, prefer the thick round muscles found next to the spine above the walking muscles of the fore or hind legs. But whatever you choose, prepare it well. Cut it so that it is even and longish, but not more than at most eight pounds in weight – a weight of three or four pounds is probably best. Lighter pieces will dry out too quickly. Remove carefully every piece of sinew you can see. It is not necessary to remove all the outside fat as well; a certain amount of fat round part of the biltong is actually recommended.

Once a piece is cut and dried a little, beat it a bit with a piece of wood – that will bruise the outside tissue somewhat so that the pickle can penetrate better. Rub with a mixture of salt, pepper, saltpetre, coriander seed, nutmeg, mace, and a pinch of ground ginger. My old recipes say 'with saltpetre, salt, brown sugar and anise'. The brown sugar I will go along with – the anise never!

Is the pickle necessary? Opinions differ. The best beef biltong I ever had was pickled biltong. The *tannie* who made it – and she was a master of the art – let it lie for days in the mixture already described, which she moistened with brandy and vinegar. Every day she rubbed the biltong well; every third day she squeezed it a bit and then put it back into the pickle. Then she dried it well, covered it with cheesecloth and hung it in the chimney, where it stayed for nearly three months. Now that was real biltong. It was as hard as a stone on the outside, and inside it was as soft and tender as lamb. A slice of it was like a cut ruby, red and transparent, and so beautiful and even that you could look at it with delight even while your mouth was watering to taste it.

Let me add this. Of all the meats, biltong is possibly the easiest to digest, and the best food. I do not know why. But it is a fact that thin slices of beef biltong (and the same holds for grated game biltong) almost melt away in your stomach. They are digested without using much energy. This makes biltong, if it is first-class, one of the best foods for sick people. But then a bad, and especially a dirty, fly-bespeckled biltong is an inferior food, and much more so if a quarter of it consists of indigestible sinew.

26 November 1943

24
Delicious Snail Dishes

In *Oom* Danie's vineyard there are many snails. 'They don't really do any harm, *Neef*,' Oom Danie said to me, 'but if the workers don't get rid of them, they may multiply.'

'*Ag nee*,' said Oom Danie a bit later, when I told him that his own forefathers had imported the snails from European vineyards, 'that is too terrible for words.'

'No, really *Oom*. They made only one mistake. They wanted to have the large, Italian snail here, but it perished on board ship and only the vineyard snail survived the journey.'

'And what on earth did they want to do with them?' *Oom* Danie wanted to know. 'Was it to get rid of some or other louse? But vines don't have lice!'

'No, no, it was to eat them, *Oom*.'

And to *Oom* Danie's dismay, I took a few dozen of his vineyard snails to the kitchen and made a snail dish. It took quite a bit of persuasion to get the old fellow to try them, but after the children and even *Tant* Hessie had declared it to be '*lekker*',[1] he did. Now *Tant* Hessie makes a snail dish every now and then.

For the vineyard snail is a real delicacy. Well prepared, it is one of the most delicious foods there is.

It is also called the garden snail, and its scientific name is *Helix aspersa*. Here in South Africa we have over six hundred of its nephews and nieces, and some of them I consider to be much more delicious. There are, for instance, the beautiful large veld snails of the Bushveld – the striped one, *Achatina zebra*, yields nearly one and a half ounces of meat. The largest is *Achatina immaculata*, which sometimes weighs more than a pound, but that is unfortunately only found in the dense parts along the coast of St Lucia Bay. There is *Metachatina kraussi* from Pondoland, and also the tasty white-yellow veld snail from the Richtersveld, with the long scientific name of *Trigonephrus porphyrostoma*. Then there are literally hundreds of smaller snails, of which the tiniest (and from a culinary point of view worthless), *Opeas sublineare*, was discovered by the late Dr Purcell in Namaqualand. It is a longish snail barely as large as a thin *naartjie* pip. All these smaller kinds are possibly edible, but not worth the effort to clean.

---

1 Delicious.

Snails usually eat vegetables – there are a few carnivorous types, but they need not be considered. Some are regarded as inedible because they cause sickness in the eater. This is due to the fact that they feed on poisonous plants such as black nightshade and hellebore, and also, in the case of the vineyard snail, because they sometimes, without any harm to themselves, feed on young leaves sprayed with some or other poison. It is well known that snails can tolerate chemical poisons that are deadly to other animals.

With a bit of care, however, it is easy enough to collect snails that are completely harmless. The snail is one of the oldest of foods. Our forefathers ate them raw – it was only later that cooks discovered how to prepare them in a refined manner for the table. The vineyard snail was always the most popular, but the Roman snail, which is larger, was the more famous. Today snails are still a popular food in Europe, where they are fattened artificially by snail farmers who prepare them for the market and see that they are given only the finest vine leaves and salad or cabbage to feed on. Nice juicy snails, fattened for market, are quite expensive. Their price before the war was about two shillings a dozen, which was good value.

It is perhaps too much to hope for that snails will become popular here in South Africa, but they are still a nutritious, useful food; and where there are vineyards or vegetable gardens we will always be able to gather enough of them for a good snail dish almost all year round. But take care that the snails have not fed on certain plants they love, such as the agapanthus or bush marigolds found in the garden. It is best to take snails from vine leaves, for then you can be sure they are healthy and harmless.

Say you have collected a dozen beautiful medium to large snails. How should you prepare them?

There are many options, but one recipe that can serve as a model for all the others is the following. It is none other than the recipe preferred by the famous Carême.

'Wash the snails well in salt water; then put them in lukewarm water – never use boiling water, as this congeals the jelly-like substance in them. Take them one by one in your hand and remove the snail with a bent piece of wire from its shell, placing it in a saucepan with some cold water. Boil the shells well in water with a bit of soda, until they are cooked clean. Then remove them from the water, brush them inside and out with a small brush, and place them on a piece of paper to dry.

'Now take the saucepan with the snails and cover them with a glassful of white wine and a few spoonfuls of strong meat *bouillon* or meat soup; add a sliced onion, a blade of mace, a teaspoon of chopped parsley, a scraping of garlic, and salt and pepper to taste. Stew slowly over a not-too-rapid fire – it usually takes no more than twenty minutes for the snails to become nice and soft. Now remove them and replace each one in its shell. Thicken the sauce in the saucepan with some fine flour or maizena and an egg yolk, and pour some in each snail shell, so that the shell is nicely filled to the top. Finally, close the door of each snail house with a layer of butter. Place the shells in the oven to warm well, and serve covered with what remains of the sauce. Your guest takes a little wooden lance, picks every snail out of its shell, and eats it with relish. Six snails are usually more than enough for each guest as they are quite rich.'

There are several other methods – *comtesse Riguidi, à l'arlésienne, à la bourguignonne* (supposed to be the favourite of our Huguenot forefathers), *à la chablaisienne; à la poulette; à la Brimont*, and so forth, that – if you feel like it – you could look up in *Larousse*. But the recipe given above is one of the best – it brings out the genuine, unspoiled taste of the little creature, and I speak from experience when I say that it really is delicious.

Have it preferably without any accompaniment – it is worth it. But if you really wish to have something with it, eat it with some toast and butter that can be soaked in the sauce. What to drink with it is a matter each must resolve according to his own taste. I prefer a not-too-strong red wine – therefore not a Burgundy, but rather a claret. Some connoisseurs declare that you can only have a swig of Bols with snails; others again prefer a sweet white wine. It is all a matter of taste.

7 January 1944

25
The Pawpaw

When I was young, we never used the word 'pawpaw'. We always called it a *'bobotie* fruit', or simply a *'bobotie'*. It grew here and there on the farms, but was rarely found on the Cape market and therefore regarded as something of a scarcity. Today everyone calls it *papaya* or 'pawpaw', and the bobotie that we get to eat is mostly not the real thing.

We regard the pawpaw as a fruit and usually eat it raw. But it is as good, or even better, as a vegetable.

No one really knows where it comes from. The botanists claim that *Carica papaya* (as it has been scientifically baptised, and the American *papaya* that we are not familiar with is not even its cousin) originally hails from South America, whence it was carried across the Pacific Ocean to a multitude of islands found in that great sea, so that it became naturalised in each and every tropical or semi-tropical country. The tree grows wild in the tropical jungle, but seldom bears the beautiful large fruit that we find on our cultivated trees. In its wild state the pawpaw is not much to write home about. It is edible, but that is about all. *Oubaas* Lindley,[1] who knows his jungles well, wrote somewhere: 'All tropical fruit are edible, but there are few that are really worth eating'. He probably had the wild pawpaw in mind when he made this pessimistic remark.

The tame pawpaw is found, on the market and in the fruit shops, when it is already ripened until soft. It is then full of fruit sugar, and you can serve it on its own as a sweet dish. Even in this state, it is not to be missed as a *hors d'oeuvre* or dessert, with or without lemon and sugar. When ripe and soft, you cannot do much more with it. It is then only suitable as an ingredient for a fruit-salad, although a good cook will on occasion, for instance when he has a wild duck or coot, whip it up with mace, breadcrumbs, an egg yolk and a pinch of nutmeg as a first-class filling. When less ripe, you can stew it. Cut it into neat squares, after peeling, and place the pieces in a saucepan with a cup of brown sugar, a glass of brandy, a piece of *naartjie* peel, and a shard of stick cinnamon. Stew slowly but well. Serve with whipped cream. My old *tannie* always used to add a glass of Van der Hum, but that does not really make much difference if there is already some cinnamon and *naartjie* peel in the syrup. The less ripe, the better this recipe will be. I prefer to make my stewed pawpaw with hard, not-at-all-ripe fruit. Then it comes out beautifully white when stewed carefully and well – stewing it too quickly makes it go brown.

---

1 John Lindley (1799-1865), a famous botanist and horticulturalist.

Both taste good, but I prefer the nice white one.

You can also make a pudding of it. Grind the flesh of the fruit to a pulp, and mix with sugar, spice (choose according to your own taste, but possibly ginger, cinnamon and a pinch of allspice is best – nutmeg will not do, nor will cloves or *naartjie* peel), the yolks of a few eggs, and a few spoons of finely sifted flour. Some people also add finely chopped grapefruit peel, a few raisins, and ground almonds. You can stuff this pudding with just about anything, Carême said, but as overloading does not ennoble the end result, I would advise you not to be too extravagant with the flavours. Place in a mould or in a cloth sprinkled with flour, and steam slowly. Serve with a sweet-sour butter sauce. Or even better, if you want to be very Afrikaans, make a sweet sauce from *skilpadbessies*[2] or, if you can get them (this is alas no longer so easy), from wild apricot berries,[3] and pour it over the pudding. The beautiful red colour goes well with the creamy yellow pudding, and enhances the taste.

You can also make pawpaw ice cream. Beat together, this time with cream, sugar syrup, grated lemon peel, egg yolk, and a few drops of orange oil. Place in the fridge and, as soon as it starts stiffening, beat again and add a squeeze of lemon juice. Freeze well, and serve with sweet cookies or rusks. You can decorate your ice cream – which is by no means to improve it – by pouring over it an iced thick sweet sauce, made from strawberries or raspberries. That is what the American cooks call a 'sundae', although they indulge in it every day of the week.

Preserved and crystallised pawpaw is something I have seldom come across, although there is no reason to be scornful of it. The fruit needs to be quite green, and the preparation is as for *spanspek*[4] preserve. I have also come across pawpaw jam, but this was made from dried pawpaw, which is unknown here, although it is sold in America.

I esteem the pawpaw more highly as a vegetable than a fruit. But then it needs to be barely full-grown and the pips still need to be quite white. Steamed in water and served with a sour butter sauce, it is a fine dish. You can also make a first-class soup and a tasty *purée* with it. For the soup, take a medium-to-large green fruit, peel and remove the pips. Cut into pieces. Chop up a large

---

2 Literally 'tortoiseberries'; the fruit of *Nylandtia spinosa*.
3 Probably the fruit of *Dovyalis caffra*, the Kei apple.
4 Musk-melon.

onion and fry along with the pawpaw in butter, without spoiling the colour. Add some chopped parsley. Pour onto it four cups of water (or meat soup, if you prefer), move the saucepan to where there is less heat, and let it cook for an hour and a half. Strain through a colander, forcing the vegetable through it. Then place it back in the saucepan, with a blade of mace, and salt and pepper to taste. Allow it to boil, rub a tablespoon of maizena into a cup of sweet milk, and add the mixture to the soup. Stir well, and allow it to cook for a few minutes. Serve with toast. This soup can be made richer by adding half a cup of cream and a lump of butter.

A tasty way of serving pawpaw is that of my old *tannie*. She diced her peeled green pawpaw and steamed it softly for twenty minutes, adding salt. Then she took a deep earthenware dish, greased it with butter or fat, and decked it out with a layer of cooked pawpaw, a layer of peeled tomatoes and chopped onions on top of that, then another layer of pawpaw, and so on until the dish was full. Over that she poured a cup of meat-roast sauce, and put the dish in the oven to bake. I can tell you, it was a feast. But as far as I remember, her masterpiece was the filled pawpaw. She cut it in two, took out the pips, and boiled it for ten minutes in salt water. Then she took it out, let it drip, and filled it with a *frikkadel*[5] filling made of minced ham, mushroom sauce, and egg yolk to bind it. She put a sail yarn around it, baked it in the oven, and served it with a white or sour sauce. Delicious!

My memory of this last dish is not quite as pleasant as my recollection of its taste, for it was while eating it that I – then still wet behind the ears – decided to make known to the world my knowledge of nature. I enquired whether the *bobotie* tree in my *oom's* garden was male or female, which *tannie* found 'unedifying' – with the result that my *oom* and I were soon visiting the garden where there was a quince-hedge.[6] Whenever I eat filled pawpaw today I can still smell the borrie quinces.

21 January 1944

---

5 Meatball.

6 Canes for administering corporal punishment to errant boys, *kweperlatte*, were selected from the quince hedge.

26
Mielies

Of all our imported vegetables the *mielie*[1] has probably become naturalised the best. We are very much a *mielie*-eating nation. Whether or not this is an advantage we can defer until later. I do not, for the moment, wish to expound on the nutritional value of *mielie*-meal – that I will leave to the Food Council, which can inform us according to latest scientific hypotheses. I merely wish to say something about the *mielie* as a vegetable for the table.

This happens to be what it is really well suited for. What can be more delicious, soft and appetising than young corn on the cob, properly done, creamy-white or golden-yellow, each 'pip' as round and fat as if it were chiselled on the cob? What genuinely Afrikaans dish do we have that can compete with a Transvaal *tannie's mielie* bread? Anyone who has eaten either, or both, will savour the experience deep in his memory.

But when dealing with *mielies*, as with any other kind of vegetable, one should not go about it as though neither art nor taste is required to make a delicious dish of it. Choose the *mielies* carefully, bearing in mind what a healthy, well-cultivated *mielie* should look like when commandeered for use. I emphasise that one should pick 'healthy' *mielies*. So many of those we are offered today – and that at two hundred per cent more than we used to pay for them – are not as healthy as they should be. The *mielie* is the seed of a grass, of which the 'beard' represents the *stamens*. Pollination takes place with the help of the wind, and the quality of the *mielie* pip depends upon whether pollination has taken place properly or only partly. Furthermore, the appearance and juiciness of the *mielie* pips are influenced by the nutrition the *mielie* plant has extracted from the earth and the air – both before it 'flowered', and after pollination. Just like people, all vegetables require certain minerals for their health – phosphates, calcium, iron, and probably many other elements as well. They only need a little, but when even that is lacking they cannot develop into healthy vegetables, and the bulbs or seeds that we use are then not completely first-class. The first thing you will notice is a lack of firmness – the *mielie* pip, for instance, will no longer have the beautiful, round, shiny appearance it should have. This is the result of too little moisture. The second is a change in colour – the pip will no longer be an even white or yellow but will have a greyish appearance and the leaves will be wilted, with yellow or brown freckles. The older the *mielie*, the worse it gets, but you may also find noticeable signs of undernourishment and unhealthiness in young *mielies*.

---

1 Maize.

Avoid such *mielies*. Choose only young ones with proper pips arranged in even rows. You will of course not find them in completely straight rows – nothing in the *mielie* world is completely straight – those rows that look straight are really growing in a spiral. At least, this is what my friends who know something of botany tell me – and who am I to express 'clever remarks' on the subject?

Should one cook the *mielie* with or without the inside leaves? The Americans always cook it with the inside leaves, which are removed along with the beard when the *mielie* is done. Our way, which I happen to prefer, is to peel off the leaves, to rid the *mielie* of every strand of beard, to immerse it in boiling water for a few minutes, and then to cook it slowly with some salt in the water. Maria then sees to it that it does not cook for too long. It is difficult to know exactly when to stop. Cooking for too long will remove the juiciness from the pips – they are then no longer nice and round, but develop sides, and the one no longer huddles shoulder-to-shoulder with the other as it should, but leans over a bit, as if shy to maintain its place in the row. I admit wholeheartedly that I have not yet mastered the art – as every Ayah appears to have done – of cooking *mielies* perfectly. Therefore I appreciate them all the more when I come across them on the farm in the *mielie* season, especially when they are still the old-fashioned 'bread *mielies*'. They compare to the smaller sweetcorn that has become fashionable as the old-fashioned *spanspek*[2] compares to the modern small ones you first have to keep in your fridge before you can enjoy them properly.

Leave the *mielies* to dry in a colander as soon as they are done, without letting them cool down, and serve – not with just anything, of course. A good green *mielie* can stand on its own legs – or pips. If there is butter on the table, those who want to spread it on their *mielie* may do so. But please do not serve molten butter in a little saucepan with your mielies. And please, not the affected '*mielie* sauce' I have come across on occasion, of butter, nutmeg and egg yolk. This is an insult and an affront! The taste of a well-cooked green *mielie* is too delicate and too fine to be blended with any other taste or flavour. And for precisely that reason one should also not have any wine with one's *mielie*. Wait until you have dealt with it properly before you reach for your glass. And of course, it must be eaten 'off the cob'. To cut away the pips and devour them with a spoon or fork – well, that is about as abominable as serving it with nutmeg and a sour sauce.

---

2 Musk-melon.

Mielies also make an excellent *purée* that can be used as the foundation of a delicious soup. One of the best recipes is the American corn soup with mussels; another is *mielie* and green bean soup. The vegetarian can also bake all sorts of *mielie* cakes if he wishes. This is, however, not the best way of using *mielies*. The cooked green *mielie* on its own is the best way to have it.

The one exception is our delicious Afrikaans *mielie* bread. Made from young *mielies*, it is one of the best dishes I know – even when made from *mielies* that are past their best, it is a work of art that deserves to be more widely known. I find it nowhere in the recipe books of other countries – even the all-knowing *Larousse*, who has plenty to say about the most insignificant of things, is silent about it. But in South America, home of the *mielie*, it is well known and popular enough, although it is seldom found in restaurants. Our own Afrikaans recipes differ in some respects from each other. In the older ones, eggs are seldom used. The boiled green *mielies* are cut from the cob, ground, beaten up with milk, cream, a touch of sugar, a pinch of salt, nutmeg – some recipes say mace – and salt to taste, then placed in a mould and steamed. The addition of eggs makes the 'bread' richer and binds it somewhat more, but this is not really necessary and the old people preferred it without eggs. When it has been properly steamed, the 'bread' is cut into slices and served as a vegetable dish with meat. It can also be served with a sweet sauce as a desert. Either way, it is a delicious delicacy and can be regarded as one of our genuinely Afrikaans dishes, one that tastes as good warm as it does cold.

17 March 1944

27
Cooking with Grapes

'No, what are you talking about? You can't cook grapes!'

The young woman had learnt domestic science in a modern school – I believe she even did it for matric, something that further lowered my already declining respect for examinations, as the woman cannot even cook a potato properly. She can go on about vitamins and nutrition until the cows come home, but she is ignorant of the art of cooking.

Imagine saying that one cannot cook grapes!

Going back to my childhood, I can see old Ayah Hanna, the cook at the White House in Strand Street, standing at the kitchen table. I can hear, coming from the yard, where *Oubaas* Haylett kept some kind of zoo, the clacking of pheasants and the cooing of tufted pigeons, as from the kitchen you could see the cages and admire the game. It is February again, but not like today – for Strand Street was not then a place where the life of a pedestrian was in danger, and the horse-tram that went by was a decent, controlled mode of transport unlike the hazardous commotion one experiences nowadays. On the table was a basketful of Canaan grapes, enormous bunches such as are seldom seen today. The Ayah was busy peeling the grapes and carefully removing the pips.

'It's for the fish, *Basie*,' she explained, and when I later had some fish it became as clear to me as daylight that you could indeed in certain instances cook grapes with great success.

The Ayah's recipe for grapes with fish is well known to cooks. What Carême has to say about it is that the grapes should not be too sweet, although he uses muscadel grapes that I find far too sweet. As we no longer get the Canaan type of grape, I would recommend one of the newer Algerian kinds, or perhaps a Waltham Cross or Raisin Blanc, but any table or wine grape can actually be used. They have to be peeled carefully and the pips removed, then you steam them without water – they are juicy enough for that. They can then be used in a variety of dishes.

One of them is sole. Fillets of sole, with mussels stewed in white wine, a blade of mace, a pinch of salt and a touch of anchovy, served on a layer of grapes (cooked as described above), is a beautiful dish that is still too little known. The same can be achieved with steamed hake or shad. The strange aftertaste given to the fish is something one has to get used to, but it is well worth the effort.

Peeled grapes, even peeled black grapes, are, with a few exceptions, never coloured, but always white or light green, transparent and nicely soft. The colour of a grape – which is actually a highly complex sugary combination, a glucoside – is due only to the skin; and only when the grape is very old or bruised will some of the colour permeate the flesh of the grape. When you cook black grapes, the flesh will also acquire something of the colour – as for instance with Isabella or Katalba grapes, that are otherwise very nicely green when cooked. The pips contain tannin, which leaves a bitter taste when cooked with the fruit. One should therefore get rid of both pips and skins.

It is rather strange that here in our winelands, where we regard grapes as the most important fruit for a quarter of the year, the product of the vine is so seldom used in the kitchen. Take vine leaves. You never find them in the home, except perhaps to decorate a bunch of grapes. Yet there are many ways in which they can be used. From young leaves you can make soup, a sort of *julienne* with a delicate taste. You can wrap *frikkadels*[1] in vine leaves, then roast or braise them. Quails in vine leaves is a well-known dish in Europe, and is well worth trying here. The young stalks of the vine can be steamed and served as a kind of spinach or asparagus; in Germany they are eaten like that, as are the young stalks of hop plants. Older leaves can be used as a wrapping for chops stewed in butter.

We do not use grapes for sweets either, although it is one of the best fruits to serve stewed or steamed, with or without the addition of sugar and spices, either hot or cold. In America grapes are often used in a dessert of sugared fruit. Here we seldom find a dessert like that containing grapes. Perhaps this is due to the fact that the preparation is a lot of trouble and requires some patience. The skins have to be taken off and the pips removed, which is a bother and takes time. But without a little trouble you will not get far when it comes to the art of cooking.

There are some so-called table grapes, especially those destined for the export market, that cannot really be eaten in any way other than cooked or as an addition to another dish, as far as I can tell. One of them is the beautiful Flaming Tokai – that is oh-so-grandly coloured and perfect in appearance, but tastes a bit like chaff. Try cooking with it, adding a bit of nutmeg, when you do a nice fat leg of lamb. Or in a fruit salad consisting of orange, pineapple and pawpaw. For that it should be steamed first, for as it stands it

---

1 Meatballs.

is not a particularly nice grape. When my friends give me a basketful as a gift, I shell the grapes and cook them (without first taking out the pips) with sugar, cinnamon and white wine, and make of it a *macédoine*[2] with the help of some seaweed. Better kinds of grape do not require this cumbersome treatment. Hanepoot, for instance, can be added to a fruit salad just like that, or steamed and served with fish or meat.

I once treated the domestic science *niggie* to dove breast – called 'supremes' by well-read cooks – with a little mound of steamed hanepoot grapes, served on a piece of toast dipped into a meat sauce with a dash of brandy in it. She later asked me whether it was something out of a tin. And this is what we call a matriculated girl! Why on earth do we waste so much money on what we call 'education'?

31 March 1944

---

2 Fruit in jelly.

28
Vegetable Dishes

In the end, after all is said and done, we get our nourishment from the ground. The scientifically enlightened person will rightly object: 'With respect, Mr Bonade, that is wrong. We get it from the sun.' But what matter, for sunshine – at any rate the life energy radiated by the sun – is gathered by plants, and anyone who eats the plants uses the energy of the sun. Cattle eat grass and crops; meat-eating people eat cattle, and get their energy that way. But we can just as easily go direct to the source of the energy, eating the vegetables themselves.

I am not proposing that we should all become vegetarians. There is no reason at all for giving up meat completely, although as a nation we tend to eat more meat than we really need for our nourishment and health. But we can mix meat and vegetables, and so enjoy the best of both.

Green, uncooked vegetables are only used in salads – and far too sparingly. It is not clear whether such uncooked vegetables really transfer all their energy to the body. The human body is not really equipped, like that of a sheep or a hamster, to extract the last bit of nutrition from a lettuce leaf. But we manage to get enough for our daily requirements, which makes it worthwhile eating vegetables raw.

To get more out of them they should be cooked in such a way that the nutritional value is improved, not lessened. My niece, who completed a course in domestic science at university, tells me that cooking vegetables often destroys their 'vitamin value'.

'Don't cry, sweetheart,' I told her, 'for vitamin value is not something the good cook bothers about. He knows only too well that it is a minor consideration, and that the main thing is to serve the vegetables in a way that makes them tasty and digestible.' She prefers not to believe me, quoting learned experts and newspaper articles that proclaim there is more treasure in a guava than a gold mine. This kind of 'learning' makes me despair of the future of our nation.

Do not therefore make too much of vitamins when you are dealing with vegetables. A carrot, a turnip, an onion, a cabbage, a cauliflower, spinach, *mielies*, maracas, sweet potatoes, runner beans or cucumbers – whatever you can get hold of – is something greatly improved by proper cooking, and just as easily spoiled by careless handling in the kitchen. Preserve the flavour of the vegetables, where possible preserve the juicy crispness that makes them 'snap between your teeth', and preserve especially the valuable minerals.

Do not therefore 'boil them up in cold water'. That is a good method for making vegetable soup, but it is not how you cook vegetables properly. Cook them in water that is already boiling if you must, but rather steam them in their own juices, with the lid tightly on. Very juicy vegetables, like cucumbers and brinjals, are done in a few minutes; others, that may look as juicy but are not – like pumpkin and marrows, which have more fibre – take longer.

And please do not add any bicarbonate of soda. Bicarbonate of soda has a specific purpose in cooking, to curb sourness, but never to preserve the colour – be it green or yellow – of cooked vegetables. Use it, therefore, when you need a *purée* of tomatoes or a tomato soup, and then with great skill and care. But do not simply add it when cooking beans, peas, cabbage, or any other green vegetable. There is one exception, steamed purslane – a vegetable used all too rarely by us, although it is found in every garden and farmyard – with sorrel: this requires a pinch of bicarbonate of soda.

Spice, salt and pepper – well, this is a matter of taste. I find that we tend to overdo the salt. Most vegetables need little salt and, especially when they have a delicate flavour, just as little spice. My old teacher in the culinary art always used to add herbs, and there is a lot to be said for it if the flavour of the herbs does not drown but enhances that of the vegetable. I do not like cooking young peas with mint because the mint overwhelms the shy, delicate taste of the peas; a leaf of rosemary, on the other hand, brings out their taste as does a dash of sugar. In the case of a vegetable with a strong flavour like asparagus, herbs and spices are neither necessary nor advisable, although I have had this vegetable stewed with ginger and nutmeg – sheer barbarity, such as one would expect from my niece with her theoretical training! It was her concoction, after she treated us to 'cocktails' *nogal*.

Of all our vegetables, cabbage is perhaps treated with the least respect. And yet it is one of the best, and also one of the most delicious when prepared properly. There are literally hundreds of different kinds, and every year a new one is cultivated that can in one way or another claim to have advantages not possessed by its predecessors. But in the end one kind does not differ very much from another. They all have strange, juicy leaves, rich in mineral salts and vegetable acids, and a pleasant taste.

The best way of cooking a cabbage is that described in our old recipes. Steam the cabbage, after washing it thoroughly in cold water. (Some recipes say: 'let it lie in cold water for a few hours', but that does not improve the taste.)

As soon as the cabbage is soft, which usually takes fifteen to twenty minutes – depending on whether you have to do with a very young head or one already going grey, put it, as my oldest recipe says, 'in a colander and pour cold water over it. Shake dry, place in a saucepan with butter, nutmeg and pepper, and allow to steam slowly.' In this way you preserve the green of the leaves, if that is what you want. The greenest cabbage is *boerekool*,[1] with its frummeled leaves, but its taste is not the best. Brussels sprouts, a refined type of cabbage, require careful, one might almost say loving, treatment. When cooked just a little too much, their fibres lose their juicy crispness.

Another vegetable we do not treat well is the turnip. The taste and flavour of a turnip are regarded as being less than aristocratic, and only rarely will you find a dish of well-cooked turnips. Yet there are few root vegetables that taste better than young turnips, steamed quickly and then '*gefruit*',[2] as the old Dutch cookbooks say, in butter. You have to use young turnips, as an old turnip root that has become spongy should never appear on a civilised table.

And what a delicious treasure we neglect by using cucumbers only for salads. Here and there I find them with a filling of mince meat that is suitable neither for them nor for the guest, who deserves something better. A young steamed cucumber is a fine dish, but it needs to be prepared skilfully lest it become too soggy. One has to go to work with the same care one would use on all the different kinds of marrow. The old Cape way of dicing them and roasting them in the oven with cinnamon and sugar is a variation we should not forget. But the best, apart from simply steaming, with or without butter and nutmeg, is the Italian way – very young marrows that are still milky are cut in thin slices and cooked in boiling oil.

28 April 1944

---

1 Kale.
2 Fried until brown.

29
Baking under the Ash

The old way of preparing food by baking or roasting it under the ash is not, as many assume, a genuinely Afrikaans custom. It is found in the cooking of every nation. Those who nose around to discover everything about the habits of our forefathers maintain, albeit with some reservations, that a certain ritual meaning used to be attached to the custom of cooking food 'under the ash'. It originated, they say, from the secret gatherings of the druids, who used to roast human flesh at clandestine meetings in the lanes of the priests – lanes of oak trees. If this were true, the custom of 'roasting under the ash' would have come to us from England. In fact it came direct from France, where in the district of Perigord it is still today regarded as one of the noblest ways of preparing food. Historically we have inherited many customs from the border area that previously used to be English and where, during the time of the English occupation of the south of France, English customs became deeply entrenched.

But the historical aspect is not our primary concern. What we are interested in is the method by which it is done.

Baking or roasting under the ash used to be easy on a traditional open fireplace. Today it is very difficult. So please do not try to 'roast under the ash' with electricity – I take it that my reader is serious enough about the culinary art to regard it as something great and beautiful, and would therefore hardly wish thereby to dry out his food.

As there are no longer open fireplaces, we have to make do with the dry heat of the oven. Roasting under the ash is something we can do while on an outing in the veld – food prepared in this way is also at its best in such an environment. What is more delicious than a lamb chop braaied on a grill over rhinoceros bush[1] smoke? Or what is juicier and tastier than a pheasant roasted beneath the warm ash? Not to mention a meat dish roasted in an ant-hill oven. Many of my readers may never have had the opportunity of trying out something like that but, if they do get the chance, let me beg them to roast a sheep's head, a large Muscovy duck, a turkey or a little lamb in it. One of my not-to-be-forgotten memories is of the first time – it was on the occasion of a Dingaan's Day[2] feast – I tasted an ox-head that was roasted whole, with its horns and skin intact, in an anthill oven. The meat of the cheeks and the palate – well, I can only make a gesture like that of the Coloured elder when he spoke of the juice of the vine in his sermon!

---

1 *Renosterbos*, Elytropappus rhinocerotis.
2 A South African public holiday on 16 December, now known as the Day of Reconciliation.

With our current problems in the kitchen we do not have to completely deny 'baking under the ash' its rightful place. In a good Swedish oven, even the much more expensive new models one finds nowadays, you can 'bake' very well. I find potatoes baked in an oven like that just as tasty as those baked under the ash, and that goes for sweet potatoes too. The connoisseur will perhaps claim that it depends on the kind of ash you use. I will grant this when it comes to *taaibos*[3] ash. It may have a real, though very slight, influence on the taste of a sweet potato. But that could also just be the imagination. When you roast or bake beneath the ash, you do not get the direct blending of food flavour with smoke flavour that you would get, for instance, when you *braai* a piece of meat on the grill over a wood fire. By roasting in an anthill oven, you can of course influence the food made in it. I know of an old *tannie* who, after the oven was nice and warm, cast a handful of the leaves of a certain bush into it – the bush had a strong herb-like smell, and the meat roasted in that anthill oven was particularly delicious. I never managed to find out what bush it was as the *tannie* was very secretive about it.

Another way is to 'pot' cook. Put the food in an earthenware or iron pot after first stewing or cooking it a little, and while the fire is burning beneath it, place hot coals on the lid. In this way you will get heat from above and below. It is an imitation of 'baking under the ash', but too tedious and bothersome, and the heat cannot be controlled. The schooled cook uses a 'salamander' to give his food – such as soufflés – a brown colour on top. This also is not the genuine way of roasting under the ash.

We should 'roast under the ash' much more than we do. Take potatoes, for instance. I maintain – and I can support this with all sorts of wonderful scientific arguments – that potatoes are never worth more than two *oulap*[4] a pound; at a higher price they are simply not worth eating as they have very little nutritional value – about as much as milk. If you peel and cook them, they are worth even less. You should therefore always cook them in their skins. Potatoes that are cooked unpeeled are, however, not to everyone's taste and require further treatment before being served. But when they are roasted under the ash, you get everything that is in them. The same goes for sweet potatoes. Remember also that this way of cooking clearly shows whether the potatoes are first-class or not. A second-rate potato will not bake evenly and will never be mealy, while the least bit of *vrotpootjie*[5] will also be immediately apparent.

---

3   *Rhus*. The leaves of some species are resinous.
4   Pennies.
5   Blackleg

One can use this method of cooking food for a number of other vegetables, and of course also for any kind of fish or meat. Larger fish do not even have to be wrapped in paper or dough – just as in the case of the ox-head, its skin can be used to temper the heat. Perhaps the best *galjoen* I have ever tasted was one – an enormous one – that had been freshly caught and was baked on the beach under seaweed ash. Time and again I have tried to make as delicious a *galjoen* in my own kitchen, but always without success – possibly because it is only under such conditions that one is able to achieve the same taste, flavour and juiciness.

To cover the meat or fish first with clay is a way of cooking I have very seldom seen among our people, but it is worth remembering. Another wonderful memory is how I once had *jakkalskos* that was *braaied*; the fruit – it is really the seed tube of an underground parasite – was first folded up in pumpkin leaves, then placed under the ash until the outside peel was charred. As far as chestnuts and *barsmielies*[6] are concerned, I need say nothing – they are more or less child's play in comparison with the serious preparation of food under the influence of dry heat from above, below and around. This is what 'roasting or baking under the ash' means, and it is one of the very best ways of cooking food.

28 July 1944

---

6 Bursting mielies.

30
Greens

Greens are, briefly (remembering that, as Multatuli declared, all definitions are problematic, and this one is therefore also disputable), the green leaves of garden vegetables, or sometimes the as yet undeveloped fruit or seed that contains the green plant colour, called chlorophyll by learned people. It is therefore largely leaf-fibre consisting of cellulose, in which all sorts of chemical substances are to be found. These chemical substances are what give greens their nutritional value.

It goes without saying that chemical substances, no matter what their nature, can be transformed by heat or by interacting with other chemical substances. This happens daily when we boil, braise or in some or other way prepare our vegetables for eating. In most cases the change the vegetable undergoes is not so drastic that its nutritional value is greatly reduced, but it is enough for the cooked green to differ from the raw version. The tubes within the tissue of the leaves hold vegetable juice that contains amino acids and mineral solutions, and the most important changes brought about by cooking the vegetable take place in these juices. Some of them are coagulated or stiffened by the heat; others are transformed into more complex substances; yet others are destroyed, either by the heat itself or by being dissolved in the water in which we cook the vegetables. The last of these is something the good cook will deliberately try to achieve when dealing with a vegetable containing bad-tasting or even poisonous ingredients. Sorrel, for instance, which is loaded with the poisonous sorrel acid, loses most of it when boiled because the poison dissolves in the boiling water and is thereby removed. Similarly the first boiling of *waterblommetjies* rids that delicious vegetable of the aftertaste left by the chemical substance that gives the boiling water its reddish colour. And in the same way young potatoes boiled in water lose the dangerously poisonous solanine they contain.

Most greens can be enjoyed without such preparation, and it is possibly a good thing to eat some raw vegetables every day. They have a crispness that is pleasant and tasty. Who does not enjoy a beautiful head of garden lettuce, with or without a salad dressing of oil and vinegar? It is a pity that we only regard lettuce as good enough to serve uncooked – there are many other grasses and vegetables that could be served in the same way. Purslane, for instance, which you find shooting up as a weed in every garden after the winter rains, is excellent eaten raw as a green – even though it is not all that green – and it is even better when stewed with butter and cream. Cabbage that is not too old is another good green; and some pulses, such as young beans and peas, can be served up raw as a table salad.

GREENS

The nutritional value of raw greens was appreciated by our forefathers long before the discovery of vitamins. When the Dutch East India Company's homeward bound fleet dropped anchor in Table Bay, one of the first duties of the captains was to send their sailors to go and pick basketsful of 'mountain sorrel', which was then known to be a first-class prophylactic against the dreaded scurvy. We now know that nearly all vegetable juices, without exception, contain amino acids and vitamins, and that it is healthy to include raw vegetables and fruit in our diet.

But please do not go on about it. Keep a clear head. The human being is not a grass-eating animal. He cannot digest grass as easily as sheep or cattle do. They have stomachs specially designed for that – they can heat the grass in a way that would give you or me a high fever. We do not have the requisite internal laboratory; and although we eat raw vegetables daily, for the sake of our health, for the taste and for variation in our diet, it is highly questionable whether we would remain healthy if we lived only on raw vegetables. I know that there are people who say that they do just that, but I have never come across any that are shining examples of health. I therefore prefer to eat my vegetables properly prepared and cooked.

This can be done in more than one way. You can boil the vegetables (as is most commonly done) in water, but this is not the best way and it always seems a bit extravagant to me. Each vegetable contains enough water to be cooked in its own moisture. All you need do is apply the heat in such a way that it will not burn, and will preserve its taste, where possible its colour, and its nutritional value. As far as colour is concerned, there are many superstitions among cooks. In one of my oldest cookbooks, I find the following: 'to preserve the colour of green peas, use a teaspoonful of bicarbonate of soda'; and elsewhere: 'the beautiful green of Brussels sprouts is preserved if you boil them with a bit of alum'. I reject both – the alum no less than the bicarb. We need them as little as we need boiling water to cook our vegetables in. Cook vegetables in their own juices, braise them with the help of a little butter or fat, and if you want to be lavish add a spoonful of whatever you wish – wine, vinegar, brandy or fruit juice – but do not add it for the purpose of boiling the vegetables.

Reserve boiling for vegetables you wish to drain first. In this case, put the vegetable in lukewarm water with a pinch of salt, boil quickly, and drain in a colander; then prepare further – for example, as a stew in the case of *waterblommetjies*. But as a rule, cook your vegetable in its own vegetable juice, with the lid tightly on, and just long enough to make the fibres soft and juicy. Only then should you get going with the salt and spice. Prepared in this way, the most common vegetable is a delicacy. I know of no more delicious vegetable than a cabbage, cut in four, steamed and then stewed with a bit of butter, nutmeg, salt and pepper. When well prepared it preserves its green-white colour, and as for its crispness – the quality prized so highly by Chinese cooks – it is just one step behind the raw cabbage we use as a salad. There is no need at all for bicarbonate of soda, or whatever. As long as it is braised slowly and consistently, and the vegetable is not exposed to the air but kept braising in the warm steam of its own environment, its colour will not change much. And it will taste a thousand times better than cabbage boiled in water.

15 September 1944

31
Herbs in the Kitchen

I recently enjoyed lunch on a Boer farm. It was a normal, simple Boer lunch. This was the menu: bean soup, roast leg of mutton, soft-boiled rice, boiled potatoes, stewed green beans and beetroot salad, followed by stewed dried peaches with custard and coffee.

Quite as ordinary a lunch as I have enjoyed probably hundreds of times on other Boer farms. But this one was memorable because the *tannie* who prepared it was a real culinary artist. Seldom have I enjoyed food that was cooked and prepared as well as that afternoon. The soup had bacon in it, was salted just right, and also had a bit of leek leaf added to it. The beetroot salad, although without oil, had some finely chopped parsley in it. The potatoes, nice and mealy, had been given just the right kiss of butter and nutmeg. The beans came with a delicious egg sauce. The stewed dried peaches were prepared in the traditional way, with a piece of cinnamon, a scraping of *naartjie* peel and a glass of sweet wine. Even the rice was first-class, with just enough salt not to spoil it. What really made an impression was the roast leg of mutton. It had a particularly pleasant aftertaste and was so juicy that, had I not seen the bone, I really would have thought it a very young little lamb. But it was the leg of a full-grown sheep, and not too fat either.

'*Nee, Meneer Bonade*,' the *tannie* said to me later, 'it is not a matter of hanging it. I don't like hanging my meat for too long, especially not mutton. It was roasted in the roasting pot after being rubbed with coriander and sage. My late mother always used a bit of fine flour, and I also like adding some herbs where possible.'

Later on she showed me her herb garden. Under an old apple tree in the vegetable garden, exactly where it belonged, next to the broad beans, the cucumbers and the marrows. There were about a dozen and a half herbs: parsley, tame sorrel and grey fennel, even rosemary and thyme, not to mention a bunch of *swartstorm*[1] that appeared to be a bit starved, I could not help noticing.

'*Ja*,' said the *tannie*, 'it needs sea air and sand, and I'm not sure it's worth the effort – it isn't much good for cooking.'

---

1 *Cadaba aphylla*, a usually leafless shrub from arid areas.

I agree fully. *Swartstorm* can be good for headaches – my doctor friends question this, but I know of a *niggie* who swears by it and prefers it to aspirin – but its value to the cook is minimal.

I take off my hat to that *tannie*. She realises the value of herbs in the kitchen. Today's cook does not know much about herbs. When he does use them, it is likely to be dried herbs like pepper, saffron, turmeric or coriander. A hundred times not half as good as freshly picked herbs from the garden. Just try. See what a bit of sage does for a coot, rubbed into it after you have first skinned it; or what effect rosemary can have on a chop. I do not even have to mention a lemon leaf in brawn or *sosaties*, or the value of a bay leaf as a surrogate for it. One of my friends tells me that the leaf of the Cape Pittosporum[2] – not the Australian kind, which has a sharper smell – is excellent in a *bobotie*. I have not tried it, but I can imagine that it would have an interesting effect on the taste. Here I am merely pleading for the common or garden kitchen herbs that can be planted and cultivated in every vegetable garden. It is a pleasant hobby to keep a herb garden. There are those who collect postage stamps and manage to find great pleasure in it. For the housewife I would recommend collecting herbs – live herbs – and seeing how many different kinds she can find. It is surprising to hear how many different kinds there actually are. Most girls do not even know half a dozen – even when they have negotiated the matric exam.

How the addition of herbs transforms our food, or at least its taste, has not been ascertained. It is possible that in some cases the herb oils have a chemical reaction with the outer tissues of meat, perhaps also of vegetables, but that is not something we know much about yet. Another explanation is that the soluble ingredients of the herbs blend with the juices of the food and thereby change the taste. We know far too little to be dogmatic about that either. As a practical cook and lover of good food, I only know that the use of herbs makes a considerable contribution to making food tastier, more delicious, and perhaps even more nutritious.

It goes without saying, however, that one should not overdo the use of herbs. Moderation in everything is a rule that holds for the modest cook as well. Some garden herbs are used for just about everything. Parsley is an excellent example; mint another. These are unfortunately the only two that most cooks have any intimate knowledge of, and they therefore have to suffice for all

---

2 *Pittosporum viridiflorum*.

purposes. I recommend giving them a desperately needed holiday from the kitchen, and in their absence some rosemary, fennel and a few nephews and nieces could be invited to assist us.

Herbs are not spices. Do not therefore confuse the taste of cinnamon, a spice, with that of coriander, which is actually a herb, although we use its seed more than its leaf. The good cook combines, where necessary, herbs and spices. Without both you will not be able to create a good curry, or for that matter a *bobotie*. When the food is sweet, spices are normally used – exactly why I cannot tell. And a meat dish sometimes benefits from a concoction of mixed herbs and spices. Ginger with pork, allspice with quails, and similar combinations are well known. In the culinary art of our forefathers it was a common thing to add spices to meat; today it is the exception rather than the rule.

To return to the herb garden – take good care of it. Nearly all herbs are fond of shade, with only a few exceptions – among them tame sorrel, which needs a lot of sun. Therefore protect the others against sunburn. It is good to water them well – that brings out the quality of the herb. We will probably get to know more about herbs in time, because it is quite likely that South Africa will produce some important new herbs that will sell well – especially for use in the manufacture of perfumes. Then our kitchen herbs will perhaps regain the respect that is their due.

22 September 1944

32
Kambro and Baroe

At the end of the previous century,[1] when Cape Town still had its beautiful vegetable market, that tourist attraction and bargain-shop for every housekeeper – a pleasure we no longer have in spite of our more civilised lifestyle and increased municipal rates, there was still a chance of buying some *kambro*[2] and *baroe*[3] in the capital city. Today this is no longer possible and one has to travel sixty or eighty miles to get hold of these delicacies. First-class *kambro* is to be found growing on the Worcester common. It is also abundant in the Karoo veld near Citrusdal, but I know of no other place where it can be found – at least of a sufficient quality to be used by the cook. In our Cape Peninsula you will find nephews and nieces that have tiny, insignificant little bulbs. But the real, genuine *kambro* is found in Karoo soil, clay, where it grows best.

It is a frail, delicate creeper with tiny, yellow-grey flowers and milk in its stalks. For that reason livestock do not feed on it, although they do chew off the leaves in times of drought. The plant contains the food in its bulb, which can range in size from a little cucumber to a medium-sized watermelon. One of the largest I have come across was displayed on the stoep of the old White House in Strand Street where it was admired by Cecil Rhodes, *Oubaas* Merriman and Jan Hendrik Hofmeyr when they were there for lunch one afternoon. It was nearly three foot long and about eighteen inches in diameter. Last year a friend sent me one that was nearly as big, but it was spongy and not worth cooking.

As in the case of the sweet potato, it is the subterranean bulb that is regarded as a delicacy by the connoisseur. It is in fact nothing more than a fusion of plant fibres containing water, or rather a solution of all sorts of ingredients, that gives the *kambro* bulb its odd flavour. My old friend Dr Marloth analysed it and told me that the nutritional value consisted largely of a certain plant sugar, called inulin, the same as is found in artichokes and in the *veldpatats*[4] that grow on the *Springbokvlakte*. In the tissue itself there is, however, as with sweet potatoes and potatoes, a lot of starch, and I would say that the bulb is therefore just as nutritious as those two cultivated garden bulb vegetables. However, it also contains an ingredient that has a somewhat bitter taste, which is why some people are prejudiced against the *kambro*. With the right

---

1 The nineteenth century.
2 *Fockea* spp. The plant Leipoldt describes was probably *Fockea edulis*, although the 'nephews and nieces' may have been *Cyphia incisa*, which was also called 'kambro'.
3 *Cyphea* spp., probably *Cyphea volubilis*.
4 Veld sweet potatoes, the rootstock of *Commicarpus pentandrus*.

treatment, however, the cook can remove this bitter taste and get the best out of the bulb.

Kambro can be prepared just like sweet potatoes. Peel it, and slice or dice it. Then put it in some salt water for an hour or so – this will draw off some of the bitter taste. Then cook it in its own steam and water. Pour off the first water. When it is soft, add sugar, cinnamon, *naartjie* peel or whatever you prefer if you would like a sweet *kambro* dish. I have also had *kambro* stew, made with bacon, sorrel and mutton-chop. It tasted a bit too watery-mealy, and I do not consider the bulb to be suitable for a vegetable dish either. It is as a jam that it comes into its own. *Kambro* jam is a rarity today, but when the old *tannies* still made it, it was often seen at the agricultural shows and church bazaars, and it was always first-class and well worth eating. Some recipes say that the slices should lie in limewater – as is the custom with green figs when making jam – but that is not necessary. The most important thing is that it should be cooked soft rapidly and evenly at first, so that there are no raw pieces among the slices. Then dry them and place in a boiling sugar syrup (old *tannies* always used to add a large tablespoonful of *bossiestroop*,[5] and I must say that it gives the jam a really nice taste) that should not be too thick, because the slices need to be completely soaked in it. Cook until the slices are nicely transparent, and bottle immediately while still warm. If the syrup is too thick, the jam will crystallise quickly and this will spoil the taste. When it is properly thin it can be preserved for years in a bottle without the slightest change. As for the flavour, most recipes say that ginger, cinnamon and almonds are also used, but my own choice is for a bit of wild fennel bulb, boiled with the *kambro*, a bay leaf, and a shaving of grated lemon peel.

Baroe is something completely different and it is, I am afraid to say, no longer available. The authorities on plants call it by a wonderful name. The bulbs are also not as large as those of the *kambro* – they are sometimes as small as allspice or peppercorns, and they do not really have a pleasant taste. *Baroe* is found almost wherever there is clay, but the largest and best bulbs are, once again, found in Karoo soil. The little flowers are pink, and the stems contain no milk. To prepare it you do exactly as you would for onions, but in fact I think onions are more worth the effort than *baroe*. There is another kind of veld food of the same name that comes from the north-western districts, especially from Namaqualand. Of that I have no experience, and it is also not something that can be cooked or baked.

---

5 Sugarbush syrup, the nectar of *Protea repens*.

There are probably other bulbous plants in the Suurveld and the Karoo that will reward experimentation. In the Transvaal we also have a subterranean bulb with a taste as delicate as that of an artichoke, and just as much plant sugar. In Namaqualand we have subterranean *fungi* that are highly regarded by connoisseurs, but this kind of veld food warrants another discussion.

13 October 1944

33
Milk Food

One of my readers wrote to ask whether I was not 'a bit mistaken' when I said the other day that 'the nutritional value of potatoes is very little – about as much as that of milk'. He asks: 'Is milk then not the food containing vitamins A, C, B and D, just about all the minerals, 3 per cent protein, 4 per cent sugar, 3 per cent fat, and just about everything the body needs? To compare that with potatoes, which consist of not much more than starch, is, as far as I can see, not quite right.'

I speak only as a cook, not as an expert on the health value of foods. From the point of view of the cook, vitamins do not mean a thing – they are not something the cook is concerned with, nor do they matter to the guest for whom he is preparing the food. As far as I know, most of the so-called vitamins are transformed when exposed to heat; therefore, again from the perspective of the cook, they are only of use when the food is eaten raw or half-raw.

But nutritional value is something every cook should know and understand something about, and there is no difference of opinion at all about the poor nutritional value of potatoes and milk: a hundred grams of milk has a nutritional value of exactly 65 calories; a hundred grams of potato has exactly 76 calories. There is therefore little difference. In 100 grams of potato there is 78 per cent water, 1,8 per cent protein, 17,2 per cent carbohydrate, 1,1 per cent ether extracts (fats), 13 milligrams of iron salts, 0,51 milligrams of phosphorous salts, and other similar mineral salts. In 100 grams of milk there is 87 per cent water, 3,3 per cent protein, 4,6 per cent carbohydrate, 3,2 per cent fat, 120 milligrams of lime salts, 0,1 milligrams of iron salts, and 0,95 milligrams of phosphorous salts. There is therefore very little difference between the two, except that the phosphorus in milk is found in a fat compound and milk therefore contains a larger quantity of fatty acids. That is all.

Milk is something without which no cook can survive, as it is one of the best emulsions we have. But it is also one of the most expensive foods we can use, a food that moreover, especially in the cities, is extremely difficult to keep pure because such an emulsion is a first-class breeding ground for all kinds of airborne germs. On the farm, direct from the cow, uncooked milk is something anyone can drink and enjoy quite safely; in the trade even pasteurised milk is not always completely pure and free of germs. The only way of making it pure and safe is to boil it first, and in the process – at least so the district surgeon, who of course knows much more about the subject than I do, tells us – its vitamins are damaged.

I repeat that as a cook I am not too concerned with vitamin values. *Neef* Kerneels, who recently had a job working with tanks somewhere in the far north, tells me that they were given many vitamins, but that he benefited much more from chewing a piece of old-fashioned dried peach roll. If only we could get more of that today. It must be about ten years since I last saw peach roll in a Cape Town shop. The sweets that *Neef* Kerneels gave me are a poor substitute.

But let us return to the subject of milk. In the kitchen it has three main uses. One is to thicken and give body to soup, sauce and such-like. You can just as well use oil beaten up in warm water, but milk is always at hand and well suited to the purpose. The second use is for mixing with flour and using it to bind. And the third is to use it as a food in itself. I am now dealing only with the third use of milk.

What we call *melkkos*[1] is usually some or other farinaceous food (like *frummeltjies*, dumplings or macaroni) boiled in milk and then served in it, sometimes after it has been thickened with butter or cream or something else. Who does not recall cold winter's evenings as a child when Mother served a soup tureen full of delicious, soft white-flour dumplings swimming in thickened milk, with cinnamon, mace and perhaps a bit of allspice? Today's government flour is not suitable for such dumplings, but we can still make them with fine buckwheat flour or even sifted cornflour. The serious concern for the cook, when preparing such a dish, is to get the dumplings light. Recipes differ on this, but old *Tant* Alie always reckoned that it was definitely necessary for the cook to have an ice-cold hand and for the milk to be boiling hot as every dumpling was drowned in it. The art of making good dumplings has all but disappeared, but it is worth resuscitating – the milk dumpling is one of the best foods we have and, when well made, one of the easiest to digest.

A second milk food is custard. By this I do not mean those milk puddings that are stiffened with the help of additives of starch or something similar. They are sold in little packets and, although I admit that they save time and can taste good enough when nothing better is available, I cannot – with the very

---

1 Milk-food.

best of intentions – even think of beginning to compare them with a homemade milk-custard in which you can taste the egg and cream. Such custard – whether steamed, cooked or baked – has its own characteristic softness that is unique and incomparable. No other food can give you this soft yet firm substance. You can try starch, gelatine, roux – everything that is used to bind – without ever succeeding in getting as delicious a combination as milk mixed with eggs. The only thing you have to be careful of is that it must be well mixed and the heat must be as even as possible so that it does not curdle. Curdled custard is a monstrosity one might expect from an electric oven!

And do be careful with spices and flavours. Milk does not tolerate excessive use of them. It requires only the slightest, microscopical whiff and vapour, and one can spoil it with too much cinnamon, too much *naartjie* peel and, especially, too much ginger. The almond and vanilla flavourings that are so often used usually overwhelm the delicate taste of the milk and eggs. A bitter almond and a sweet almond, peeled and boiled in milk, is really all you need. We Bonades have never had much time for vanilla – it is, despite all that can be said for it, a grossly over-estimated flavour.

Another way of enjoying milk is as ice cream. You can make ice cream without milk, but that would never be first-rate. Milk, eggs and cream, beaten up as for milk custard, is the basis of every good ice cream.

I prefer to use milk powder to cook with. It is completely safe, pure and clean, and in the long run much cheaper than the milk you have to buy from a dairy for more than its economic value. There are different kinds on the market, and they are now all made in South Africa, so you can rest assured that you are supporting the industry of the fatherland. Just be careful and follow the instructions meticulously when making milk from milk powder. It is not difficult, but requires a degree of time, patience and effort – all of which are fully repaid.

27 October 1944

34
Seafood I

For those with any imagination, it is always a source of wonder how much there is for which to thank the sea – the sea that many of us have never seen and know only from hearsay, the sea sometimes depicted as a cruel monster that devours all and gives nothing in return, and yet the sea without which we would not be able to exist – that is companion to and, to an extent, lord of our steadfast world.

What on earth, the reader with a logical mind might ask, does the sea have to do with our kitchen or our cellar?[1]

Just think back. Our earliest forefathers, who went without clothes and knew nothing of the art of cookery as we understand it today, obtained all their food from the sea. Shell-fish and seafood of all kinds were what they lived on. You only have to dig in the dunes along our coast and you will find shell middens – the remains of our forefathers' dinners, discarded after their contents had been eaten by them and their guests.

Today there is still a great deal of food to be found in the sea. Men of learning, who think so far into the future that they can foresee the world being unable to produce enough food to feed its increasing population, already anticipate that we will have to better exploit the sea as a source of sustenance. What they have in mind, first and foremost, is the sea's wealth of plankton, that enormous supply of small plant-animals on which the huge whales thrive. It is exceptionally difficult to prepare a meal from plankton. We have tried, but up to now the results have been unpalatable, even though the nutritional value is high. I am sure that in time we will manage to fashion plankton in a form the cook will find useful and cheap, but it has not happened yet.

There are, however, many other types of seafood that we know well and should make better use of than we do at present. Some are already popular; others are less well known and still regarded with a measure of suspicion – which is not fair, for the accomplished cook is able to turn them into tasty dishes that deserve respect, especially in these times of controlled food.

Take, for instance, periwinkles. Every child knows them after playing on the beach once or twice. They are crustaceans with about as much nutritional value as chicken's eggs. You can eat them raw, with or without a sour sauce. You can stew them, with or without spices, onions or whatever you prefer,

---

[1] The original Afrikaans articles were originally published under the title *Kelder en Kombuis*, in English 'Cellar and Kitchen'.

into a tasty ragout. The more aristocratic members of their family – mussels, oysters, *perlemoen*[2] and about twenty other kinds – are perhaps not so abundant, but with a little effort and patience one can get hold of them as well. I remember how as a child I used to see more than a dozen kinds in the old fish and vegetable market in Cape Town. In those days seafood was something the old people really liked. On Fridays you could enjoy it to your heart's content at the White House in Strand Street, and in Kalk Bay there was a place where the cook used to prepare it excellently.

Some people regard seafood with distaste. It is too mushy for them. But the accomplished cook knows just how to neutralise this mushiness so that it loses its unattractiveness. An oyster eaten raw with lemon and pepper cannot but be mushy but, baked in a crust of dough that has been rolled out ten times, it is a completely different matter. Similarly when it is turned into a delicious oyster soup, with cream and milk and sprinkled with grated cheese. However, the connoisseur prefers eating his oysters raw. Only in this way, he declares, can he fully appreciate their delicate taste. This does not, however, prevent the cook from making all kinds of mixed dishes from oysters, and there are hundreds of oyster recipes that are well worth trying.

The same goes for mussels. We have different kinds of mussels, of which the large blue ones and the nearly square white ones are the most popular. Today they cost more than they did a few years ago, when it was still possible to get them for a hundred a shilling at the fish market. But even at the higher price they are an economical food because their nutritional value is high and they can be prepared in a variety of ways to make an exceptionally tasty dish. There is also no fear of them being detrimental to your health if well boiled, taken from a part of the sea that is not polluted with sewage, and fresh – that is to say still alive, with their shells closed tight.

Put them in some fresh water, and wash off all sand and slime. Then place them in boiling sea or salt water, and boil well for five to ten minutes. This will kill the shellfish, and open the shell. All the sand and dirt inside the shell will then enter the water. Now take the mussels and keep them warm. Pour the water in which they have been boiled through a cloth to purify it of sand and other dirt. This water can then be used as the basis of the sauce in which they are served, which can be prepared according to a variety of recipes. Most require onions, a slice of garlic, parsley and pepper, with or without a glass of

---

2 Mother-of-pearl.

brandy or wine. Pour the sauce over the mussels and serve them in their shells. There will be no sign of any mushiness – mussels prepared in this way are soft, tasty and nutritious.

Our old Cape cooks also used to take the cooked mussels from the shells, mince them with a sausage machine, and prepare the minced mussels in various ways. First as a powerful and tasty mussel soup, with milk, cream, some grated cheese and nutmeg. Then as mussel *frikkadels*,[3] with parsley, some vinegar and wine, a lot of pepper (some cooks add turmeric, or even curry powder), and fried in boiling fat. Or baked in a dough tartlet which the French cooks call *vol-au-vent*. Another way is to make mussel bobotie. Follow the usual recipe for meat bobotie, mix the mussel meat with a little ginger, a lot of pepper, a bay leaf, parsley, vinegar and a spoonful of finely chopped pickles of the old type. Add half a dozen seeded raisins and a few blanched almonds, cover with egg-custard, and bake in the oven. It becomes, in a word, delicious.

15 December 1944

---

3 Meatballs.

35
Seafood II

Under seafood we should also include seaweed. This is something we tend to use far too little. 'It's a shame,' the old *tannie* said to me, 'that people no longer know how to eat seaweed creepers!' This is the kind that grows on sea-bamboo. Its colour is brilliant red in the deep-sea water, but when washed up and bleached by the sun it is a dirty grey or yellow. There are many other kinds that are edible, but for the moment I shall concentrate on the creeper.

Collect some – it is easy enough, especially after the south-easter has been blowing, because then it washes up on the beach *en masse* – and take it home. Store it in a tightly closed jar. When using it, take a few handfuls, soak it in cold water, wash it well, then place it in a saucepan with enough water to cover it completely. Boil slowly until it starts swelling and becoming soft, then take the saucepan away from the fire and let it draw slowly, stirring well every now and then. Strain it through a cloth after a few hours, and what you get is the decoction of the seaweed that serves as the basis for a jelly or custard. For a simple jelly, mix the decoction with sugar, spices, lemon juice and a glass of sweet wine. Pour into moulds, preferably small moulds, and place in a cool spot or in the fridge. Pour it out as soon as it is nicely stiff, and serve with cream or a sauce. It should not, however, stand for long when taken out of the mould, as it can easily become runny.

The decoction can also serve as the base for a fish soup, made from the bones and heads of any type of fish, and thickened according to taste with minced fish or crayfish. The famous Chinese soup made from birds' nests is nothing more than such a seaweed soup. It is made with the decoction served boiling hot, well peppered, and flavoured with all sorts of additives. The ingredient of the seaweed that gives it its gelatinous quality, a pectin called *agar-agar*, is quite similar to the fruit pectin we use for making fruit jelly. We used to be under the impression that the pectin, like gelatine, does not have much nutritional value, but now we know better. In some countries seaweed is used as a peasant food, and there are many different kinds that are suitable. It is braised, with or without spices and butter or fat, then served as a stew. It is sometimes mixed with vegetables, but the connoisseur prefers it without any intrusive accompaniment and finds the taste attractive on its own.

Let us return to our very best seafood. This is the *perlemoen* (abalone) or *klipkous*, known to scientists as a kind of *Haliotis* or pearl mussel. Stewed *klipkous* is a South African dish that has achieved well-deserved fame among connoisseurs. It is a dish we can regard as genuinely indigenous, for we prepare it according to recipes that differ significantly from the way in which

Haliotis types are prepared in other parts of the world – for example in Australia, where it is also a popular food, now even available in tinned form.

To get hold of *klipkous* is about as difficult as finding first-class beef. It used to be sold for next to nothing on the fish market in Cape Town. For a few oulap,¹ you could get three or four large *perlemoen*. Now you have to order them days in advance, and then wait for the tide and the weather to play along with the fisherman's comfort in getting them from the rocks where they live.

But say you have managed to get hold of a few large *klipkous*. Put them in cold water and let them lie there for a good half-hour. Then brush thoroughly the bottom, the sucker, with a strong brush – rub hard and remove as much of the green slime as possible. If that cannot be done with the brush, use a blunt knife and scrape it well. Now take the animal from its shell. Cut away the beard, remove the innards and throw them away. What remains is the hard, white body of the animal. Place that on a block and pound it with a piece of wood until the gristly edge is flat and soft. Pound it evenly and carefully, taking care not to break it, but make sure that every part of the gristly outer wall is soft. Then dry it well with a moist cloth, and cut it into two or three equal pieces. Place them in a saucepan with a cupful of tail- or kidney-fat, and add a blade of mace, nutmeg or ginger, as you please. Place on the fire, which should not be too hot, and close the lid tightly. Shake now and then while stewing for ten to fifteen minutes, no longer. Remove the lid and test the *klipkous* to see if it is nicely soft. It should be soft enough for a normal table fork to penetrate easily under its own weight without having to exert any pressure. If it is not yet soft enough, close again and allow it to steam in the fat a few minutes longer. How long is something only the experienced cook will be able to judge. If heat is applied too long, the danger is that the meat will be too tough – and when it comes to *klipkous* this would be an unforgivable traversty.

When it is nicely soft, take the saucepan from the fire and remove the pieces of meat. Place them in a dish, sprinkle a little salt, pepper and nutmeg over them, and keep them warm. Now make a sauce with the fat, or butter if you prefer. For that you will need a small quantity of fine flour, a glass of good brandy, and a cup of sour milk or curds and whey. First make a fat or butter sauce with the flour, stirring it constantly so that lumps do not form, then add some fine salt and a pinch of pepper. Remove the mace or ginger, and stir in

---

1 Pennies.

the curds and whey. Finally, add the brandy. Serve separately in a sauce dish. The *klipkous*, which should be nicely white and soft as marrow, can be served either in its own dish or on a slice of toast covered with some of the sauce. It is one of the most delicious seafoods I know.

The most important thing is to cook the *klipkous* without a drop of water or a grain of salt. Either would make it tough, whereas the butter or fat makes it nicely soft. It is hardly necessary to add that the *klipkous* should be fresh – the slightest hint of aftertaste will spoil it.

What to serve with it? This depends on your own preference. The Bonades have the habit, probably inherited from the time when our farm was still a beach farm and the old *tannies* could serve *klipkous* every day, to have it with dry rice or mealy potatoes only. I have also had it with yellow rice and raisins, and that was not bad. Another old *tannie* served it with cooked cauliflower, as white as the *klipkous* itself. But if you ask me, it does not really matter what you eat it with. *Klipkous* is a dish that needs nothing but itself. It stands on its own merit, and there is no need to add anything.

What to drink with it is completely a different matter. *Perlemoen* has its own unique taste, quite a strong taste at that. It cannot easily be smothered by anything else, and it is so very soft that in itself it will not overwhelm any good wine. The choice of wine is therefore wide open. Some connoisseurs prefer a light, somewhat sweet wine, like the different kinds of what we now call Sauternes. Others prefer red wines, jerepigos or pontacs, if they are not too sweet. I myself tend to prefer a dry white wine with *klipkous*, but in the end it is a matter of individual taste.

Just one piece of advice. When you have finished the *klipkous*, take a *pimpeltjie*[2] of good brandy. Now that '*het smaakt*',[3] as our forefathers used to say.

12 January 1945

---

2 Tot.

3 Tastes good, literally 'has taste'.

36
Seafood III

Of all the favourite *strandkos*[1] of my youth, *perdevoetjies*[2] were perhaps one of the most popular. They used to be prepared at least once a week at all the old beach and holiday places that were then fashionable. *Perdevoetjies* were easy to obtain – you could find them, large or small, without much trouble, and prise them with a blunt knife or a piece of barbed wire from every rock that was accessible at low tide. The *outas* and Ayahs used to sell them for thruppence a half-bucket, and for an extra penny they would clean them for the cook.

Nowadays it is not so easy to get hold of edible *perdevoetjies* – I mean those found in the sea. The other kind, found on rocks alongside rivers, cannot be regarded as edible – they are succulents, not animals. The sea *perdevoetjie* is a shellfish with quite a thick sucker, and it is this sucker that one eats. The animal is taken out of its shell, the innards are scraped out, and the sucker is then pounded with a piece of wood until soft. The procedure for preparing it is more or less the same as for *klipkous (perlemoen)*, the only difference being that all sorts of spices are added to stewed *perdevoetjies* and they are sometimes served with vegetables – such as purslane, which makes a first-class accompaniment. The old Ayahs maintained that a cutting of wild fennel root[3] was indispensable when making the real thing. I must admit that it does give stewed *perdevoetjie* a unique flavour that improves it, but where do you find wild fennel root today? Certainly not in a city or *dorp*. You would have to find it and dig it out yourself and, believe me, getting it out of the ground is no child's play.

A *perdevoetjie* stew needs to be cooked long and slow, for perhaps two or three hours on a mild fire, but not for too long. In this respect also it differs from *klipkous*. And again, add no water or salt before the *perdevoetjies* are soft. Well cooked, they are wonderfully soft and about as good as thick offal stewed in milk. Poorly done, they are inedible – tough as leather and delectable as a stone. Take special care not to have sick *perdevoetjies* in the saucepan – these are the old animals that have gone yellow, have shrunk inside the shell, and are easily removed. Their suckers are always rather soft and they '*kook rafeltjies*',[4] as the old *tannies* used to say – a sure sign that they are not completely healthy. And do not take any shells from rocks in the immediate vicinity of an urban sewage system – they will not really be polluted (and in

---

1 Beach food.
2 Possibly the 'Horse's hoof' slipper limpet, *Hipponix conicus*.
3 *Chamarea* sp.
4 Literally, 'cook fronds'.

the heat that the *perdevoetjies* are exposed to during the process of cooking, no germ will have much chance of survival), but they easily acquire an unfortunate flavour that may just spoil the dish.

Of course we also count fish and other marine animals as seafood, but I have written about fish elsewhere and, although there is much to add, I need not do so now. The kind of seafood we have been hearing about so much recently, whale meat, will also have to wait for a later discussion. Having said something about shellfish, I will restrict myself to two particular kinds of seafood, the value of which has not been adequately recognised simply because there is a strong prejudice against them. I refer to octopus and squid.

Both are traditional foods in other countries. In Lourenço Marques,[5] for instance, both are eagerly snapped up when they arrive at the fish market, and here at the Cape too there are people who like both. When properly prepared an octopus is one of the most delicious dishes that can be served. The cook has to know, however, what parts of the animal to select if he does not want tough pieces in the octopus stew. The octopus should not be too large, and only the tentacles should be used. Skin it and cut off the suckers with a pair of scissors. Then pound well with a piece of wood, so that the meat is bruised but not broken. Discard the thin end of the tentacle – it consists mainly of sinews that are tough when cooked. Now stew slowly, once again without water, in fat or butter, and add what you wish, according to taste. Some old Ayahs added potatoes and made quite a thick, dry stew, almost like braised snoek and potato stew, which is also the usual way in which Chinese octopus is prepared. But others prefer a juicier stew, which actually amounts to a kind of thick soup. It is served with toast sprinkled with some grated cheese, and is not to be missed. Another way of preparing it is to stew the octopus with similar pieces of fish in a curry sauce.

The squid, which seems to be more popular than the octopus, is a cousin. It is known as *tjokka* at the fish markets and is a favourite food of the Coloured people, who know from experience how good it tastes when properly prepared. It is, however, by no means an easy task to prepare it properly. Mrs Aagot Stromsoe provides a few recipes for preparing it in her first-class little book on fish and fish dishes, *Do You Know How to Cook Fish?* and I do not have anything to add except to say that the cook who has not tried to make squid stew is advised first to have a chat with one of the old Ayahs at the fish

---

5 Since renamed Maputo.

market and to ask how you tell whether a squid is fresh or not. Because a dead squid deteriorates rapidly in taste and texture, and the 'ink' contained in the squirting-pouch is the first thing to undergo a change.[6] This ink is regarded by the expert cook as an indispensable ingredient of the sauce with which the squid is served. It has an odd taste, which can be tempered by adding coriander and a glass of brandy. First fry some sliced onion in butter or fat, then stew the squid in it until nicely soft. Stir in the 'ink' with some cream and flour, to make a thick sauce, and stew slowly, with the lid on the saucepan, until everything is soaked through and through. Different spices can be added. The best is a little ground ginger, mace and rosemary, but all sorts of other spices can be used according to taste. Serve with mushy rice.

As a table drink to go with it beer is perhaps the best, but any good table wine would be agreeable. Currying squid is not really recommended, for the curry overwhelms the unique, delicate flavour, rendering it almost unrecognisable.

9 February 1945

---

6 In Afrikaans the squid is known as an *inkvis*.

37
Green Peas

Pulses are perhaps the oldest food known to humankind.

My old *tannie*, who is glancing over my shoulder as I write, just shakes her head.

'As far as I know,' she says, in that dreadful, oh-so-sweet manner she adopts when she wants to criticise me, 'our dear Lord said that for food He gave us the plants that have seeds and all the trees that bear fruit. Is that not what is said in Genesis 1 verse 29?'

'Absolutely right, *Tannie*,' I answer, not at all put out, 'but *Tannie* is forgetting that pulses also have seeds, and the scientific know-alls maintain that pulses like lentils and peas, not grasses like wheat and rye, were our very first food.'

'They have a lot to say,' *Tannie* snaps at me. 'Today they talk of vitamins that the Holy Scripture doesn't even mention. All just talk.'

'I agree completely when it comes to the vitamins, *Tannie*. But please … I have to have this piece ready before this evening …'

By the way, *Tannie* is one of the few cooks of my acquaintance who knows how to do things with peas. I have her to thank for being able to distinguish between peas and peas, for having learned the difference between peas that honour their name and peas that could just as well have been acorns.

Cooking peas – peas suitable for the table – are young peas, not those usually passed off as cooking peas that you have to pay a fortune for in these days of controlled vegetables. Real cooking peas are young, soft, virgin-green, juicy and plump. You usually only get them if you have a row of peas in your own garden. Do not wait until the pods are thick and fat – the less they look like a water-loving creature's thighs the better they are for the pot. Watch your peas closely, therefore, and as soon as the pods show signs of bulging, pick and shell them. Then you will get the young peas the connoisseur prefers; and, believe me, there is no vegetable that comes close!

To prepare such young peas requires expertise and what *Tannie* calls *'n slag*.[1] When it comes to expertise, I agree. Concerning *'n slag* – well, one could argue endlessly about that without coming to any worthwhile conclusion. I know of

---

1 A knack.

an old Ayah who, according to the general testimony of the families she cooked for, had a remarkable 'knack' of colouring tartlets a beautiful golden yellow. When she told me her secret, however ... well, since that day I have always been a bit nervous when presented with a golden yellow tartlet.

To return to the young peas, for heaven's sake do not wash them. It is possible that a worm might hide in the pod, in which case just show him that he does not belong there. That is all that is really necessary. Place the peas in a saucepan, with just enough water – or preferably a bit of meat soup – to quench their thirst when it starts getting hot. Close the lid and let them cook in their own steam without adding anything whatsoever. To add mint, lemon peel, nutmeg, or whatever is an affront to them and an insult to your own taste. And do not cook them for too long. Very young peas – I am dealing only with them – do not require more than a quarter of an hour in the saucepan. As soon as they are soft and mushy, take them from the fire, sprinkle with a pinch of sugar and salt, and add a lump of butter – the best available, of course. Shake the saucepan, without taking off the lid, until the peas are well oiled by the butter. Serve immediately. My, now that is really an excellent dish to serve a guest.

When peas are older, swollen with more body, the cook can still prepare them in this way. Indeed it is the usual way of cooking peas. But the connoisseur will not like it. The fully-grown pea does not have the soft juiciness of the baby pea, and this is why it is smothered with mint that overwhelms the taste of the pea. No, use the full-grown pea for making soup or *purée*. An excellent soup can be made of it – the so-called *Potage St Germain*. Its basis is a good *consommé*, preferably made from chicken bones and veal. Cook the peas in the manner mentioned above and mash them. Then cook them for half an hour in the soup, strain through a colander, and heat until the soup is velvety and even. Add spice, salt and pepper, and bring to the boil again. When it starts bubbling, add a cup of cream or two cups of milk and serve immediately with toast.

Some cookbooks suggest that one should colour this soup by adding spinach juice to give it a nice green appearance, but I disagree – just as I oppose the idea of insulting peas or indeed any green vegetable by cooking them with bicarbonate of soda. Green pea soup does not have to be leaf-green. The more cream or milk you add, the less green it will be – but it will not taste any less good.

My old *tannie* interrupts me again. 'But who would make pea soup without onions? You don't seem to have the faintest idea of what is appropriate. Why don't you tell the people ...'

Well, there are cooks who start by frying sliced onion, sliced leek, a slice of sour apple and a snippet of mace in butter, adding it to the pea *purée* and then boiling it all up together as a soup. This is purely a matter of taste, and I am liberal and tolerant enough not to regard this as heretical. But I prefer my *Potage St Germain* without onion, celery or mace. A combined vegetable soup is something I esteem very highly – but this is something different from a green pea soup.

Speaking of heretics, heresy is – according to the dictionaries – the wilful rejection of a generally accepted doctrine of faith. There are no such doctrines in the art of cooking, for otherwise there would be no culinary art. Cooking is learned through experimentation and experience, and sometimes by accident. If *Oom* Karools – who was in France during the last war[2] and there acquired the habit of sprinkling cheese over his soup – always wishes to eat his pea soup with cheese over it, I shall not feel obliged to drag him to the pyre in a chequered *sanbenito*. The fellow has his own life to lead and his own taste, and that is that. But the taste of green peas has a character of its own, and I regard it as worthless and unnecessary to try to improve it by adding and supplementing all sorts of things. It is a different matter when you are dealing with dried peas, but that is a separate topic.

16 March 1945

---

2 World War I.

38
Dried peas

Dried peas, like other dried pulses, need to be prepared in a completely different manner. Dried pulses are the seeds of ripe pulses in which the food for the seedling – called the germ proteid by men of learning – has developed so far that it contains a number of ingredients that the young pea does not have. Unfortunately we have not advanced far enough to know exactly how the change takes place inside the pea, or inside any other pulse such as lentils or beans. For the cook, however, it is enough to know that such changes have taken place, and he does not need a chemist to point this out to him. Experience and common sense reveal that dried peas contain much less juice and liquid than green peas, and that they need to be soaked before use; also that they are much harder, much more wooden than when they were in the pod. The knowledgeable cook will also have learned, using his sense of taste, that dried peas have a completely different taste and flavour from green peas.

Do not think, therefore, that you will be able to make green pea soup from dried peas. I know only too well that this is done. The holy saint – well, I cannot for the moment recall his name, and it is too much bother to leave my typewriter in order to go and look it up in *Larousse* – once made cabbage stew using partridge. This was on a day of fasting, and there was reason enough for the transformation. But I am bold enough to imagine that the partridge remained a partridge, and my colleagues in the culinary art fully agree – today we still have partridge cabbage stew, and it is a first-class dish. I am only trying to say that you cannot make a green pea soup from dried peas, even if you call it – coloured as it might be with spinach juice or one or other green colouring from the chemist – *Potage St Germain*. It would simply be bad pea soup, for if you want to make soup from dried peas they need to be prepared completely differently.

Not that I wish to compare the two. No good cook would do that, for he would know that every food has its own characteristics and that it is unfair to compare one dish with another. Such comparison would in the end amount to nothing more than a matter of taste. Thus while I have waxed lyrical about the real *Potage St Germain*, I would not hesitate to join in the refrain if someone else were to sing the praises of dried-pea soup.

It is, indeed, one of the soups on which the poetic imagination can be given free rein, as is the case with onion soup or the much more aristocratic *bortsch* of our Russian friends. But to merit such praise, a dried-pea soup needs to be prepared, served and eaten properly.

DRIED PEAS

First the dried peas themselves. They can be green or yellow. That, again, is purely a matter of taste, but most cooks prefer the yellow kind, whole or split. Look them over well. Pick out the bits of dirt from among them. Then put them in cold water and wash them thoroughly to remove any dust that may still cling to them, also to select those that have been eaten by weevils and are spongy – to be fed to the chickens. Wash them under the tap, and when they are clean and shiny put them in a saucepan with enough water to cover them completely. Leave them to soak for a few hours.

In addition, take a piece of salted bacon, a piece of leftover ham still containing the bone, a piece of celery stalk, sliced onions and leeks (here I am in complete agreement with my old *tannie*), a bunch of herbs (I use bay leaf, sage, thyme and rosemary, but there are of course many other combinations), white pepper and a small teaspoon of brown sugar. No salt, as there is enough in the bacon and ham leftovers to pickle the soup. If necessary the cook can add a bit of fine salt just before the soup is served.

Brown the sliced onions and leek in a saucepan, and add a few cups of good chicken or meat soup. Allow it to boil and bubble. Add the other ingredients, along with the soaked peas, and pull them aside so that they can cook slowly – very slowly. Scoop off the foam, but keep the lid on so that the soup will not evaporate. Cook slowly but well – this is the art of obtaining a good, well-cooked dried-pea soup. When the peas are mushy, pour the soup through a colander, take away the bone, and after the peas have been mashed fine – a *purée* made of it, to use the fancy term – put the rest back in the saucepan and boil well once again. Some cooks now add a new piece of bacon or dice an earlier piece, which is braised until soft before adding it. But the soup will already be strong and tasty enough without it. Stir well to ensure that the soup is velvety and even, as in the case of green pea soup. Nothing more is required. Serve it with diced bread baked in fat.

'Ja-nee,' says my old *tannie*, 'the Bonades like a *klitsel*. Say something about the *klitsel*.'[1]

This is true. The Bonades, spoiled by habits formed in times when the cook still held sway in the kitchen and could make decisions without supervision, always tried to gild the lily and perfume the violet. I add this purely for the sake of interest, for as a connoisseur I feel that it is unnecessary,

---

1 Mixture beaten together.

even unartistic, to further enrich dried-pea soup that is properly cooked with good bacon and ham bones. But those who insist on having their soup so strong and tasty that they do not require anything further to eat might like a *klitsel*.

The cook pours – into the warmed soup tureen in which the pea soup will be served – a cup of cream and the yolks of a few eggs, which are then beaten up, with or without adding a glass of brandy. The boiling-hot pea soup is then poured onto it and served immediately after being stirred. My own opinion on the matter, although I know only too well that *ou-tannie* will regard me as a heretic, is that this is completely unnecessary. Well prepared dried-pea soup can stand, unassisted, on its own merits.

With a *purée* of dried peas – as also with one of green peas – the cook can get up to all sorts of tricks for his vegetarian guests. The vegetarian 'meat dishes' all have such a *purée* as a basis, with or without the addition of ground beans, peanuts or nuts. In a vegetarian restaurant in Cologne I once had a baked 'duck' that was made completely from dried peas. The *purée* is then usually shaped into neat triangular pieces, a chicken bone is stuck into the one side, a paper collar is folded around it, and the piece is then fried and served as *cotelette à la Maintenon* – in imitation of the well-known lamb chops that derive their name from the lady friend of Louis XIV. That gentleman was not particularly refined when it came to table manners as he had the habit of eating chops with his fingers and then wiping them on the table cloth. Hence the paper collar that was originally attached to keep the royal fingers clean.

16 February 1945

39
Tameletjies

The bell ringer who used to come and pull the bell-rope at the market three times a day was an old half-caste. Everyone called him *Stomparmpie*.[1] His right arm had been blasted off years before when he let the fuse on a dynamite shell burn too quickly when they were busy breaking stones out of a quarry. This incident dates from my youngest childhood, and I cannot remember whether he got *voldoening*[2] for the accident as the law would stipulate nowadays. But what I do remember well is how the old fellow taught us children to make *tameletjies*.[3]

In those days sugar was quite expensive. It had to be imported from the East and West Indian islands and came in grass bags, so that when we spoke about a sugar bag, it was always a grass bag – beautiful and neatly woven – that we meant. When a new batch of sugar arrived, the shopkeeper used to send out samples in paper envelopes, each with about one and a half ounces of sugar and the price marked on it. The samples came to us children and were most welcome. Usually, especially when it was that moist, dark-brown Demarara sugar, we tucked in immediately. But there were times when we had enough self-control to keep it for making sweets – which were equally attractive to us young ones. How wonderful it was to beat up molten sugar until it formed white *kapok*,[4] a *kapok* that you could knead and twist into little sugar men, oxen, wagonwheels or whatever your childish imagination inspired you to. The artistic cooks call it '*fondant*' – we always called it *witkleisuiker*.[5]

Coffee samples also used to arrive in the same way. It might be news to my reader to hear that South Africa used to import coffee, tons of it every year. Now do not look at me as though I am plucking it from my imagination and presenting it on a tray decorated with poplar leaves. I am speaking the gospel truth, but to give an explanation would be beyond my ability. It had something to do with a foreign law, a trade agreement, and a clever way of making money by picking up each other's acorns. But it is a fact. What is more to the point concerning the coffee is that it came in envelopes as raw beans. And there was no pleasure in chewing raw coffee beans. We therefore had to roast them first. Some kinds – especially Java, paper-bag number three – would then taste quite good, especially when chewed with pine nuts.

---

1 Little stump-arm.
2 Satisfaction.
3 Sugar candy.
4 Snow.
5 White clay sugar.

Old *Stomparmpie* taught us how to make *tameletjies* the old-fashioned way. It is a kind of sweet that you do not find anymore. But, strangely enough, I came across the old recipe in one of my mediaeval cookbooks. The cooks of the Middle Ages – about 1400 to 1550 – had a tough time with sweetness. Sugar was a scarce commodity for them and they could not afford be too extravagant with it. Honey and fruit juices had to be made use of to add to the sugar supply, and egg white had to be incorporated to make the sugar look more than it really was. Nuts were also added, which is how we came to have marzipan – one of the greatest aids in the mediaeval kitchen.

The *tameletjie* is therefore one of the oldest sweets known to us and most definitely comes from China, where sugar was well known from the earliest times. The traditional way of preparing it was exactly as old *Stomparmpie* taught us.

First make sure that you have a mould. We used to use the lid of a shoebox. It was handy and could be used over and over again. It was greased with butter or fat on the inside to make sure that the *tameletjie* did not stick to the paper. The sugar would be melted in a little pan, usually seized from the kitchen without parental permission. It would then be prepared over a little fire in the garden made with appropriate care and some token of solemn ceremony under the large medlar tree. Next to the fire there would be three flat stones on which the little pan could be placed with safety, no matter how furiously the flames would leap up around it. Old *Stomparmpie* would determine the exact moment for taking the pan from the fire by poking a pointed stick into the molten sugar and rubbing a drop of it carefully between his fingers. It is, however, better to let the drop of molten sugar plunge into a cup of water; then you will not risk blistering your fingers. But the former was his way of doing it, and whenever I make *tameletjies* I still do it without thinking, even though I know only too well that it is against the rules. The aim is to judge whether the sugar has reached '*tameletjie* point', which is slightly higher than '*fondant* point' and a bit below 'caramel or burning point'. For a good *tameletjie* there should, however, be a touch of caramel or burnt sugar in the end result, and it is therefore a task for the connoisseur to determine when it is just right.

In the meantime we would crack open the pine nuts, take out the nuts, get rid of their shells, and split each nut in half. Sometimes also a few almonds if they could be found. But the almonds had to be blanched first, which was easy enough if you first put them in warm water, but took much longer if you had to use your teeth or fingers. Our tutor always used to have a pinch of ground stick-cinnamon at hand – I now suspect that it might in fact have been cassia and not real stick-cinnamon, for that was then very expensive – and if we could get *Ouma* to give us a few 'green almonds' (pistachios) out of her pantry (which we sometimes managed to do, even though they were then more or less priceless), we added them as well.

When the molten sugar was exactly right, *Stomparmpie* would hold the pan over the shoebox lid and drip a thin layer into it. 'Quick now with the nuts,' he would urge, and we would sprinkle some of our preparation on the layer of sugar, over which we then sprinkled some stick-cinnamon (or cassia). Then we waited, with the pan over the fire again, to keep the sugar in check. Then another layer of sugar, this time to the top, and on top of that the rest of the nuts. In a few minutes the *tameletjie* would be hard as a stone. It could now be taken out of the shoebox lid – a beautifully transparent sweet, the colour of topaz, with the pine nuts in it like white streaks in a piece of Amàndola marble. And it tasted as good as only a *tameletjie* could.

Today we have sweets that are made by the ton. Machines mould them and cut them up. All sorts of chemical products colour and flavour them. It is mass production, a boring repetition of the same taste and the same appearance. Very seldom do we find our traditional sweets, unadulterated *tameletjies*, true to the old recipe. And yet they are so easy to make. Every cook can beat up his own fondant sugar, and make a number of elegant sweets for the meal or thereafter. It really requires no special knack – it is one of the cook's easiest conjuring tricks. And many combinations are possible. Mix some butter with the *tameletjie* sugar and you will get a more brittle product; add a spoonful of cream and you have a juicy *tameletjie*; add a few drops of fruit juice, Van der Hum, or whatever, and immediately you have something else, although not necessarily something better.

To my mind the traditional pine-nut *tameletjie* is still one of the finest sweets our country has produced. It is just a pity they are now so hard to find.

25 May 1945

40
Sausage

There is perhaps no single dish so well known and so widespread throughout the world as the sausage. It happens to be one of the oldest dishes in the history of the art of cooking. In the first printed cookbook known to us, that of Scappi,[1] the cook of a famous Pope, you will find various recipes for making sausage. Scappi was Italian, and it is actually Italy that we have to thank for our culinary art. Today so much is made of French cooking, but in the end French cooking is nothing more than a refined form of the Italian art, and here and there it even misses something of the taste and juiciness that is so characteristic of Italian cooking.

But to return to the sausage. In today's Italy, despite all the changes it has been through, the art of sausage-making is still well known, and there are literally hundreds of kinds, from the frail, fine *solticchi* to the enormously large *mortadella*. The sausages differ greatly as to their ingredients and taste, but none that would qualify as a good sausage is made exclusively from one kind of meat. A proper sausage is a mixture of meat, spices and sometimes other ingredients, but it is also a mixture of different kinds of meat. Minced meat of one kind, even when stuffed into an intestine, is by no means a sausage – that is what you would call *sosys*,[2] which again is nothing other than the old Latin *salsisia*. This *salsisia*, which is described by Petronius, is minced meat rolled out, salted – hence the name, derived from *sal*[3] – and then fried on a warm plate. Today we call it *frikkadel*.[4] Only when two kinds of meat are minced and mixed together, properly spiced, and then stuffed into an intestine do you have our contemporary sausage. Who came upon the idea first, heaven alone knows.

An old Chinese cookbook, from a thousand years before Scappi, tells of minced food fried in wrappings that consisted mostly of vegetables, groundnuts or fruit. The Latin writers talk of *sosys-es* that must definitely have been real sausage. One recipe for it says: 'Take the breast meat of quails, the fat meat of a young lamb, the leg of a hare, lean pork, grind it, and mix with honey, salt, garlic, aniseed, coriander and a handful of bran. Stuff the mixture into little bags and roast them under warm ash.' What the little bags may be is left to the reader's imagination. Carême thinks that they were vine leaves sown together; another expert is of the opinion that they must actually have

---

1 Bartolomeo Scappi, author of *Cuoco Secreto di Papa Pio Quinto* (1570).
2 Not a real sausage, an Afrikaans word parodying the sound of the English word.
3 Salt.
4 Meatball.

been cleaned intestines. I have tried the recipe twice, and the result is excellent – if one is not too liberal with the honey, that is.

Cooking food in little bags is probably one of the oldest methods experimented with in the art of cooking. It is easy to understand why. Our forefathers did not have metal pans and saucepans in abundance. It is indeed odd to read today that an important Roman household did not have a frying pan – it only came into use much later, at more or less the same time as the fork. Earthenware pots were too expensive for poorer people, and they therefore had to make do with leaves and the innards of the animals they slaughtered. One of the traditional dishes still highly regarded today by genuine Scots is *haggis*, a pudding of minced meat cooked in a sheep's stomach – or, to put it more precisely, wrapped in the cleaned stomach of a slaughtered sheep.

Every country, and just about every district, in Europe has its unique kind of sausage. Some are world famous. The tiny pork sausages of Vienna, which we now import in tins from Argentina (not nearly as nice as those in Austria) have become truly cosmopolitan. The same holds for different kinds of salami, which should really be made with horsemeat. The salami we buy in shops has a bit of sugar added to imitate the taste of horsemeat, which is slightly sweet. There are all sorts of recipes for preparing sausage, and of such a variety that you could write a voluminous book about it all.

For us, there is one kind of sausage that stands out from the rest. This is our traditional *boerewors*,[5] which is alas seldom found in its genuine, noble, unmatched, inimitable form. What passes under that name is usually a mill-ground meat of the toughest kind, mixed with far too many breadcrumbs, and some coriander, salt and pepper. I am in complete agreement with my old *tannie* who was given some the other day at a *braaivleis* and pushed it aside in disgust, saying: '*Dis mos nie wors nie, dis sommer gemors!*' ('This isn't boerewors; it's just rubbish!') You see, she herself is a first-class sausage-maker. When I know I am going to eat her sausage, I fast the day before, confident that I will be indulging in the priceless dish she will serve me, along with homemade white bread (in her house you never find government bread, only the genuine white farm bread, crumbly, soft and easily digestible) or a portion of mushy rice.

---

5 Literally, 'farmer's sausage'.

'You know, my child,' she says, '*boerewors* must be made with mincemeat, very finely minced, except for the bacon. The bacon should be diced and added to the mince. Then, my child, when it is *braaied* on the plate, the fat will melt out and keep the sausage nice and moist. Yes, my child, it should be moist but crispy, so crispy that the outside cracks as you eat it.'

Exactly. And that goes not only for the finely minced meat. My old aunt always adds a bit of pork and mutton, although the basis of her *boerewors* is beef. And no leftover meat either. No – only selected thick, soft, round sirloin, and first-class pork. The meat is finely minced, well ground, and sometimes even pounded with a mortar. The pork is diced and frayed, then mixed with the rest of the meat. The mixture then gets its *opskiksels*[6] – a glass of wine, a glass of vinegar, a tablespoonful of brandy and salt to taste. (Always a bit more than is really necessary, in my opinion, since too much salt influences the taste of the herbs, but on this point *Tannie* simply will not listen to me. When I quote from my cookbooks, she simply says: 'My child, I keep to the commandment of Moses, who says: "You should not go with the majority in things that are wrong".' What can one say?) And then coriander (clean, new seed, without the slightest trace of weevils), pepper, a pinch of ground ginger, a leaf of sage rubbed to pieces, bruised rosemary, and – be careful with this one – a suspicion of garlic. Everything is well stirred, so that it all clings together – something that is not easy, and requires a strong arm. Then it is stuffed into the well-cleaned intestines, with the help of *Tannie's* old fashioned little copper sausage-stuffer, and hung up in a cool room until it is used.

This kind of sausage is a pleasure to eat. It is the apotheosis of sausage when it is braaied on a grill over a rhinoceros-bush fire in the open air. Or even in an iron pan on a common Swedish stove, or an Aga if you are a millionaire. I can also recommend it strongly when wind-dried while hunting. No biltong tastes better, and I know of very few dried sausages abroad that can compete with it.

But the stuff that now passes for *boerewors*! Ichabod - three times Ichabod![7]

1 June 1945

---

6 Trimmings.

7 The glory has departed. Biblical, the name given by Phinehas's wife to her son to mourn the loss of the ark.

41
Sosaties

There is perhaps no other single dish that can be regarded as more genuinely Afrikaans than *sosaties*.[1] Yet it is by no means unique to South Africa, and it is known in many different countries around the world. In Russia, for instance, you will find pieces of veal, pork, onions or preserved cucumber skewered together on a stick and roasted on the grill. The pieces of meat are first soaked in sour milk, then rolled in salt and pepper, rubbed with a clove of garlic, and roasted. The taste is of course not like that of *sosaties*, but the method of preparing it is more or less the same. In the south of France, in that beautiful Ardour valley – whence we get some of our dishes – you will find another kind of *sosatie*. The meat is first ground, then mixed with bacon and stuffed into a little gut. These sausages are then pickled, after which they are strung up on wooden pegs and roasted under the ash or on a grill.

Tant Alie says: 'Those are by no means *sosaties* – they are just some of that French rubbish you get in their restaurants.' She knows all about it because when she was still young enough to be courted by her male contemporaries, she paid a visit to Paris. According to her it was then a very strange place, certainly not what it is today or was in my time. I never had the misfortune of eating any rubbish there, although I must agree that I never came across any genuine *sosaties*.

'No,' says *Tant* Alie, 'to tell the truth, child, you don't get *sosaties* like our late *Ouma* Liesbet used to make any more. Now those were real *sosaties*.'

She explained to me at length exactly what kind of sosaties they were. And since I must say that *Ouma* Liesbet – I never knew her, as when I was born she had already exchanged her earthly existence for a heavenly equivalent, and all that remained was the memory of her unrivalled cooking, especially when it came to making *pannas*,[2] brawn and Spanish-reed chops, about which I may have something to say at a later stage – that *Ouma* Liesbet used to be exceptionally orthodox in following the rules when making her *sosaties*, I can do no better than tell the reader how she went about it.

First, the meat. The basis, the foundation, the cornerstone of a decent *sosatie* is pork. And not just any old pork. Today we tend to cut *sosaties* from whatever piece of meat we get hold of, and we are only too pleased to get some. But on the farm it used to be different. When a pig was slaughtered,

---

1 Kebabs.
2 Scrapple.

which happened regularly every month because *Oupa* Hermaans was very fond of it, they carefully cut the *hasievleis*[3] from the vertebrae just below the ribs – long, soft strips, with quite a lot of fat between the fibres, but not enough to make it rancid. The strips were then cut into even pieces, dried well, and placed in an earthenware bowl on a layer of orange leaves. Then a moist cloth was draped over it and the bowl was placed in a cool spot, where the large mulberry tree cast its shade upon the windowsill. Then pieces of mutton, about a third of the amount of pork, and preferably from the leg of the lamb, but sometimes also the fillet, were cut up and a few pieces of good, thick, soft bacon added to it. This too was dried and then mixed with the pork in the bowl.

Then onions were cut into thin, even slices – medium, fresh, strong onions that had not been dunked in boiling water to lose part of their manliness, onions strong and juicy. A layer of onion slices was placed in another bowl, and on top of it a layer of the meat, with a raisin (freed of its pips) here and there, a dried apricot or sliced *platperske*[4] and, like little red jewels amongst it all, some small chillies. Then a layer of brown sugar, mixed with some curry powder, salt, pepper, and good coriander seed that the weevils had not got hold of. Then another layer of sliced onion, this time with a small piece of onion leaf (*Ouma*, as far as I know, never used garlic for her *sosaties*) and a few of the orange leaves on which the meat had previously been laid. Then another layer of meat, sprinkled once again with the curry powder, brown sugar and the rest. All of this was then covered with a last layer of sliced onion. Now it was ready for the sauce or curry pickle.

For this *Ouma* used a cup of red wine, two cups of good wine-vinegar – she would never have dreamed of using white or malt vinegar, and I would not recommend it either, for that would merely amount to diluted acetic acid with no trace of a wine flavour – a cup of water, a teaspoonful of salt, a few peppercorns and a tablespoonful of good curry powder. She put it all together in a saucepan on the fire and warmed it up slowly, stirring it to give the curry powder the opportunity of learning to swim in it evenly. The moment it began to bubble she took it off the heat and poured it over the *sosaties*, always enough to cover the meat properly. The *sosaties* were then placed back in the cool spot where they remained until morning. Perhaps they would be stirred with a wooden spoon during the night, but it was better just to leave them

---

3 Fillet.

4 Dried peach.

alone until morning. Then it was stirred, and *Ouma* would always add a cup of sour milk or cream. I consider this worth doing, but on this point many people differ – holding the view that *sosaties* do not need milk. In any event, the meat and the onions had to be stirred and mixed well, then left until the meat had absorbed enough of the flavour of the other ingredients. How long is a problem that every cook has to solve for himself. Personally, I prefer less than twenty-four hours; otherwise the meat becomes pickled and loses its childlike innocence.

Then the sticks had to be cut, preferably from green bamboo, although I admit that nowadays this might be virtually impossible to find. And take care, for if you are not used to doing it you risk inflicting some terrible wounds on your fingers. See to it that each of them has a sharp point, then spear the meat onto the sticks, with a piece of bacon between every two or three pieces of meat. The *sosaties* are now ready for *braaing*, which should be done on a hot grill or over glowing coals – I prefer the coals. Some *braai* it in a pan in the oven, but that is not advisable.

While the *sosaties* are *braaing*, pour the sauce through a colander. The strained fluid is then heated in a saucepan; and what remains in the colander is put in a pan with a bit of fat, baked until soft, then stirred into the warm sauce once more. Boil the sauce until it starts thickening and serve it with the *sosaties*, but in a separate gravy boat. Do not of course forget about the rice or, if you prefer, the mealy boiled potatoes. And with this meal one drinks a good red farm wine – not the best, since the *sosaties* have too sharp a taste to complement a truly first-class wine.

13 June 1945

42
Brinjals

In my youth we used to speak of *eiervrugte*,[1] a literal translation of the English 'egg-plant'. My Dutch friends use the French word '*aubergine*'. In Afrikaans we say *brinjal*. But whatever you call it, it is a beautiful vegetable. Hardly a 'fruit', even in the sense in which an avocado is a fruit, or a tomato. Because, although there are those who eat brinjals raw, just as there are those who chew cabbage, turnips and onions, it is not really a vegetable I would recommend for a salad. No matter how pretty it may look, you first have to tame the brinjal with heat before it can be enjoyed.

Properly prepared for human consumption, however, it is one of the most delicious vegetables the garden or the veld has to offer. One knowledgeable cook maintains that it is in fact the most delicious, and devotes a whole chapter to its virtues. Well, taste is not really something you can argue about. It simply varies too much. No two people will have exactly the same preference for a 'taste'. It is, of course, completely true that there will be a measure of concurrence about which foods are tasty and which are not, or which are sour, salty or sweet. The scientific know-alls tell us that these are the only three distinctions a sensible person can make – sour, salty and sweet – but the knowledgeable cook knows better. He understands only too well that there are all sorts of subtle tastes, mixtures of those three, blended so fine that you would never tell them apart unless you have refined and 'educated' your sense of taste.

So please do not try to make a brinjal salad. Raw bringils could be better used as trimmings on the table. I recently met an old *oom* who planted some persimmons. 'I don't eat the stuff,' he told me, 'but the wife says they look beautiful among the other fruit.' He knew what he was talking about.

Select your brinjals with care. Discard those that are wrinkled, wilted or a bit dried out. Also those that are too large or too old – they will be spongy and tasteless, even with the best treatment a cook can give them. Take young ones that are firm, juicy, and display their youthfulness. There are different types. The best are probably those that are really white or cream-coloured, but you seldom find them on the market. If you do not grow them yourself, they will be very difficult to get hold of. The second best is the medium-to-long kind, purplish-blue, with hues of reddish-brown here and there. Then come the medium-sized round ones with a brown colouring. Last come the large brown or purplish-red round ones, sometimes as large as a football.

---

1 Egg fruit.

Peel the brinjal neatly. The cookbooks say you should do it with a sharp knife, which is possible but rather difficult. You can also put it in boiling water and then pull off the skin, something that is not quite as easily done as it is, for instance, with a tomato. And if you wish, you could also cook it with its peel. But whatever you do, the peel will always be hard. I would therefore make a case for using the sharp knife.

Now cut the brinjal into slices and lay them on a dry cloth. Sprinkle with some fine salt and allow them to lie in peace for half an hour. By that time they will be sweating and coated with moisture. Dry them well, and they will then be ready for cooking.

But how? Frying? Well, then you would need boiling fat or oil to dunk them in, preferably in a wire basket, and let them fry until nice and crisp. This is how the Italian cooks many of his juicy vegetables – marrows, brinjals, cucumbers, pumpkins. The result is a thin, crisp slice, just like a potato chip, that is fried until it is cracklingly crisp. Sprinkle with fine salt and serve on a napkin. You could also fry the slices in butter or fat in a pan. They will be a little less crisp, but have more flavour. Sprinkle finely snipped parsley and a puff of white pepper over it.

These are both simple methods, but neither really brings out the very subtle taste of the brinjal. That you will only get when you stew them slowly, with or without butter. Put the slices in a pot or deep pan – an earthenware saucepan is perhaps best – with salt to taste, a pinch of fine ginger, a shred of mace, as much pepper as you like, and a large lump of butter. Then stew slowly over a moderate fire until nicely soft. Some people stir it; some add a tablespoon of thick cream. Again this is a matter of taste. Brinjals stewed in this way are delicious enough without anything added. A refined way of serving them is to make little tartlets from the best cake dough, fill them with stewed brinjal, then bake them in the oven until nicely brown. But these days you do not find good flour for making tartlets, and a tartlet made from government flour is a monstrosity as far as I am concerned.

I have, however, had brinjal tart – the open kind the Americans are so fond of. The brinjal is cooked, mashed and mixed with sugar, a glass of wine, cinnamon and a pinch of salt, then used as a tart filling. One can also dice the brinjal, then bake it in the oven with butter, cinnamon and sugar, as is the old-fashioned way with marrows.

There is also stuffed brinjal, where the poor thing is filled with mincemeat – or, if you are a vegetarian, with a surrogate made from ground walnuts, carrots and breadcrumbs – and then baked in fat. But none of these is as good as stewed brinjals.

What about the pips? Well, if the brinjals are young and virginal, you really do not have to worry about the pips, and an old brinjal with hard pips is hardly suitable for the table. Middle-aged ones with pips that are still reasonably soft can be fried or stewed, pips and all. If you are fussy you can cut away the pips, but in the process you will also lose something of the flavour that gives the brinjal its characteristic taste.

3 August 1945

43
Cold Soup

It is purely a matter of habit that makes us always eat our soup warm, and preferably boiling hot. There are many delicious cold soups that are very handy when you need to put a meal together quickly. Cold consommé is well known. It is simply meat soup, preferably made from mutton, beef and pork, that has been kept in the fridge for a while until it has formed a jelly. If it is a weak soup, like you often find in hotels, it will not have the ability to gel. All you will then get is an ice-cold, sometimes utterly tasteless, watery kind of food, with possibly even a bit of hard fat floating on top.

This is the ultimate in ignorant cooking. A cold soup should have no fat whatsoever, floating or otherwise. The fat should be carefully scooped off. An oil soup, as I will describe in a moment, is something different. There the fattiness is so interwoven with the other ingredients that it becomes an integral part of the soup.

There is a first-class cold *bortsch*, or beetroot soup. It is simply boiled chicken soup with beetroot cut up and added. They are cooked together until the chicken soup has acquired a beetroot flavour, put on one side and, when cold, strained through a cloth, and the expressed juice of a few young beetroot then added. This makes the soup wonderfully red. Spice and salt, and place in the fridge, but do not allow it to gel. That will only happen if the chicken soup is strong and hearty – as it should be. As soon as it shows signs of wanting to gel, remove it from the fridge and beat it a little with an eggbeater. It should be fluid when served, with just a touch of crispness.

Sweet cold soup is always a fruit soup, and can be made in different ways. A good orange soup is made by taking a few spoonfuls of maizena, a few spoonfuls of sugar, a blade of mace, cinnamon and a cup of water, putting them all together on the fire and stirring until the mixture becomes thick. Move the pot away from the heat, remove the cinnamon and mace, add four cups of orange juice and a pinch of grated orange peel, and boil it up once more. Remove from the heat and add – carefully while stirring slowly, lest it curdle – the yolks of three eggs. Remove from the heat once more and beat repeatedly; and when too thick, dilute with water. Put it in the fridge and serve with almond rusks when nice and cold. This soup is easy enough to make, but whenever I have not made it myself it has always been a complete flop. It requires a special knack for beating in the eggs.

During my travels overseas I came across an interesting soup. They call it a *gazpacho*, but it is actually a mix. I really like it, especially on the farm in winter, when there is the opportunity to add all sorts of veld food. But I must admit that it is an acquired taste. Still, those who are willing to attempt something new can try it, as follows.

Take a handful of any kind of herbs available – the greater the variety the better. You could for example use the following: thyme, mint, rosemary, beetroot leaves, lettuce leaves, mustard leaves, sorrel leaves, the inside leaves of a cabbage – in short, any kind that can be used for a salad, including young onions or leeks, young carrots, and a mealy potato. Cut up or grate it all very fine, and mix. Stir in, drop by drop, a mixture of two spoonfuls of good salad oil and a tablespoonful of wine-vinegar (never use the white shop vinegar – it is pure acetic acid, probably made from wood) in which you have first dissolved a teaspoonful of fine salt. Stir it all thoroughly – the more it is stirred, the better. Then pour over it four cups of water and stir well once more. Place it in the fridge and serve with pieces of toast, or – my preference – cheesecake. A bit more oil can sometimes be added to give the soup body. But the big secret is to crush all the herbs, all the elements in it, to such an extent that they will impart their flavour and an enjoyable juiciness to the soup. If one of the ingredients tends to dominate too much, this is because the stirring and the mixing have not been thorough enough. It should be a properly 'blended' mixture in which all the flavours can be tasted without any of them being dominant.

There are those who first cook this mixture, strain it through a cloth, and only then place it in the fridge. But then it amounts to nothing more than a meatless vegetable soup, of which there is an infinite variety. The novelty lies precisely in the fact that it is not cooked. It is, in other words, a more or less watery salad. In America it is always made with the addition of cream cheese, sometimes also with shelled nuts, like Brazil nuts or almonds, but this is a somewhat refined touch that really does not belong here. A cold nut soup is something else for which there are many recipes. It is made more or less like the abovementioned orange soup – the basis is always a custard of maizena or rice flour, whichever you wish, and the nuts, eggs and spices are also added according to taste. Sometimes raisins or fruit preserves are also mixed in. The permutations are as varied as for ice cream.

9 November 1945

44
Christmas Drinks

'Merry Christmas' implies cheerfulness and a mood of homely, convivial cosiness. I admit that this may be possible when food is not plentiful and there is no chance of any liquor, but I realise equally that it is more easily achieved when the festivities are celebrated around a table well laden and when the host has seen to it that a suitable quantity of drink is provided.

We Bonades are not teetotallers. We are moderate people, farming folk with a tradition of viniculture, based on the *dictum* of old King Solomon that 'he is a fool who allows wine to dumbfound him'. And we honour that tradition as much on Christmas day as we do on any other day of the year. We know that wine can make you cheerful, cosy and convivial. The scripture says so, and we agree.

As a young upstart I used to help *Oupa* Jan fill four or five bottles of sweet wine on Christmas morning. Unfortunately we no longer get that type of natural, unadulterated farm wine. I vividly remember its colour – not quite red and also not quite gold, the colour of a fire opal with the shine of a *naartjie* peel. In my mind's eye I can still see a few drops on the little tap, me carefully transferring them with my forefinger to my tongue, and I can still hear *Oupa* saying: 'That is not done – you will get your glass at table this afternoon.' These days, unfortunately, I no longer get such a glass of wine. According to law our wine farmers have to blend their sweet wine with spirits when it contains more than so much sugar, or whatever. Heaven knows why, but this is what the law stipulates, and as long the law dictates, I see no way in which we will ever again, even at Christmas, be able to enjoy a first-class sweet wine – as fine as that decanted by my oupa.

And yet, sweet wine is just about indispensable at the Christmas meal. Therefore we have to make do with what we can get, and even with the added sixteen per cent of spirits there are still good, palatable sweet wines to be found. They are mostly red or reddish-yellow fortified wines, of the class we call 'Port', although they really are not port wines at all. They are blended wines, sweet and heavy, with a fairly high spirit content and rarely an exceptionally good bouquet, although they sometimes have a passably good taste. As heavy wine they should be used in moderation, preferably after the meal when coffee is served. It is not advisable to drink them earlier.

No wine farmer, if he is a good wine farmer, will allow his Christmas guests to spoil their palates and their appetites before the Christmas meal with the now fashionable mixtures called 'cocktails'. A glass of good sherry – either

completely without sweetness, with the genuine bitter, 'nutty' taste that the *'flor'* gives it, or for those who are more partial to something with a grain of sweetness, the darker, sweeter type – is, however, something that can always be recommended as an appetiser before the meal. It can even accompany the soup, especially a hearty meat soup. Even when there is already some sherry in the soup – and my old *tannie* never served a meat soup for Christmas without adding a few tablespoons of good sherry before the soup tureen was taken to the table – a glass of sherry will go with it admirably.

Since we usually have our Christmas meal in the afternoon and Christmas day tends to be rather hot, the table wine should be light, chilled and delicious. There are quite a few good white wines to choose from. Those cultivated from the Riesling grape are regarded as being the best, simply because they are at present made and blended with care. They are the lightest wines on the market and can safely be enjoyed with most of the dishes served at the Christmas table. It is sometimes argued that they are too sour, but that complaint is completely unfounded as our white wines contain less acidity than most of the imported ones. They should be served as cold as possible. Half an hour in the fridge is the best way of chilling them, and when there is no fridge at hand they can be opened, wrapped in a wet cloth and placed in front of an open window to catch the draft for half an hour before being brought to table.

A red wine should not be chilled, but can also be opened half an hour before the meal. There is perhaps less to choose from among the red wines. There are the lighter types with more or less the same alcohol content as the white wines, then there are the heavier Cabernet types, with a darker colour, a much better bouquet and a stronger flavour. Some of those now being sold are first-class wines that do not have to stand back for imported table wines, and they are all healthy, unadulterated wines that no one need be afraid of. One of the greatest benefactors of mankind, the famous Pasteur, expressly declared: 'Table wine is the best, the safest and the healthiest drink one can drink'. The Bonades underwrite this pronouncement, on the authority of generations of experience.

But what about sparkling wine? It is fashionable in certain circles to present sparkling wine as something special. This fashion is simply a form of snobbishness, for sparkling wine is never a natural wine and the wine connoisseur will never prefer it to the real thing. While champagne is an imported sparkling wine, and the imitations that we get here cannot by any means be compared to it, we have among our own natural wines many that are far superior to the imported sparkling ones. In time we will probably find a sparkling wine of our own that will be able to compete with the Italian sparkling wines – which are, of course, not champagnes – but as yet we have none. We do have wines, white and red, that sparkle and that the wine merchants sell for more than our good wines. We can mix our red and white wines with sparkling water if we wish – that makes a very useful drink for those who like it, and on a warm summer's day such a mixture is refreshing and delicious. But this is not the best way to drink wine at table. It is equally inappropriate to add a block of ice to your wine glass.

For the after-dinner party, in the afternoon or in the evening, and for the younger generation who have not yet come to understand the seriousness of drinking wine, one can make all sorts of drinks in which light wine plays a large role. The most popular mixtures are those consisting of a light wine, fruit juice, spice and something that lends a distinctive taste or attraction to the mixture, such as flowers, ripe fruit or herbs. Such mixtures can be sweetened by adding sugar, syrup or *moskonfyt*.[1] For a heavier mixture some brandy or a glass of liqueur can be added, but then it needs to be drunk with care, for a mixture like that can be extremely seductive. My old *tannie* left handwritten recipes for several such mixtures – they were served to us young people on birthdays and festive occasions. The two that follow are copied from them.

Mulberry drink. 'Take two cups of fresh mulberries, cleaned, and grind in the mortar with two tablespoons of brown sugar; pour over it a bottle of red wine. Stir well and place in front of the window (or preferably in the fridge). For use, put in a can and stir in a pinch of nutmeg, ginger and mace; add six bottles of soda water and serve in glasses with a mulberry in each.'

I would use more sugar, but this is a matter of taste. It is a good, enjoyable drink that is as pleasing to the taste as it is to the eye.

The other recipe is not really for children, and is more or less a kind of punch that most people will find far too sweet.

Apricot drink. 'Peel and de-pip three dozen medium-size apricots; crack open half a dozen of the pips and take the white part, bruise it, and add it to the

---

1 Grape syrup.

peeled apricots; add a cup of good brandy; mix with two cups of white sugar and beat together well; let it stand for a few hours and then add two bottles of white wine, a cup of ginger syrup, a glass of Van der Hum and two glasses of sweet wine. Beat well and let it stand until it settles. Decant without disturbing the precipitate at the bottom and mix with two bottles of soda water. Serve with a piece of ice in each glass. This tastes even better when made with dried apricots.'

There are many such fruit-wine mixtures, but it is questionable whether in the end they taste any better than a good glass of wine by itself. But as the host and hostess have to cater for everyone on Christmas day, it is advisable for them to be well acquainted with the art of making such mixtures. When you have among your guests some who are so opposed to wine that they refuse to try it even on Christmas day, the wine can be left out of the mixture, and a clean fruit 'bowl' concocted.[2]

23 November 1945

---

2 See Chapter 8 on 'Grog and Bowl'.

45
Oysters

Brother Jan's eldest finished matric with a first-class pass, and is now enrolled as a first-year medical student. Would I please keep an eye on him, wrote Brother Jan, and see to it that everything was all right?

My memory of the little chap – it had been about ten years since I last saw him – was of a bolt-upright, skinny as a fishbone, short-pants, barefoot youngster with mischievous little eyes, a turned-up nose pointing skywards to such an extent that it always seemed to be smelling something unpleasant, and front teeth that a yappy little dog would be proud of. Now I am confronted with a fellow stretching an inch and a half further into the air than I would be able to myself if my rheumatism would allow me to straighten up – a fellow with smoothly plastered hair, the foreshadowing of a moustache on his upper lip, the even more suggestive blue-black along the jaw, and the inkling of that cheeky, half-embarrassed attitude his generation is afflicted with when confronted by older people for the first time. The turned-up nose was just as turned-up, and the teeth just as white as before, but the young man was now grown-up and no longer gave the impression of a hungry, moulting chicken. The yellow tie swaying in the wind – convincing evidence of his rank as a first-year student – and the grey blazer had nothing in common with the short-pants of ten years before.

It did not take us long to leave behind the protocol-like relationship between uncle and nephew, as *Kleinjan* at his best is quite adaptable. Within an hour I had got to know everything about the family, the farm and his school adventures. It was apparent that *Neef* already felt at home in his new environment, especially after the initiation ceremony that – it pains me to say – is still the habit at institutions we recklessly still call 'universities'. It was just as apparent that he would not let himself be intimidated by anything that *Omie*, or whoever, said, taught or advised.

When it was time for lunch I took him to a place where I sometimes enjoy the midday meal. There the waiter came straight towards us with the news that they had oysters in stock. I ordered two dozen without thinking. *Kleinjan*, his couldn't-care-less, 'you won't impress me' attitude notwithstanding, was in awe of the scene at the club, and his lively banter quietened down somewhat. When the oysters came, he stared at them like a Kalahari Bushman seeing a motorbike for the first time.

'Now what on earth is this, *Omie*?' he asked, and I imagined that I saw his turned-up nose flipping a centimetre higher.

'Oysters, man, the very best! We're fortunate to get them today. They're usually flown to Johannesburg, and it's seldom we get the opportunity of eating them here.'

'Eat, *Omie*? ... *Si* ...' His politeness made him bite off the word in his mouth[1] just as I swallowed my first oyster, appropriately baptised with a drop of lemon juice.

'Of course. Look, you take them like this,' and I showed him how. Unfortunately, just as I was busy baptising it, his oyster went into a spasmodic convulsion.

'But what the ... *Omie*, this thing is still alive ...'

'I should think so. You'd never eat dead oysters – that would be far too dangerous. Come now, don't be so childish. If you want to be a doctor, you'll have to get used to trying everything, and I give you my word that you'll enjoy this. There now, swallow it down ...'

'Please ... no ... *Omie* ... *Omie* must excuse me. It looks ... it looks just like *dermskraapsels*.'[2]

'Well then, have your *dermskraapsels*, or have you never eaten sausage? If you don't want your oysters, give them to me. I'll eat them for you, and you can order yourself some soup. But I must say, *Kleinjan*, I thought that Brother Jan's son would be able to show he's a man, even when it comes to oysters.'

Kleinjan did not order soup. He took a swig of his beer and followed me with his eyes – no longer mischievous but really afraid, as if he had come across a cannibalistic *omie* – as I devoured one oyster after the other. Only at the end, after I had encouraged him several times to order something for himself, did he ask me in a whisper, '*Omie*, is that really nice?'

I regard it as a civilising task to teach someone to eat oysters, and though I am by nature – like all of us Bonades – impatient, especially with people who are full of themselves (that is to say, who do not agree with me), I did my best to bring my nephew around in a most avuncular way to try just one oyster. And then just one more. There were, however, only half a dozen left, and we could not order any more, oysters being so rare these days. My reward was *Kleinjan's*

---

1 *Kleinjan* was about to say '*sies*', which expresses disgust.
2 Scrapings of gut.

well-considered opinion: 'Yes, I must admit, *Omie*, they really are not bad.'

Yes, *nefies and niggies*,³ oysters really are not bad. That is, if you eat them properly – without all sorts of additions that end up spoiling the pure, undefiled, immaculately innocent, genuine oyster taste with other tastes and flavours that are a real sin to the oyster connoisseur. Serve it in its shell. Open it yourself if you have the slightest fear the waiter will let the point of his knife slip into the creature's tender flesh. Make sure that you at least get it served with its muscle still functioning so that it can shrink. And do not come and speak of cruelty or barbaric treatment of a defenceless little animal. Such ultra-ultra-humanitarian excuses do not hold for a cook. Will he who gives in to them ever dare eat duck liver *pâté* or tortoise soup or crayfish salad or stewed eel? I would ask whoever holds forth along such lines to honestly guarantee that the *mielie* feels no pain when you strip off its leaves or the watermelon when you cut it open. Was it not the portly *Oubaas* Chesterton who put his vegetarian friend in his place by asking: 'And why should only the salt and the mustard suffer?'

Therefore see to it that your oysters are still alive and eat them either (and preferably) in their virginal innocence without adding anything, or with a drop of lemon juice to soften slightly the saltiness still clinging to them. Do not fry them – that is to do them an injustice. Make no soup from them – that is to adulterate something delicious and pure into something complex and artificial. Eat them with a piece of bread and butter. If you have the opportunity, try them with a bit of caviar in a sandwich. But never with red pepper or onions or anything else that could spoil the fine taste of the oyster. You should therefore also be careful about what you drink with them. You do not actually have to drink anything, since they contain enough water themselves. But if you must, then choose between a good beer, preferably a dark type, and a white wine that is not too sugarless and that should, of course, not be sparkling. For us older Bonades – since, as you see, the younger generation still has much to learn – champagne with oysters is from the devil and not mentioned in front of Christian children – *inter Christianos non nominanda sunt*, as the Old Father says. And never think that, if you bear these tips in mind, you will ever be in danger when eating oysters. They are the most innocent and delicious animals ever to come out of the sea.

21 December 1945

---

3 Nephews and nieces.

46
Our Daily Bread

Now that the war is over, we might be getting bread again. What we have been getting instead is … well, the Bonades are not in the habit of using bad language – they rather suffer in silence. For does Solomon not say: 'A fool lets his anger rail, but the wise one calms it down'?

I do, though, still manage to eat good bread from time to time. When my petrol ration justifies it, I drive to the farm. *Tannie* still has the pure, genuine farm flour that is ground in the old mule mill – a contraption that is now as rare as a young woman who is satisfied with the nails that our dear Lord gave her. And she – I mean *Tannie*, of course, not our oh-so-stylish young woman – still sifts it from time to time to produce a first-class fine flour. I am not sure whether it is unlawful or punishable, but if I were in her shoes I would do exactly the same. Because I simply refuse to eat bread made from war flour. That is … but what did Solomon say?

And what is there more delicious, tasty, healthy and attractive than a loaf of freshly baked farm bread? With farm butter or soft fat on it – I prefer the beautiful, yellow-brown soft fat remaining in the saucepan after a plump chicken has been turned into a blessed food offering. It has a taste that is unique, and with a sliver of biltong on top – what more on this earth could the most refined gourmet want? Bread made from sifted flour is always nice and white – its colour is different to that made from unsifted flour. *Tannie's* is usually grey-yellow and grainy, with a crust – ah, that crust!! It commands more than one exclamation mark. For the crust is surely one of the most important parts of a good loaf of bread, like the crisp skin of a roasted sucking pig – at least it should be. Alas, in the city bread we have been getting, it is like … but let me not forget the old king's admonition.

Tannie has her own secret method of baking bread, and I will not give it away here. But I once tried baking my own bread. The oven was nice and hot, there were no unwelcome visitors in the kitchen, and there was a bowl full of sifted flour. For one with some talent and an inclination towards preparing food, the temptation was very great indeed. I nearly succumbed, but fortunately my sense of honesty prevailed over my spirit of inquiry. And I received my just reward for that restraint in the face of the devil of temptation when *Tannie* later asked me if I would not show her how 'a learned chap' makes bread. I fear the invitation was meant somewhat sarcastically, as she knew only too well that I have no 'knack' with baking cake or kneading dough, but challenges are there to be taken up by a knight, and so I tried. The result was first-class, and *Tannie* graciously complimented me, although I know she prefers her

own method to mine. She maintains that farm bread requires no milk, and she prefers old leaven to the bought yeast that I use. Well, each according to his taste.

I take ten cups of sifted flour – not sifted from the rubbish you get today, but from pure farm flour – three cups of milk, four tablespoons of sugar, two tablespoons of sifted salt, a lump of butter and a cup of warm water. The milk is boiled up with the sugar, salt and butter and, when lukewarm, I stir into it a packet of that shop yeast that *Tannie* dislikes. Then comes the lukewarm water, and some beating mixes it all together nicely. I slowly add the sifted flour and stir until I have a good dough. This dough is then kneaded – and I admit that this is something I do not do half as well as *Tannie* or even Ayah Rosa, but it is an indispensable requirement – why, I really do not know. One of these days, as soon as I have my own sifted flour, I shall experiment and see what happens when you bake without kneading. But my recipe says: 'Knead … knead until it is properly soft and plump'. Then it is covered with a damp cloth until it has 'risen' properly. This normally takes six to seven hours, and it is therefore best to make the dough in the evening and to let it rise overnight. As soon as it has risen nice and high, the breads should be shaped, either long or round, as you please, and greased with some butter or fat. They should then be left to stand until they are twice as large as when they left your fingers, then baked in a hot oven. My first batch was not like *Tannie's* white bread, but in my opinion it was first-class. The Ayah said it would have been better 'if *Baas* had added a mealy potato'. I will try that one of these days.

But when will that be? How much longer will the aftermath of war linger, and when will we have flour to bake with again?

11 January 1946

47
Tongue

There are different types of tongue, like the malicious tongue and the false tongue, but that is not my present concern, although I would like to say that the Bonades have had to endure much bother and discomfort from that kind of tongue. However that may be, the tongues I would like to deal with are the kind you can touch with your own tongue without being hurt by them.

There are also different tongues of this kind for, as *Neef* Frans tells me, every animal in existence has a tongue. *Neef* Frans wrote a thesis on lizard tongues for his doctorate at one of our universities and, listening to him, it must be the most wonderful, strange and scientifically interesting tongue in the world. But I have never heard of cooking gecko or rock lizard tongue as a dish for the table. A crocodile tongue is so tough and disgusting to look at that when I once had the opportunity of trying to practice some culinary art on it, it all became too much and I abandoned the attempt.

To come to my topic: the tongues we normally bring to the kitchen are those of oxen and sheep, of which only the former is really worthy of the culinary art. Smaller tongues – those of sheep, pigs and even smaller animals – are usually cut up and used for brawn or a *ragout*. (It is, by the way, high time that we found a good Afrikaans word for 'ragout': in its original French it means something that is tasted again, for a second or subsequent time, *ragouter*. In French cooking it is a meat stew made from already roasted or cooked meat with vegetables and spice – thus a kind of warmed-up second-hand stew. Even we Bonades do not have a family word for it. My grandmother on my mother's side used to say *ragoe*, with the g pronounced very softly. The Dutch members of our linguistic family do not have a suitable name for it either. But once I set off on a side trail, I never manage to outspan – so let me leave etymological puzzles on one side.)

It is only when you go along on a hunting expedition that you discover how delicious other varieties of animal tongue are. The tongue is, for instance, the only part of a *wildebeest* that is to my mind suitable for the connoisseur's table. The same holds for the tongue of a zebra and, although my hunting friends will not agree, the tongue of every kind of grass-eating game, as opposed to that of game like kudu or impala that eat leaves and branches. A camel's tongue looks quite delicious, but it is too tough, has a thick skin, and does not taste at all good. I may have been unlucky with the only camel tongue I ever had the opportunity of eating, but I remember being as disappointed with the camel bone marrow, which was a really awful oil. My experience in this area is admittedly limited, and I will not place myself in the pulpit on the subject. We Bonades only stick to a belief in the face of being burned at the stake when we definitely know more about the matter than those who dare to contradict us. And since my readers will more than likely not have had much to do with the tongue of game, I need say no more about it.

I will therefore restrict myself to ox tongue, which when all is said and done is still the only kind of tongue the cook can shed a tear about when it is not properly prepared for the table. We use it fresh, when it is at its best, but it is also good salted and pickled, and when dried and smoked it has an exotic appeal that I find quite fascinating. All the cookbooks describe at length how to prepare it in those different guises, and it would take up many pages to repeat it all here. One or two things that every cook should know about cooking ox tongue may, however, be appropriate and even educational at this stage, simply because one usually finds, if the tongue dishes served in hotels are anything to go by, that this knowledge is rarely acquired.

As regards fresh tongue, the first and most important point is that when cooked, roasted or stewed, it must be genuinely fresh. The least cause for concern should be taken as proof of guilt, and a fresh tongue that is the slightest bit 'gamey' will not do. Even when you try and overcome the problem with vinegar, spice or other ways of making it smell or taste different, in the end the result will be a complete failure. And a fresh tongue spoils very quickly, especially when the air is warm and humid. Therefore put it in the fridge, or in a cool place, as soon as it comes from the butcher, and use it as soon as possible. Cook by dunking it in boiling water, then letting it cook slowly for an hour where the fire is not too hot, with a bit of lemon juice, or vinegar, and some salt in the water. Some also add herbs, a carrot and an onion, but this is not necessary. A cooked tongue is something very tasty in itself, so flavoursome and soft that it could almost be served without further preparation. However, most cooks prefer to peel off the skin and refine its outer appearance by removing any superfluous pieces of meat and some of the cartilage and sinews in it. When tongue is served cold, it is put in the fridge with a weight on top of it in some of the water in which it was cooked, which then forms a jelly around it. Before it is put in the pot, it should be properly prepared – all the fat should be cut away, the bones inside should be taken out, and it should be rolled up and fastened with a little peg to keep it together. It should not be cooked for too long or it will become mushy; but it must be cooked sufficiently or it will be tough.

Cooked tongue serves as a basis for many first-class tongue dishes, to which French cooks have given wonderful names. You can slice it up, dice it, cut it into round pieces, or just do as you please; and it can then be fried or stewed. The dish is given its particular name according to the kind of sauce used. The best of the many tongue dishes are perhaps those in which quite thick slices of cooked tongue are stewed in a sweet wine with herbs, almonds and raisins. The sauce is thickened with some fine flour and a beaten egg yolk. A small spoon of lemon juice is added, and the dish is served as hot as possible.

A salted tongue is first soaked in fresh water for a few hours, preferably all night long, then slowly cooked in unsalted water that is replaced at least once. It should be cooked quickly the first time, then again 'lukewarm'. The result is a tongue that is baby-soft, and that requires nothing more than mustard and a good soft-boiled potato, with nutmeg and butter of course, and a glass or two of red farm wine. Many different dishes can be made with salted tongue, but most of them seem to involve unnecessary trouble. For cooked, salted tongue is a dish in itself – a delicious dish that, if well prepared, will honour any cook.

Dried tongue is a completely different matter, so different that my views on this subject must wait for another occasion.

22 February 1946

48
Camp Food I

If there is one kind of cooking we farm people understand, it is the art of preparing good food where we camp or outspan. It is actually an art that we Bonades should know well but, to tell you the genuine, gospel truth, our family has somewhat lost the touch. In the old days, as my grandfather often told me, it was the custom to spend New Year's Day somewhere in the veld. They would take the large tent-wagon with a team of oxen, and *Ouma* and the girls would collect provisions for days before the great outing. They would take three of the farmworkers with them – *Outa* Doors, April, who was in charge of the oxen and had to look after them, carry wood, do odd jobs, clean fish, and on occasion look for bait for *Oupa* in the rock crevices, and Toontjies, who had to assist *Ouma* in making food for the men. I have a vague memory of one of these outings, but I was far too young to remember much. With the arrival of the motor car, the tent wagon made way for the lorry and – I do not really know why – we became more civilised, urban, refined – spoilt I would say – and we seldom undertook anything more challenging or old-fashioned than half a day's picnic somewhere on the farm.

But old-fashioned camp life, as I later rediscovered it in the Transvaal at a Dingaan's Day[1] festival in the Lowveld, was a revelation of what Boer women can achieve. I speak not of the kind of food we took along with us – brawn, sausage, bacon, koeksisters, buttermilk cake, sosaties, pickles, pickled fish, and dried fruit. Those we still take along today when we Bonades go for a picnic in the motor car, along with all sorts of tinned food that are not to be frowned upon. What I am talking about is the food prepared at the campsite, more or less fresh from the veld.

There are, for instance, the meat dishes. The game or birds that the men shot would hang for a day or two. The exception was partridge and *dikkop*, that were immediately cleaned and put into an iron pot along with bacon, salt, herbs and a bit of farm wine to stew, with the fire below it and coals on top, until it was time to eat. Prepared in this way, even an African coot is a delicacy.

Hare was always served in the farm style. This, I believe, is a variation on one of the very oldest recipes, but it definitely differs from the 'jugged hare' and stewed hare recipes you find in the cookbooks. We always used to cook the hare in shreds, or rather braise it, with onions, herbs and a glass of wine, and done in this way it was as tender and tasty as you could wish it to be. The game was always roasted in the iron pot, in more or less the same way as the fowl.

---

1 South African public holiday on 16 December, now known as the Day of Reconciliation.

In the Transvaal I saw *tannies* bake in an anthill oven, but this did not appeal to me and they also tended not to lard the meat properly. Our game is almost always too lean to eat without lard, and the more thoroughly it is larded the better.

Tame meat, whether mutton or pork, is, when it comes to camping, always at its best in the form of chops. To *braai* them properly, you need a hot fire, made of leadwood[2] or thorn-tree[3] wood in the Transvaal, and in the southern parts any wood that makes good coals. Here in the Cape Province we are privileged to be able to place a layer of rhinoceros bush over the coals, which imparts to the chops a peculiar, fragrant taste, but this is a refinement lacking at most campsites – instead you can rub the meat with herbs according to taste. But choose your chops well and see to it that they are soft and tender. First give them a tap with a clean stone or a piece of wood – not too hard, for you do not want to break the fibres – you should only bruise them a little to get rid of the stiffness. Salt them – a pinch of fine ginger in the salt is delicious, and some people are very fond of coriander or aniseed. Dry them well – a wet chop will never braai as well as it should. Then place them on the grill. If you have not brought one along, you could make do with one improvised from *Oom's* wire fence, but it is generally preferable to take your own along. First grease the grill with a bit of fat, and make sure that it is nice and hot before laying the meat on it. Three or four chops can withstand the fire ordeal together, but look after them well and see to it that you turn them over as soon as they are well browned on the one side. When done, serve immediately with or without a lump of butter. If you have such civilised implements as knives and forks with you, a lump of butter is recommended, but a chop should actually be eaten just like King Louis XIV enjoyed his – with the fingers. His Majesty did that at table, however, and not when out camping. His favourite, *Tannie* De Maintenon, found it so unbearably rude the way he always used to dirty his jacket – the one with the golden fleece on it, *nogal* – with dripping fat that she ordered the cook always to serve the king's chops with a piece of paper lace around the bone. That is how we came to have *Cotelette à la Maintenon* – mutton chops with frumpled pieces of paper around the bone. The way they are usually served in hotels, there is – if the truth be told – not much difference between the meat and the paper when it comes to taste and juiciness.

Therefore see to it that your camp chops will not suffer such reproach. They should have good flavour, and be soft and tasty. It is no small matter to

---

2 *Combretum imberbe.*

3 *Acacia* sp.

achieve all this with a grill, which is why some people prefer to *braai* them in a pan. I have nothing against that – a chop fried in a pan can be delicious – but it can also be the opposite. It all depends on the way it is *braaied*. A proper chop should retain all its juiciness, so the fire should be glowing hot to scorch the surface of the meat, which should then be roasted right through. The result is a piece of juicy meat that almost melts in your mouth.

What to eat with it? As far as I am concerned, I can imagine nothing nicer than a piece of white farm bread, well plastered with farm butter, its inside just as soft as the meat should be with a beautiful golden brown crust into which your teeth, be they natural or false, can bite with relish. Vegetables and other additions? I know that camp hospitality ensures that they are always close at hand, but I really think them superfluous. A good slice of bread and a chop – they go together like husband and wife, and to separate them from each other is an offence and a sin.

29 March 1946

49
Camp Food II

On our veld picnics we never used to make soup. In the hunter's camp, however, soup is one of the most popular dishes enjoyed by the light of the campfire. Nowhere have I tasted a better camp soup than in the Lowveld at a bushveld camp where the hunters knew what they were doing.

Camp soup is much more than just a normal soup. Carême, one of the greatest experts in the history of cooking, maintains – and I think he is absolutely correct – that soup should only be used as an appetiser. Therefore it should, according to him, consist of a thin, preferably clear solution of cooked vegetable or meat juices. Meat extract has a stimulating effect on the mucous membrane of the stomach, just like a glass of good sherry. It therefore improves the appetite and the digestion, even though it has no great nutritional value in its own right. You could give it nutritional value by mixing it with flour, milk, wine or anything else that provides nutrition, but a solution of meat or vegetable extract is not really what you would call food. And when food is added to it, as in thick soups, it becomes a dish that should not be served merely as an appetising prelude to the meal, but as a part of the meal itself, and it is then used as much for its food value as for its taste.

This view of soup is not shared by Chinese cooks, who sometimes serve a nutritious soup between or after other dishes, but not beforehand. They would, however, agree with me that hunter's camp soup is the most appropriate evening meal for the open veld.

Such a soup is cooked slowly all day long. Early in the morning a large iron pot is filled with water. In it is put whatever vegetables are available – usually potatoes, onions, dry beans, lentils or peas – and whatever remains of the hunters' booty in the form of bones with a fair amount of meat still on them. Salt and pepper are added at an early stage – other spices are not usually at hand, although someone who is familiar with the bush can add a lot of flavour to soup by adding some of the leaves and herbs usually found in the immediate vicinity of the campsite. There you will usually also find some root vegetables that can be used. The soup is cooked slowly and stirred from time to time with a spoon or a piece of clean thorn-tree wood. A civilised cook will try and scoop off the foam, and especially the fat that may be floating on top, but in my experience this is never done, and it is precisely for this reason that the result is so remarkably hearty and tasty when you have it the same evening. It is a thick, doughy soup that is served along with the marrowbones and the meat, and it is a meal in itself. After such a bowl of soup you need hardly touch the *braaivleis* that invariably follows – it is so nourishing that nothing more is required but the usual *aposteltjie*[1] with coffee, and then your pipe.

Another camp dish that is unfortunately no longer fashionable is *askoek*.[2] This is the old-fashioned name for any kind of *roosterkoek*,[3] which has been called by many names. There is a collection of recipes written by an old *tannie* in 1815, the year Napoleon was defeated at Waterloo. The reason I mention Napoleon is that he, according to one of his contemporaries, was very fond of *askoek*, which he always used to devour with goat or chicken fat in such a greedy fashion that it would leave him suffering from indigestion. Well-prepared *askoek* will never give you indigestion when chewed properly. The old *tannie* agrees with me on this point. She starts by telling us that the flour does not really need to be sifted flour, but that it should be 'new' flour, 'stone-ground fresh', from which I gather that she means common *boer*-meal that has not yet been spoilt by weevils. Such flour is then mixed with salt and bicarbonate of soda and slowly stirred into a mixture of water and milk until you get quite a stiff dough, which can be left under a damp cloth until it is time to bake the *askoek*. Pieces of dough are then plucked from the lump and flattened into cakes 'about a hand's breadth wide and as thick as a thumb'. They are laid on a layer of warm ash with a coal or two still showing here and there, covered with more warm ash and left like that until both sides, top and bottom, are nice and hard. Then they are taken out, as much of the ash as possible wiped away, and served immediately. The camp guest cuts open each cake with his pocket knife – with his *herneuter*, as the old people used to call it – and spreads butter on the inside, if he has some; otherwise it can be had with sauce.

These days we use a grill for *askoek*, with the result that the little cakes are not evenly baked, but it does not really matter. The important thing is that the outside of the cake should be brittle while the inside remains soft, dry and delicate. Some recipes say that the dough should be made with milk – this makes the inside a bit moist, but perhaps tastier. It is, however, not at all necessary to add fat or egg yolk, as then the *askoek* would no longer be an *askoek* but an ash bun, something too refined for the campsite ambience, where simplicity is the paramount virtue.

---

1 A round, hollow tea cake with a 'lid'.
2 Literally, 'ash-scone'.
3 Griddle cake.

There is perhaps no better dessert to round off a campfire meal than a pancake. The pancake dough is easy enough to make: a bit of fine flour, a pinch of salt, a few eggs beaten up, and enough milk – you can use tinned milk if no fresh milk is available – to make a thin dough, thin enough to drip easily from the spoon. The pan should preferably be small, no more than nine inches wide, and the fire warm enough. Put enough fat in the pan to grease its surface when molten and allow it to heat up well, until it starts smoking. Then place a tablespoon of the thin dough in it and swirl the pan so that the dough covers the whole of the bottom evenly. If the fire is hot, the pancake will be ready in barely a minute, and if the layer of dough is thin enough, as it should be, it will not even be necessary to turn it over. This the artful pancake-maker does easily enough, either with a knife or by giving the pan a deft flick, but that requires skill and experience, and if you are not good at it the pancake will more than likely end up in the fire. Therefore make your pancake thin, as thin as possible, and be content with having it baked nice and golden-yellow from below. Sprinkle with sugar, put on a plate next to the fire, and cover with a warm plate. Continue the work – and it should be done quickly, with haste, so that you can have a dozen pancakes piled up within a quarter of an hour. Then you can ask someone to hand them round while you continue making more. A bit of nutmeg and cinnamon mixed with the sugar is always delicious, and if syrup or honey is available it will go well with this simple camp pancake. You could even leave out the eggs, but then it is advisable to add a pinch of bicarbonate of soda to the dough, and it is possible that the pancake may then be a bit tough.

5 April 1946

50
Our White Wines I

A few correspondents have asked me to say something about our white wines. They would like to know which is the best wine to buy, why it is the best, and in what respect it differs from others that are available.

It is not for me to recommend particular wines, for by doing so I would open myself to the criticism of being partial and, which would be much worse for us Bonades, the accusation that I rate my own taste higher than that of my readers. Fortunately I do not suffer from this form of snobbishness. And I always remember, when writing these articles about food and drink, what a great Frenchman said about another Frenchman who is still regarded as a more famous chap than the one who gossiped about him.

The criticising Frenchman – his name was Baudelaire and there are those, some of the Bonades amongst them, who regard him as an excellent poet who also had good taste when it came to food and drink – was bold enough to say that Brillat-Savarin, who is admired by all Frenchmen as the high priest of the table, was nothing but a puffed-up, ignorant, uncouth, uneducated, inexperienced braggart who denounced himself in his own words as someone who knows nothing at all about the holy science of the art of cooking and eating. All the stupid Brillat-Savarin had to say about wine in his widely read and world-famous book on the art of eating was a single sentence: 'Concerning wine, it is an invention of Noah and is made from the juice of the grape'.

Just imagine. A thick tome dedicated to the art of cooking by someone who claimed to be a connoisseur and professor of the art of eating, a man who spent his whole life in a wine country – and such a banal summary.

I could easily go along with Baudelaire's scoffing at such an expert, but I like to be fair and therefore I did some research of my own. My literary investigations revealed that the famous Brillat-Savarin, well acquainted as he was with the kitchen, knew nothing whatsoever about the cellar, and that on one awful day he treated his guests to some not so clear white wine. Now French white wine is never really first-class, and if it is not a sparkling wine there is normally not much to be said for it. But still, neither Brillat-Savarin nor his guests had the right to conclude from this one unfortunate incident that French white wine cannot sometimes be good.

The same goes for our white wines. At present they are not yet as good as our red wines. We have red wines that can compete with the best European red wines.

We have blended Cabernets with a flavour next to which even a *Nuits St George* cannot hold its own, with a sparkle and a colour that compares well with that of the best brands. Our white wines, however, are not as good as they ought to be, or could easily be if only our winemakers would take more care and our infernal legislation would allow them to be treated in the modern way.

Our white wines are inferior when it comes to flavour and what the French call *velouté*, which means velvety plumpness, something that, as it were, allows the tongue to perceive the taste of a watery solution. This is their greatest deficiency, but there are also others, for instance their too high alcohol content.

The lack of flavour is to a certain extent due to the fact that our white wines are less acidic than the European ones. Yes, I realise that this statement is contrary to the accepted view. Just the other day I treated one of my friends to a choice Riesling, as soft and palatable as you could wish for, but after the first sip my guest said: 'Oh no, this always gives me acidity in my stomach – I would rather have a whisky and soda'. I did not tell him what old Dr Hahn said about imported whisky in his evidence before the select committee of Parliament – he would simply not have believed it. And when he told me that the only white wine he could drink without getting heartburn was *Liebfraumilch*, I realised that it would be quite impossible to instruct him in the most elementary oenology. For I agree completely with Multatuli, who said: '*Er is moed nodig tot het voeren van den strijd tegen misverstand*'.[1]

The more acid a wine contains, the easier it is to preserve the flavour that comes originally from the leaves of the vine. In the trade it is no longer a secret that leaf extracts are sometimes, with the greatest care of course, added to European wines for the export market. I also see no ethical reason why not, on condition that we know that such doctored wines are, like champagne, no longer natural. I would not however recommend this method to improve the flavour of our white wines. We should rather select carefully the grapes to be used for making our best white wines. Not that we should wait to get *edelvrot*[2] grapes, although I look forward to the day when one of our wine farmers will make a real *auslese* white, but a bit more attention could be given to the selection of the grapes and especially to the fermentation of the must in the vats. One of the most flavoursome white wines I have tasted here was a

---

1 'You need courage to take up the struggle against misunderstanding.'
2 Noble rot.

mixture of sémillon and sauvignon, quite a sweet wine that was not for sale in the shops because it had too low an alcohol content. There is no reason at all why our white wines cannot be given more flavour with proper treatment and without making use of extracts.

The velvetiness of our white wines depends upon the quality of that strange gelatinous substance that science calls 'pectin'. Unfortunately we have to ward off this pectin instead of encouraging it to remain in our white wine. Why? Simply because it makes our white wines murky by entering into a marriage with the iron sometimes found in the must and giving birth to an odd pair of twins. One of these composite substances is soluble in wine, the other is not and makes the wine murky. And the strangest thing about it is that the one can easily be converted into the other by being exposed to light. A bottle of murky white wine can be made clear again by placing it in the sun; and it becomes murky again when placed in the fridge. The French call it *casse* – not really a sickness but a quality of white wine that is not good for the trade. If the law were to allow us to prepare white wine according to modern methods, for instance by adding prussic acid, we would probably never have to complain about *casse*. It would allow more pectin in our white wine and thereby give us a plumper wine that tastes more like jelly.

It is also possible to make a natural white wine without adding alcohol. On our wine shows we get such wines – I can remember tasting a first-class natural wine on the last show – flavoursome, soft, lovely, not sweet, and yet with a certain pectin quality that made it somewhat oily. A few weeks ago I tasted it again, in the form of a white wine sold over the counter with a certain amount of alcohol added, and – well, what would you expect? According to the law you cannot sell wine containing more than 20 grams of sugar per litre if it is not strengthened to more than 16,6 per cent with alcohol. According to law we are not allowed to sell a natural sweet wine over the counter, and the law will not allow us to get rid of *casse* by preparing our young wines properly.

24 May 1946

51
Our White Wines II

In my previous article I quoted a saying of Multatuli about misunderstanding, not with any intention of implying that it is not necessary to fight misunderstanding but simply to indicate that I had no appetite for getting involved in an argument with a headstrong fellow after a fine midday meal. Our wine farmers should, in their own interests as much as that of the public, stand together and bravely go on the offensive against misunderstanding about wine. The Bonades will support them boldly in any attempt to educate the public and inform them about wine, white as well as red.

One correspondent asks: 'What white wine should I buy?' This is a fair question that should be answered by the wine industry. In California the wine farmers and the wine merchants have joined hands to inform the public. They put an amount of money aside for systematic propaganda. What they mean by that is practical guidance like, for example, the distribution to every library of wine lists in which the brands are indicated, with information about their alcohol content and acidity level. Something like that is what we need here.

I know of only one restaurant in the country that presents its guests with a more or less complete list of indigenous wines. Even this list is not complete: a few names are missing, and the information provided is not always accurate and is open to misinterpretation. But I notice that it mentions fourteen different brands of white wine, and they are all, at least within the limitations mentioned in my previous article, good, acceptable, drinkable wines. Not one of them dates from before 1938 – they are therefore all relatively young wines, just as, to tell the truth, nearly all the wines you will find on the shelf are, although not necessarily unripe, still in their youth. It would not be appropriate for me to mention any particular wine here, for reasons that my readers will understand, but I betray no secret when I refer to the white wine of 1931, produced by the Nuy farms, and still available over the counter a few years ago. This was one of the best and most flavourfully blended white wines you could then buy. Today there are first-class brands from the districts of Tulbagh, Paarl, Stellenbosch, Somerset West and the Cape that will be as good in a few years' time.

My advice to my correspondents is to order a case of each of the different brands. Store them in a cool place in the pantry or cellar, and give them a chance to rest well before trying them out. Wine is a living thing – it gets tired quite easily. Try a glass that has been shaken about on a motor car journey and compare it with the same wine that has rested properly in the fridge for a few hours. This is one of the reasons our wines seldom make a first-class impression in the dining cars of the railways. At sea it is a different matter – there the wine is given proper rest, and the motion it is exposed to is less protracted and unsettling than it is during a journey on a gravel road.

Therefore allow your wine to rest. Then try two or three brands, one after the other, and do so under proper conditions. White wine loses much of its peculiar flavour when it does not meet the tongue chilled – only a fortified sweet white wine tastes acceptable at room temperature. The knowledgeable reader may immediately say: 'Yes, but what about sherry?' I beg your pardon. I fully agree that sherry is an exception to the rule, but then it is also an exception to many things that hold true for most wines, simply because sherry is a different kind of wine that cannot really be compared to other wines. But when it comes to white wine, drink it chilled – not quite iced, but well chilled. Twirl it round in the glass and smell the bouquet. The most important test of any kind of wine is the nose test. You can immediately tell not only whether the wine has flavour, but also whether it has an improper smell. Then, while the mouth is still half-open, taste it – not only in your mouth but also at the back of your throat, where the taste and fragrance more or less blend, and the real aroma becomes noticeable. Then the swallowing – the more or less tangible feeling when mouth, palate, tongue and throat come together to deliver judgment on what is passing over them.

It is only by establishing the brand that best appeals to your own taste that you can decide which wine will be best for you. It may not be exactly what your friends and acquaintances prefer, and it is therefore advisable to acquire half a dozen different brands for the cellar. No one has been able to establish with any certainty how much time white wines require to reach full maturity. My own experience is that they can remain in the cellar for four to six years without deteriorating, and I have tasted some of *Oubaas* Philip Rabie's white wine that was twelve years old and could still be called delicious. But it will require much research before we will be able to speak about it with any certainty. The white wines now available over the counter are still very young and could do with another two or three years in the cellar before being drunk.

I started off by saying that our wine industry could do much to clear up misconceptions about wine. Many people still have not the faintest clue. For instance, they think a red wine is made from red grapes and a white wine from white grapes, that sparkling wine is a champagne, that imported wines all contain less acid than indigenous wines, and that the label on an imported bottle of wine is as reliable as a dividend cheque from a gold-mining company.

On the contrary, the sparkle of a wine has nothing to do with its foam – a foaming wine is a wine that still contains carbon dioxide from the second fermentation, it is not a natural wine; and champagne, which is a foaming and very seldom a sparkling wine, is one of the most meddled-with wines in the trade. Our indigenous wines have less acid than any imported ones. The well-known brands of imported wines are no proof that the wine in the bottle really is what it purports to be, and the most popular brands are all blended wines. *Liebfraumilch*, for example, and *Beaune* are trade names that do not mean as much as that of even a second-rate wine. A red wine is made by letting the skins of the grapes ferment along with the must – the colour comes from the skins, and there are only a few varieties of grape that have rosy juice (Katalba, for example, and Pontac). These are all minor details that we Bonades have known since our youth. But the city youth do not know these things and grow up under the impression that wine (how few of them ever get the opportunity of drinking natural wine) is a solution of alcohol, made from grapes and discovered, to the curse of humanity, by Noah.

Heaven knows, we don't want our children growing up to become 'puffed-up, ignorant, uncouth, uneducated, inexperienced, bragging' citizens like Brillat-Savarin, do we?

I recently had quite an odd white wine, in some respects very individual. It had a unique flavour, something between that of sorrel and rosemary. It was nicely sparkling, with a 'wettish' taste, an equally lovely aftertaste, very acidic, and with a low alcohol content – I would say about eleven per cent. The colour had a light green shine to it, and I was precocious enough to think that it was made from a Furmint grape. But it was not. It was wine made of wild grapes from the Knysna forest, where the grapes are as black and large as *gros colman*, as sour as vinegar, and possessed of a pip that burns your tongue like a chilli!

7 June 1946

52
Freshwater Fish

In a farmhouse on one bank of the Groot River, I once enjoyed some very fine fish. It was a thick piece, boneless and soft, grilled over the coals, with a pleasant flavour and a somewhat sour aftertaste. When I asked what it was the *tannie* said: 'It is the fillet of the *moddermorgel, Meneer*. We cut it out, pickle it in vinegar, then bake it.'

The barbel of the Groot River – which is what we are talking about – is also found in many other rivers, and is one of our largest and most delicious freshwater fish. It can weigh up to sixty pounds, has a flat stump of a head with long outgrowths around its mouth, and a greyish-brown colour. It is not a pretty fish, and also not one that anglers are fond of, as it fights and will not easily allow itself to be hauled in. It is only its weight that makes catching it with hook and line difficult. And once you have caught it, you find yourself not really knowing what to do with it. It is so revoltingly ugly and its skin so slimy that you have to be quite resolute to regard it as food.

And yet, when prepared as described above, it does not taste bad at all. I have dealt with it in different ways and over time I have come to the conclusion that it can be regarded it as a delicious fish if one knows how to go about cooking it.

All the deep-water river and freshwater fish suffer from the apprehension that they might have a muddy taste that will be unpleasant or even disgusting to the connoisseur. One of our best freshwater fish is the carp, which is far too seldom used as its meat is first-class if cooked properly. It is not enough just to clean it, then cook it in the pot or pan or *braai* it on the grill. That way you will get the full benefit of its mud and stand little chance of enjoying the genuinely fine taste of the meat itself. The old *tannie's* method can be used for the large carp. You can cut fish chops – strips – out of the thick meat, marinade it first in a mixture of wine and vinegar with herbs, then *braai* it in the pan or on the grill. If the fish is too small for so generous a treatment, you could also, after cutting off the fins and skinning it (as the skin is not worth preserving), marinade the whole fish and then bake it, covered in breadcrumbs, in a pan. From such pieces you can then make first-class fish preserve, with the necessary addition of fried onions and a curry sauce. Therefore do not pass over the barbel or the carp.

Our best and perhaps tastiest freshwater fish is the yellowfish, well known throughout the land. As a sporting fish it is one of our best, since a yellowfish of two pounds or more can put up quite a fight and give the angler enough work landing it with a thin line. We usually *braai* it whole in the pan, but that is not the best way of doing it as it is very bony and it is a bother having to get rid of the bones during the meal. Divided into pieces, a braaied yellowfish can be pickled and, after a few days, if you have used good vinegar, the bones will be soft. But no one really wants to eat bones with their fish. For my part, therefore, I prefer to cut up a yellowfish at the outset so that I have properly formed pieces to work with, and as few bones as possible. I then salt and pepper them, and if they are not fatty enough, lard each piece with a strip of bacon, and cook them in white wine with a blade of mace or some herbs. Or I bake the pieces in a pan. One must be careful not to cook or braai them for too long, as the taste of yellowfish is very fine and the meat requires just a few minutes on the fire. The knowledgeable cook will be able to adjust this recipe in countless ways. He might braise the pieces with special sauces – tomato sauce, mushroom sauce, curry sauce, etc – and in this way prepare a very fine fish dish that will not have to stand back for sea fish at all.

In some rivers you get a small fish, barely the size of a largish tadpole, slender and grey-white. It has no proper name and, as far as I know, is not normally eaten. But it is actually a very fine little fish. I have at times got hold of dozens of them in a pillow case used as a net, and prepared them tastefully in the way European cooks prepare sardines.

It is done as follows. Dry the little fish properly so that not a drop of water remains. You do not even have to clean them or scrape off any scales. Take quite a large pot and place in it enough oil or hard fat to half-fill it. Allow the fat to heat until a blue smoke starts rising from the pot. This means that the oil or fat has reached a temperature far above that usually required to cook meat or fish. Place the dried fish in a wire basket and place the basket in the boiling fat. Keep it there until every little fish is nicely brown. Take out, sprinkle with salt and ground dry parsley, and serve promptly. You can eat them skin and all, like chestnuts. It may not be a 'large' dish, but it is definitely a welcome change and well worth trying. In Europe such small fish are counted among the tastiest dishes and, when available, they fetch high prices as connoisseurs regard the 'whitebait' of the Thames – which is nothing other than our little river fish – as one of the tastiest dishes there is. The orthodox accompaniment to such crisply fried little fish is small pieces of rye bread generously spread with butter.

Our freshwater fish are quite plentiful and we make far too little use of them. There are many kinds and, as far as I know, they are all edible, although some kinds, such as the Transvaal tigerfish that anglers are so fond of, have hardly any edible meat and are so bony that they are impossible to prepare for the table. All the recipes for sea fish can also be used for freshwater fish, and the cook will have enough opportunity of showing off his art and skill preparing river fish in different ways. I would make a special plea for cooking it in wine and adding certain herbs that improve the taste, such as rosemary, mace and fennel leaf; also, where necessary, for a proper larding of the fish when it is not fat.

27 December 1946

53
Red Wine

The sad history of *Grootoom* Gieljam is something our family prefers not to mention. When I was young it was the custom to send children out of the room when the conversation came round to *Grootoom*, which of course just made us all the more curious. It was only in my matric year that I gathered he was *kinds*[1] by the time he died. My maternal *ouma* filled me in.

'We knew he wasn't all there, my child,' she told me. 'It started with his aversion to red wine. One of the abolition missionaries came along, and Gieljam chopped down his vineyard. Can you believe it?'

The Bonades have always been fond of wine, and they are not afraid or ashamed to say so because they adhere to Scripture which, of course, states clearly: 'God makes the grass grow for the animals and plants to serve mankind, to bring forth wheat for bread from the earth, and grapes for wine to gladden the hearts of men'. And they know that as well as old Mr Pasteur, who said when the doctors inducted him as an honorary member of their Academy (he being a teacher in physical science and never legally having had the right to cut out anyone's appendix) that wine is not only the best and healthiest of drinks, but also one of the best assistants to the expert cook. In our home there was therefore always wine on the table, and in the kitchen or pantry – always red wine. I am not saying that white wine is not just as good for cooking, but red wine is the experienced cook's aid and refuge *par excellence*.

Its redness is due to ingredients that scientists have not been able to agree upon. What we do know for sure, however, is that it is a strange colouring that undergoes a remarkable change when exposed to air – as old Mr Pasteur would have said 'by oxidisation' – and that that also makes a big difference to the taste and flavour. It is precisely this change in the wine that is of so much value in the art of cooking, since it can be used to improve the taste and aroma of some dishes, especially those consisting mostly of animal proteins. Just about every kind of meat, wild or tame, is improved by red wine; tough meat soaked in it and then cooked is more tender than meat merely cooked in water. A beefsteak that has been lying in red wine for a few hours gains considerably in taste and juiciness. And this has nothing to do with the wine spirit – the alcohol – of the wine. Wine spirit causes the meat juices to coagulate and is therefore not at all suitable for softening the meat. Therefore use red wine with quite a low alcohol content – preferably farm wine that has not been fortified. Naturally, on the stove or in the oven the alcohol quickly evaporates and leaves behind the

---

[1] Senile, literally 'child-like'.

ingredients that make wine so eminently suitable for kitchen and table use – the amino and fatty acids, and the colouring that so easily changes into something new and keeps the scientists baffled.

It was, according to my maternal *ouma*, one of the proofs of *Grootoom* Gieljam being a few sandwiches short of a picnic that he objected to the use of wine in stewed mutton. 'And that is the recipe we still use today, my child,' the old lady told me. 'How on earth could we prepare it without red wine? A change of taste? But of course, my child, that is exactly what we use it for. It makes a big difference, my child, whether you first braise the meat in red wine or make do without it.'

How many farm cooks know that today? We use all sorts of bottled sauces, of which most of us cannot say with any certainty what the ingredients are, and we neglect farm wine. This is because our people just do not know any better. I am not saying that the prophet's conclusions are correct. We are not quite finished. But they are writing quite a lot in the newspapers about malnutrition that, it is said, is quite common, not only amongst the blacks in the Transkei, but also on our Boer farms.

As a cook I am bound to say, with my hand on my heart – I really do not know what this means for in truth it is an expression which, taken at its word, is not accurate, and why the assurance of an anatomical impossibility should contribute anything to the reliability of what I may say is beyond me – to say, therefore, that red wine is just about indispensable if you want to prepare good food for the table. Everyone knows that you can make do without it, just as you can manage in the kitchen without vinegar and butter and herbs and mustard and oil and nutmeg and cloves and pepper, and all those things that contribute so much to making food enjoyable and tasty instead of just edible. As with herbs and spices, red wine is one of nature's gifts that is of great assistance to the cook, enabling him to serve food in a manner that maintains nutritional value and stimulates enjoyment and relish.

Therefore try it with any recipe or dish where before you used only water. Make it an ingredient of coloured soups, of meat, vegetable and fruit soups. Stew meat in it; add some to curries and stews. Try it in all sorts of ways. The art of cooking remains in many ways an unknown domain in this country, an expanse in which you may with advantage dare to explore and try out a thing or two for yourself. I have done so many a time, and with felicitous results in most cases. There have been failures, of course, but these I do not regret.

I once stewed ghoo beans in red wine, and what came out of the pot was about as sad as the history of *Grootoom* Gieljam.

17 January 1947

54
Zebra Meat

'Not even the *volk*[1] eat zebra meat,' my Bushveld host assured me. 'They use only the fat for making soap.'

This sounded a bit strange to me, for we Bonades have always been endowed with a sense of realism. The *volk* will eat any kind of meat, and in addition many a thing you would hardly honour with that name. One simply needs to recall what happened when the last *wildebeest* was slaughtered.

I had eaten zebra meat before, years ago when *trekking* somewhere along the Magalakwyn River. And according to my memory it was definitely quite tasty, a tender meat, as *Oom* Danie told me in my young days. *Oom* Danie was a transport-rider and later made a small fortune delivering acacia for firewood to the people living in the then still embryonic Kimberley. He was one of those who contributed to the deforestation of the plains in that area, but one should grant that our people then knew very little about soil erosion – that we hear so much about today.

To cut a long story short, *Oom* Danie explained that there was no meat on earth that could hold its own against zebra meat. A young zebra, in his opinion, provided meat without equal. Years later I ate some donkey meat in the form of chops that I took for first-class lamb chops. My host assured me, however, that it was the meat of a young donkey, a very young, innocent animal that had never consumed anything but milk. It really tasted good. And why on earth should it not? Horses, donkeys and zebras are not only the most beautiful four-footed animals in existence; they are also, in respect of their eating and living habits, the cleanest. Take for instance the zebra. It only eats grass. It does not nibble, like many an antelope, at bushes with leaves that sometimes have a turpentine-like resinous oil that imparts an awful taste to the meat. It drinks a lot of water – an unbelievable amount. You have to see it drink at a dam to appreciate how much it really consumes. It is always nice and plump – what happens to underfed zebra heaven alone knows, since the animals you find in the veld are always admirably fat, as if taken care of by a stable boy. And talk about clean – you would go a long way to find a wild animal that is cleaner.

Oom Danie did not tell me anything about how to prepare zebra meat for the table. As far as I remember, he cut a piece of meat, salted and peppered it, and *braaied* it over the coals. Nor have I found anything about it in the cookbooks.

---

1 Workers, literally the 'folk'.

There are, however, many recipes that provide information on how to cook and prepare horsemeat – ragout of horsemeat, horse chops, horsemeat sausage, horsemeat salami, horse mince, grilled horsemeat, spiced, stewed, smoked horsemeat, horse ham, horse mousse, and dozens more. But when it comes to zebras and camels, the cookbooks have nothing to say. The enterprising cook has to draw on his experience and find his own way.

My first problem was to find a little zebra. You have no idea how difficult that was, but we Bonades are persevering people. I eventually convinced my host that, in this time of scarcity of soap, it was undoubtedly his duty to make zebra fat available to his workers for soap-making. He agreed to shoot an old stallion, and although I tried to explain that something like that would be quite tough, and perhaps even completely inedible, I could not get him to change his mind on that score. I naturally did everything I could to put my case as convincingly as possible. There was, for instance, the argument that a zebra, if shot when still very young, would be spared all the trouble that lay ahead – just imagine the cruel prospect of being caught and eaten by a lion, not to mention a Cape wild dog! But it was all in vain. It was an old stallion or nothing, and with that I had to be content.

The stallion was one of the largest zebras I have seen – quite old, too, since its teeth were already worn away. But it was plump, smooth and beautiful to look at. The slaughtering is not worth dwelling on. My part was the inside fillet – a large, smooth piece of meat, or rather two pieces. I tried it the very same evening. Perhaps this was not quite fair to the zebra meat. A few days in a marinade would possibly have improved it, but I wanted to use the one piece for biltong, and I wanted to see what kind of meat it would turn out to be if *braaied* immediately.

I cut my piece of inside fillet into proper 'tournedos', or round pieces, each about two inches thick and a hand wide. They were then pounded with the handle of the knife, cut nice and even, and rubbed with a mixture of salt, pepper, young *blinkblaar*[2] twigs, and some wild wormwood[3] I found growing along the river bank. Then they were *braaied* in an open pan with a spoonful of butter. After being nicely browned on both sides, I poured a glass of sweet wine over them and braised them in it for a while. The result was a dozen tournedos that, as regards their appearance and aroma, no Carême would have been ashamed of. A little sifted flour and another glass of wine made a

---

2 *Zizyphus mucronata*.

3 *Wilde-als, Artemisia afra*.

tasty sauce of what remained in the pan, to which the *blinkblaar* gave a tang. On each round chop was placed a soft, fried piece of tomato, and the sauce was poured over it all. My zebra dish was ready.

During the cooking I did what every good cook does and tasted the stuff in the pan. It was beautifully soft, with a very good taste – so tender that a fork easily sank into it. The tenderest wether-chop could not compare.

The camp guests reacted according to their nature and their sense of taste. One of the *tannies* pulled up her nose, left the bouma, and in her disgust drew comparisons that were not altogether appropriate. Another camp mate carefully took a small piece on his fork, but never got as far as tasting it. We were pleased about that later as only one piece had been provided for each guest, and we ended up with two more to divide between the rest of us. Those who were brave enough to taste it all agreed that it was first-class meat. Of course comparisons were made – with *eland*, mutton and pork – but those were all plucked out of the air. Zebra meat is *sui generis* – unique in its taste, tenderness and flavour. And the biltong, which was dried out fourteen days later, was just as delicious.

In future I will give preference, above all other Bushveld game, to zebra meat. And I will definitely, when I get the opportunity, use more than just the inside fillet.

24 January 1947

55
Brawn

Paging through an ancient recipe book – it is more than three hundred years old and unfortunately has nothing to do with our family, so I cannot really brag about it – I happened to read, with reference to brawn: 'This dish is not suitable for a high table; the commoners enjoy it, though'.

The cook, dead and buried for three hundred years and more, produced a recipe I honestly cannot recommend for a dish as beautiful as brawn. It reads: 'Cook a lamb's head, a pig's head, and five or six chicken feet ...' Peas and flour are added, and – can you believe it? – snippets of garlic and 'leftovers of salted herring ...' Now that is really a nightmare of a brawn.

Where today do you find the real, genuine brawn that *Ouma* used to make in the old days? Nowhere, I fear. It is perhaps for that reason that we find crude imitations, sometimes as hard as Cape salmon cooked to death, sometimes as tough and tasteless as vegetables cooked in the English manner. But the real thing is something completely different that melts away in your mouth and leaves you with the feeling the Israelites must have had when they tasted manna for the first time.

When a pig was slaughtered, it used to be the wedding feast of true brawn. Head, trotters and selected pieces of meat were cooked up slowly and patiently, together with orange leaves, sage, a bay leaf, allspice, nutmeg, ginger, and sometimes even a tiny piece of saffron, in enough water to cover everything but not drown it. When the meat was tender and fell from the bones, it was dished out of the pot and spread out on a clean tablecloth, and we children used to help pick out every little bone and piece of sinew. Then back in the pot. There was always a bit of a commotion between Ouma and our cook at this stage. The cook would want to 'clean up' the 'soup' that was in the pot – which was done by beating it up with a few ground egg shells, then straining it through a cloth. In this way you get a clear brawn in which the pieces of meat lie buried as if caught up in an iceberg. *Ouma* was however against this, and I think she was right. A good brawn should not be clear. If you want a clear brawn, you may as well make it like the cookbooks of today tell you, by dissolving a few spoonfuls of gelatine in water, putting snippets of meat in it and letting it gel. That is no brawn; it is an imitation meat jelly that would never make you think of manna eaten in the desert.

Therefore back to the soup, without 'cleaning it up'. Cook it slowly once more with the addition of half a cup of mixed wine and vinegar, and some lemon. The lemon is not strictly necessary, but my late *ouma* always maintained that it added just that touch of perfection. Some connoisseurs prefer a squeezed lemon cooked up with the soup and meat – it is a matter of taste.

When everything is cooked nice and evenly, the pot is taken from the fireplace and its contents worked on once more. The larger pieces of meat are reduced in size; the swimming orange leaves and sage are removed – only the bay leaf may remain, and if necessary a few new orange leaves can be introduced. Salt and pepper are now added, the whole is warmed up again, the foam taken off the top, and it is then ready for pouring into moulds. These were the old-fashioned rippled copper moulds, each one large enough to hold one and a half or two pounds of brawn. The brawn was dense enough to suspend the contents evenly during the process of stiffening. While stiffening, the fattiness floats up to form a thin layer on top that protects the brawn against penetration by unwanted germs. *Ouma's* brawn could be kept for weeks without any fear of spoiling, but the best time to eat it was two or three days after it had set.

Now that was real brawn. Soft, tasty, flavoursome, with a pleasant mixture of different tangs, a velvety smoothness like that of old wine, yet a firmness that would have pleased a Chinaman, although there was nothing crisp in it, nothing that would crunch under your teeth. That was *Ouma's* brawn for you.

I challenge anyone to come and tell me that it is unsuitable for a high table. It is the glorification of the best to be found in a pig's head and trotters, the jellied fifth essence of excellence – an unsurpassable work of art. And with that, amen.

31 January 1947

56
Atjar

Dreams of the Far East ... the smell of melatti and the many sounds of the *desa*-bazaar ... palm trees and 'kabous' ... volcanos and impenetrable jungles ... man-eaters and pirates ... headshrinkers and opium smokers.

With a bit of imagination you see and feel all of this when you hear the word atjar.[1] And I can imagine that what the word really means has contributed more to the pleasure and satisfaction of humankind than many a thing the wonderful East has provided, created and preserved.

We do not find it any more today. And, my goodness, do not come and tell me that it is still made; that in every Afrikaans cookbook and in some English ones you will find recipes for its preparation; that it is still to be found here and there; that it is not yet as dead as the dodo of Mauritius. This is all nonsense. The traditional atjar, as we Bonades used to know it – at a time when confirmation still lasted a year and a half, when it was still the custom for a civilised person to present you with his snuff-box, when girls did not yet make themselves ridiculous by making their fingers look like they had been caught in the pantry door, and when you could still sometimes find something worth reading in a newspaper – that kind of atjar has disappeared completely. It has melted away like snow on the Cederberg mountains in August.

There are those who are able to speak without emotion about the dying off and disappearance of old habits, old friends, old fashions and old things, and who would not shed a tear about the loss of something our forefathers loved and cherished. They are, as the Latin poet said bluntly, 'unfeeling stones that do not notice the slow erosion of wind and rain'. It is they who today satisfy themselves with So and So's Pickled This and That, Tom Dick and Harry's Sauce, Potdamn's Pickle, *Ouma's* little Wake-me-up, and heaven knows what else is scraped out of bottles and tins and served up with our best dishes.

We Bonades are different. We like the old stuff. We are loyal to what our forefathers cherished. And one of the *tannies* still makes the genuine, traditional atjar.

This very summer month is the right time for it. When I happened to be in the vicinity, I was sent to the garden to gather the necessary *ingrediënte* (*Tannie* would never say *bestandele*[2]).

---

1 Pickle.
2 Ingredients.

'Please don't bring old *mielies*,' she would warn, 'and the marrows must be no larger than a ha'penny.'

And what did not go into *Tannie's* atjar! Small gherkins, you could just about say with their mother's milk still on their little teeth – which is completely silly, of course, as someone with teeth would not be drinking mother's milk any more – small *mielies*, an inch and a half long, young cucumbers, as soft and juicy as they come, green beans and yellow beans, small walnuts, the insides of hard, crisp, white heads of cabbage, pieces of pure white cauliflower, green and red chillies, almonds, raisins, apricots, peaches, far from fully grown *naartjies*, small lemons, celery, carrots, little turnips, little radishes – just about everything that a garden and fruit orchard could provide. And still *Tannie* would sigh that in her great-grandmother's time still more would be used. 'Especially,' she would say with a sad smile, 'the preserved bamboo and the young nuts they got from India.'

I know for sure that this was completely correct. We still have the bills from Batavia and Colombo in which mention is made of '*bamboesen voor 'n atjahr en vogelnesten uit Tonkin*'.[3]

But we did manage to contribute this and that to help *Tannie* make an excellent and tasty atjar. Stem ginger, wild aniseed root (she got that from a girlfriend in the Hantam) and grapefruit peel. Also, of course, turmeric, a tiny bit of saffron, onions, garlic, coriander, peppercorns, and all kinds of nuts.

This was boiled up in the usual salt water until everything was nicely soft. *Tannie* always added a handful of seaweed. Then it was poured out onto a tablecloth and sorted – what was bruised and less than first-class was discarded. The 'pickle' was boiled in wine vinegar, with salt, a glass of brandy and a tablespoon of turmeric. ('Yes, I know, my child, that many people use   's curry powder, but it is really not necessary and I find that it makes the atjar murky, my child.') The boiled *ingrediënte* were placed in a large, wide-mouthed flask, the boiling pickle was poured over them, and there they stayed for a day or two. Then they were boiled up again, slowly and carefully, with *Tannie* tasting now and then, and here and there, and where necessary a tablespoonful of honey was stirred in, or sometimes brown sugar – but atjar must be full of flavour, sharp, tangy, and therefore not too sweet. ('Yes, my child, there are those who make it into a pure jam, but my late mother always

---

3 'Bamboo for an atjar and birds' nests from Tonkin.'

used to say it should bite, you know, my child, bite – especially with a roast.') Then it was put back into the flask, the pickle was poured over it, and the bottle was carefully sealed.

'After three months,' said *Tannie*, 'it is ready. But it is better to wait a year, my child, especially if the walnuts and almonds are on the old side. Then they will be nicely saturated.'

I think there is nothing finer with either a roast or a bobotie than one of the small green *mielies* out of *ou-Tannie's* atjar.

21 March 1947

Glossary

baas	master or boss
biltong	strips of dried meat
blits	(in context) spirit
boegoe	*Agathosma* species, usually shrubby with highly aromatic foliage
bredie	stew
dikkop	stone curlew
dop	drink
grootoom	great uncle
klipkous	abalone or perlemoen
kloof	ravine
koeksister	sweet, syrupy, doughnut-like delicacy
kraal	pen or outdoor enclosure for animals
kraalbossies	bushes forming part of an outdoor enclosure
kukumakranka	*Gethyllis* species
moskonfyt	grape syrup
neef	cousin (male)
niggie	cousin (female)
omie	little uncle (literally) used affectionately
oom	uncle, widely used term of respect, not limited to relatives
oubaas	old master
oupa	grandfather
outa	respected old African or Coloured male gardener or servant
perlemoen	pearl mussel or abalone
platteland	countryside
rhinoceros bush	Renosterbos (*Elytropappus rhinocerotis*)
salamander	metal plate used for browning or caramelising dishes
sambal	condiment
smoor	braise, smother
sosatie	kebab
tannie	aunt, widely used term of respect, not limited to relatives
vlei	shallow lake
waterblommetjies	water hawthorn, floating water plant (*Aponogeton distachyos*) with scented white flowers.

List of scientific names and their modern equivalents

Caryphyllus aromaticus = Syzygium aromaticum
Cinnamomum cassia = Cinnamomum aromaticum
Cyanella capensis = Cyanella hyacintoides
Eugenia acris pimento = Pimenta officinalis
Haliotis capensis = Galiotis midae
Moreae edulis = Moraea fugax
Oxalis lupinifolia = Oxalis flava
Prionium palmita = Prionium serratum

Index

à l-arlésienne, 91
à la bourguignonne, 91
à la Brimont, 91
à la chablaisienne, 91
à la poulette, 91
Aaltjie, of de Zuinige Keukenmeid, 4, 17, 45
abalone, 131
Abraham, Father, 37
achatina immaculata, 89
achatina zebra, 89
acids, amino, 11, 14, 15, 67, 110, 111
acids, volatile, 69, 70
Advokaat, 32
African coot, 56, 180
Afrikaans food, 23
Aga stove, 154
agapanthus, 90
agar-agar, 131
Algerian kinds of spinach, 1
allspice, 21, 93, 117, 121, 124, 208
almond nuts, 21, 23, 80, 93, 121, 125, 130, 150, 162, 177, 211, 214
aloe, 26, 60
alum, 111
aluminium, 27
aluminium equipment, 27
ambrosia, 18, 40
America, 16, 41, 61, 92, 93
American cocktail, the, 11
American cooking, 3, 93, 96, 100, 159, 162
American corn soup with mussels, 97
American Indians, 41
amino acids, 11, 15, 67, 110, 111
amoroso, 14
Amsterdam, 45
andoetjes, 45
anise, 88
aniseed, 32, 152, 181
anthericum, 26
ant-hill oven, 105
anyswortel, 21
Apollyon, 64
aposteltjie, 184
apple, sour, 65, 143
apricot drink, 166
Arabic word, 1
Arabs, 66
Ardour River, south of, 24
Ardour valley, 155
arrack, 66
argot, 31
Aristophanes, 2
Armagnac brandy, 20
aroma, 32, 192, 197, 204

artichokes, 60, 120
ash, baking under the, 105, 108, 109
ash bun, 184
ash, taaibos,108
askoek, 184
asparagus, 27, 100, 103
atjar, 210-214
aubergine, 158
auslese white wine, 188
Australia, 8, 134

babiana, 81
bacon, 2, 4, 46, 61, 64
baking, 42, 105, 171
bamboo, 131, 157, 211
bananas, 23
barbecue, 41
barbel fish, 194
baroe, 120-121
Barry, Dr, 2
barsmielies, 109
Batavia, 211
Baudelaire, 187
bay leaf, 33, 35, 45, 116, 121, 130, 145, 208, 209
bean, governor's, 5-6
beans, stewed dry, 55
Beaune, 193
béchamel-sauce, 49
beer, 11, 66, 140, 169, 170
beetroot leaves, 16, 162
Barry, Speaker dr, 2
beulingen, 45
bicarbonate of soda, 6, 103, 111, 112, 142, 184, 185
biltong, 84-88, 154, 171, 204, 205
bindenfleisch, 84
birds, wild, 56-65
bitter lemon liqueur, 20
bitterskil, 21
black nightshade, 90
blesbok, 50, 51
blinkblaar, 204, 205
Blum, 4
bobbejaan-uintjies, 81, 82
bobotie, 18, 23, 24, 116, 117, 130, 214
bobotie-fruit, 92, 94
bobotie, saffron, 23
boegoe, 32
boerekool, 104
boerewors, 24, 153-154
boer-meal, 184
bokuintjies, 82
Bols, 11, 91
borrie quince, 94
bortsch, 144, 161

Bosman, Professor, 1
bossiestroop, 121
Botha, General, 2, 25
bouillabaisse, 53
bowl, 27, 31-33, 156, 167, 171, 183
Brandsiekte Act, the, 2
brandy, 19-21, 31-33, 51, 66-70, 80, 83, 88, 92, 101, 111, 130, 134-135, 140, 146, 154, 166-167, 211
brandy old, 69
brawn, 116, 155, 175, 180, 208-209
Brazil nuts, 162
braaivleis, 41-43, 153, 184
bread, 46, 47, 65, 66, 79, 85, 145, 153, 170, 171, 174, 182, 195, 197
bread, mielie, 26, 80, 97
bredie, 1-4, 23, 24, 25, 76, 77, 81
bredos, 1
Brillat-Savarin, 34, 57, 187, 193
brinjals, 158-160
brinjal, stuffed, 160
brinjal tart, 159
Brussels sprouts, 104, 111
buchu, see boegoe
buckwheat meal, 36, 37, 39, 51
bush marigolds, 90
bush partridge, 60
butter, farm, 55, 171, 182

cake, plain, 24
California, 191
camp food, 180-185
camp soup, 183
Canaan grapes, 99
Cape Pittosporum, 116
Cape Town, 8, 9, 11, 23, 61, 120, 124, 127, 134
Carême, 6, 9, 35, 56, 83, 90, 93, 99, 152, 183, 204
carica papaja, 92
carne secca, 84
Carolina, South, 41
carp, 194
casse, 189
catechins, 4
caul, 76
cauliflower, wild, 26
Ceylon, 20
champagne-cup, 33
Charente region, 69
Chartreuse, 20
Chartreux Abbey, 20
cherry liqueur, 20
chervil, 27
Chesterton, oubaas, 170
chestnuts, 37, 82, 83, 109, 195

217

chicken's eggs, 47, 48, 49, 126
China, 20, 150
Chinese book of recipes, 2
Chinese cookbook, an old, 152
Chinese cooks, 80, 112, 183
Chinese octypus, 137
Chinese recipes, 2
Chinese sauce, 80
Chinese soup, 131
Chinese, the, 48, 80
chlorophyll, 16, 110
chops
    braaied, 41, 181
    cotelette á là Maintenon, 146, 181
    Spanish-reed, 155
    tame meat, 181
chop suey, 2
Christmas drinks, 163-167
Citrusdal, 120
claret-cup, 33
Cloete, Mrs, 20, 21
cocktail, the American, 11
cocktails, 103, 163
coffee, 24, 47, 67, 68, 70, 113, 147, 163, 183
coffee samples, 147
cognac, 21, 69
comtesse Riguidi, 91
conditus, 3
consommé, 60, 142, 161
consommé, cold, 161
coot, 56, 64, 92, 116
coot, African, 56, 180
Coqui francolin, 54, 60
cormorant, 61
cotelette á là Maintenon, 146, 181
crayfish, 23-80, 131, 170
crême de cacao, 20
crêmes, 20
Creole duck, 64
Cuissy, Earl of, 34
Curaçao, 20
curds and whey, 37, 39, 134, 135
currant jelly, 51
curried meat, 37-40
curry pickle, 156
curry powder, 39, 130, 156, 211
custard, 18, 113, 124, 125, 130, 131, 162
cyanella capensis, 82

Danzig liqueur, 20
decay in game, 50, 55, 57
De Maintenon, tannie, 181
Demarara sugar, 147
diet, the 'well-balanced', 47
deurmekaar, a, 2

Dijkman, Mrs, 44, 45, 84
dikkop, 60, 61, 180
Dingaan's Day, 54, 105, 180
dodo, the, 210
Do you know how to cook fish?, 137
donkey chops, 201
dop-brandy, 68
dove breast, 101
dove, green, 56
doves, bush, 53, 54
dried-pea soup, 144, 145, 146
dried peas, 143, 144-146
druids, 105
drinks, Christmas, 163-167
duck
    Creole, 64
    Muscovy, 61, 64, 65, 92, 105
    yellow-billed, 64
    liver, 64, 65, 170
Duckitt, Miss Hildagonda, 78
duiker, 50
duiwelsdrek, 84
Dumas, 84
Dutch East India Company, 24, 73, 111
Dutch scrapple, 45
Dijkman, Mrs, 44, 45, 84

eau de vie du marc, 68
eau de vie du vin, 68
Ecclesiazusae, 2
edelvrot grapes, 188
egg-plant, 158
eggs
    chicken, 47-49, 126
    coloured, 48
    crayfish, 48
    raw, 47,
eiervrugte, 158
eland, 205
elder tea, 32
elderberries, 61
English model, the, 25
Escoffier, Maître, 37
Europe, 3, 24, 25, 48, 90, 100, 153, 195

farm wine, 65, 157, 163, 177, 180, 197, 199
fennel, 8, 18, 25, 39, 113, 117, 121, 136, 196
ferweeltjies, 82
figs, wild, 56
fino, 15
fish
    barbel, 194
    carp, 194
    freshwater, 194-196

preserve, 194
tiger, 196
whitebait, 195
yellowfish, 194, 195
Florentine manner, 28
fondant, 147, 150, 151
Fourcade, Dr, 81
fowl, wild, 56
Fowler, Mr, 44
Francatelli pudding, 83
frayed meat, 50
fresh water fish, 194-196
frikkadels, 100, 130
fruit
    dried, 20, 93, 113, 124, 156, 167, 180
    juice, 33, 35, 79, 93, 111, 131, 150, 151, 161, 166, 169, 170, 176, 177
    ripe, 92, 166
    salad, 100, 101
    sugar, 92
fruit-cup, 33
fruit-wine mixtures, 167
fungi, 122

galjoen, 109
gallbladder, 57, 64
game, 23, 42, 50-55, 56, 57, 60, 61, 84, 85, 88, 99, 175, 176, 180, 181, 205
game, leg of, 50, 53
gamey, 176
gazpasho, 161
gebraaide vleis, 41
geese, wild, 56
genus Anthericum, 26
geranium leaf, 25
Gerhardt, Baas, 81, 82
germ proteid, 144
Gieljam, grootoom, 78, 79, 197, 199, 200
gin, 11, 66
glucocide, 100
goewerneursboontjie, 5-7
goose, wild, 56
Gordon's Bay, 79
governor's beans, 5-7
grapefruit peel, 93, 211
Greek Dictionary, 3
green dove, 56
green pea soup, 142, 143, 144, 145
green peas, 111, 141-143, 144, 146
greens, 110-111
grog, 31-33
gros colman, 193
gros grain, 31
grouse, sand, 60, 61
Grover, Mr, 44, 45

grysbok, 50
guava jelly, 36
guinea fowl, 61, 64
Gulf of Mexico, 4, 8
gypsum, 11

haasvleis, 85
hacher, 3
haggis, 153
Hahn, Dr Daniel, 188
hake, steamed, 99
halfkoord, 15
haliotis, 131, 134
ham, minced, dumplings of, 55
hamster, 102
hanepoot grapes, 101
Hantam, 73, 211
hare, 50, 53, 64, 152, 180
hash, 3
hash, what a, 2
hasheesh, Indian anaesthetic, 1
hashis, 3
hasievleis, 156
hawthorn, 73
Hay, Dr, 83
Haylett, oubaas, 99
heart, 45, 46, 55, 64, 199
helix aspersa, 89
hellebore, 90
herb garden, 113, 116, 117
Herbaal van meester Gerhardt, 81
herbs, 7, 20, 25, 32, 76, 83, 84, 103, 113-117, 145, 154, 162, 166, 176, 177, 180, 181, 183, 194, 195, 196, 199
hereboontjies, 5
herneuter, 184
herons, 61
Hilda, 20, 45
hock-cup, 33
Hofmeyr, Jan Hendrik, 120
hollandaise sauce, 49
homeopathic particles, 47
homeria, 81,
hors d'oeuvres, 92
horsemeat, 153, 204
hondesuring, 1
Hong So, 2
Hongaarse tarhonya, 3
hop plants, 100
Hotnotskool, 26
Hotnotsuintjies, 81
Hottentots, 8
Humansdorp-Knysna region, 81
hunter's meat, 53
hunter's pot, 50
hutspot, 53
hydnora Africana, 8
hyssop, 20

Indians, American, 41
ink (of the squid), 140
inulin, 120
iris, 81
Isabella grapes, 100
Italian cooking, 152
Italian risotto, 3
Italian snail, the large, 89
Italy, 24, 152

Jacques Perk's rainbow, 34
Jacquin, 3, 4
jakkalskos, 8, 9, 10
jakkalskos soufflé, 8-10
James I, King, 31
Java, 147
jerepigo, 9, 64, 65, 73
julienne, 100
Jurançon, 24

kafferpruime, 21
Kalk Bay, 78, 80, 127
kambro, 120-122
kambro jam, 121
kambro stew, 121
Kamies mountains, 81
Kamp, 23
kapok, 147
Karoo clay, 82
Karoo soil, 26, 120, 121
Karoo veld, 120
Katalba grapes, 100, 193
katonkel, 15
Kimberley, 20
King James I, 31
King Louis IV, 146, 181
Kleinia, 16
Kleinmond, 79
klei-uintjies, 82
klipkous, 8, 24, 131, 134, 135, 136
klitsel, 145, 146
Knysna, 81, 193
Kos vir die Kenner, Leipoldt se, 44
kraalbossies, 54
kudu, 175
kukumakranka liqueur, 21, 32
kummel, 20
KWV, 15, 69

La Chapelle, 6, 16, 36, 44, 56
Larousse gastronomique, 5
Le Cuisinier Moderne, 16
leek leaf, 113
lemon peel, 33, 39, 46, 64, 71, 83, 93, 121, 142
lexicographers, 1, 84
Lichtenstein, 1
Liddell en Scott, 3

Liebfraumilch, 188, 193
life water, 66
Lindley, Oubaas, 92
liqueur
    bitter-lemon, 20
    cherry, 20
    Danzig, 20
    kukumakranka, 21
    sugar-bush syrup, 21
    Van der Hum, 19, 20, 21, 23, 92, 151, 167
liqueurs, 11, 19-21
liver, duck, 64, 65, 170
Lourenço Marques, 137
lourie, 57
Lowveld, 54, 180, 183

macaroni, 124
macédoine, 101
Magalakwyn River, 201
maizena, 51, 91, 94, 161, 162
Malagasy, 1
malt vinegar, 156
maracas, 102
maraschino, 9, 20
marinade, 50, 51, 194, 204
marinading game, 50
market, fish and vegetable, 9, 11, 61, 120, 127, 134, 137, 140
Marloth, Dr, 9, 120
marrow, 27, 54, 76,79, 103, 104, 113, 135, 159, 175, 183, 211
marulas, 56
marzipan, 150
Mastika, 20
Mauritius, 210
meat
    curried, 37-40
    frayed, 50
    short, 64
medlar, 7, 9, 150
melkbos, 8
Merriman, Oubaas, 120
metachatina kraussi, 89
Middle Ages, 24, 150
mielies, 95-97, 102, 211, 214
mielie and green bean soup, 97
mielie bread, 80, 95, 97
mielie cakes, 97
milk, 18, 24, 32, 35, 35, 37, 39, 48, 60, 64, 66, 83, 94, 97, 108, 120, 121, 123, 127, 130, 134, 136, 142, 155, 157, 174, 183, 184, 185, 201, 211
milk frummeltjies, 124
milk tart, 24, 39
mincemeat, 154, 160
mint, 103, 116, 142, 162
misbredie, 1
Moddermorgel, 194
moepels, 57

moorhen, 64
moraea edulis, 81
moraea family, 82
mortadello, 152
mosbolletjies, 68
Mosel-Auslese, 28
moskonfyt, 83, 166
mossie, 57
mountain sorrel, 111
Muir, Dr, 81
mulberry drink, 166
Multatuli, 110, 188, 191
Muscovy duck, 61, 64, 65, 92, 105
mussel bobotie, 130
mussel frikkadels, 130
mussels, 97, 99, 127, 130
mutton chops, 181
mutton, roast leg of, 113

naartjie, 20, 21, 32, 61, 79, 89, 92, 93, 113, 125, 163, 211
naartjie peel, 21, 32, 61, 79, 92, 93, 113, 121, 125, 163
Namaqua sand grouse, 61
Namaqualand, 89, 121, 122
Napoleon, 184
Napoleon brandy, 69
natural wine, 69, 165, 166, 189, 193
North America, 16
Noyau, 19
Nuits St George, 188
nutritional value, 6, 27, 32, 48, 67, 95, 102, 108, 110, 111, 120, 123, 126, 127, 183, 199
nuts
    almond, 19, 21, 23, 80, 93, 121, 125, 130, 150, 151, 161, 162, 177, 211, 214
    chestnut, 7, 37, 82
    pine, 147, 150, 151
    pistachio, 151
    shelled, 162,
    walnut, 15, 64, 160, 211, 214
Nuy farms, the, 191

octopus, 137
oeufs, 8
oil soup, 161
oleroso-type sherry, 14, 15
Olifants River, 81
olla, 3
onion soup, 84, 144,
opeas sublineare, 89
opskiksels, 154
orange leaf, 39
orange peel, 21, 60, 161
oranges, 60, 100
ostrich biltong, 85
ostrich egg, 8
oxalis lupinfolia, 81

Oxford Dictionary, 44
ox head, 25, 105, 109
ox marrow, 76, 79
ox tongue, 176
oyster soup, 127
oysters, 80, 127, 168-170

Paarl, 191
Pacific Ocean, 92
paljas, 44
panache, 44
pancake, 23, 185
pannas, 24, 44-46
papaya, 92
papaya, American, 92
papaya carica, 92
paradox, 34
parlementslede, 2
Parmentier's fashion vegetable, 18
parsley, 7, 36, 65, 91, 94, 113, 116, 127, 130, 159, 195
partridges, 50, 56, 60, 61, 144, 180
partridge
    bush, 60
    Coqui, 54
    in red wine, 56
    recipes, one of the oldest, 56
Pasteur, 123, 165, 197
pawpaw, 60, 92-94, 100
    as a vegetable, 92
    dried, 93
    ice cream, 93
    jam, 93
    preserved and crystallised, 93
    pudding, 93
    stewed, 60, 92
    filled, 94
peach blits, 66
peach pip, 33
peach roll, 124
peacock, 50, 56, 57, 61
pearl mussel, 131
peas
    baby, 142
    dried, 143, 144-146
    green, 111, 141-143, 144, 146
pectin, 131, 189
penang, 40
penang meat, 40
penguin eggs, 48, 85
perdesuring, 1
perdevoetjie stew, 136
perdevoetjies, 136, 137
Perigord, 105
periwinkles, 126
perlemoen, 127, 131, 134, 135, 136
persimmons, 158
Petronius, 152
pheasant, 50, 54, 56, 57, 61, 99, 105
pienangvleis, 37

pierinkievol, 11
pig, sucking, 34-36, 64, 171
pigeons
    speckled rock, 60
    tufted, 99
pimpeltjie, 11, 15, 135
pine nuts, 147, 150, 151
pineapple,
    crayfish, 80
    soufflé, 10
pistachio nuts, 151
pittosporum leaf, 78, 116
plankton, 126
Plein Street, 23
plover eggs, 48
plum jam, 51
pod leaves, 60
poison, 16, 17, 26, 27, 47, 67, 68, 81, 90, 110
Pondoland, 89
pons, 31
Poole's Hotel, 14
porcupine skin, 24
Port, 163
Portugese name, 1
Potage St Germain, 142, 143, 144
potato
    baked, 18, 55
    sweet, 36, 55, 102, 108, 120, 121
potatoes, 16-18, 36, 43, 54, 64, 82, 108, 110, 113, 121, 123, 135, 137, 157, 183
potatoes a la Ayah Toontjies, 17
Pretoria herbarium, the, 81
prussic acid, 17, 67, 189
pulses, 110, 141, 144
pumpkin, 4, 103, 159
pumpkin bredie, 4
pumpkin leaves, 109
punch, 31, 32, 33, 166
Purcell, Dr, 89
purée, 4, 15, 16, 28, 83, 93, 97, 103, 142, 143, 145, 146
purée, French, 1
Queen Victoria Street, 23
Queens, 23
quince, borrie, 94

Rabie, oubaas Philip, 192
ragoe, 175
ragout, 127, 175, 204
ragouter, 175
raisins, 23, 37, 40, 93, 99, 130, 135, 156, 162, 177, 211
Raper, Mrs Elizabeth, 79
raspberries, 93
red wine, 32, 33, 36, 43, 49, 51, 52, 55, 56, 64, 65, 91, 135, 156, 165, 166, 187, 192, 193, 197-200
red-winged starling, 61

Rhine Auslese, 28, 33
rhinoceros bush fire, 154
Rhodes, Cecil, 120
rice, soggy, 55, 64, 77, 104
rice bredie, 3
Richtersveld, the, 89
Riesling grape, 165
risotto, Italian, 3
rock pigeon, speckled, 60
roosterkoek, 37, 184
rosemary, 35, 46, 76, 77, 103, 113, 116, 117, 140, 145, 154, 162, 193, 196
Roman snail, the, 90
Romans, the, 9
Rotterdam, 4
Royal, the old, 23
royal game, 57, 61
rumex, 1
rumex acetosella, 1
Russia, 155
Russian vodka, 11
Rustenburg district, 61

sage tea, 32
sal, 3, 152
salamander, 108
salami, 153, 204
salmagondis, 3
salmagundy, 3
salsisia, 152
salt, ethereal, 69
sambals, 23, 40
sand grouse, 60, 61
sanduintjies, 82
Sandveld, 82
sauce, hollandaise, 49
sausage, 152-154
   Vienna, 153
Sarah, 37
Scappi, 36, 84, 152
schmeckt sehr schoen, 46
schnapps, 66
school subject, cookery as, 4
Schreiner, Oom Theofilus, 68
Schwabe family, 20
Schwabe, Mrs, from Worcester, 32, 45, 46, 79, 85
scrapple, 44, 45
scruppel, 45
scurvy, 4, 31, 111
seafood, 126-140
Sea Point, 23
seaweed creepers, 131
seevaarders, 4
shad, 99
Shakespeare, 14
shelduck, 64
sherry, 9, 10, 11-15, 36, 163, 165, 183, 192

sherry-flor, 14
short meat, 64
silicon, 47
sirloin, 31, 154
skeepsbredies, 4
skeepsmansmoes, 4
Skeurbuikskloof, 4
skrappel, Dutch, 45
skurwegoed, 31
slaaikool, 26
slymblom-uintjie, 82
Smith, John, 41
snail dishes, 89-91
snail recipe, 90
snail
   the garden, 89
   the large Italian, 89
   the large veld, 89
   the Roman, 90
   the vineyard, 89, 90
   the white-yellow veld, 89
   à la bourguignonne, 91
   à la Brimont, 91
   à la chablaisienne, 91
   à la poulette, 91
   à l'arlésienne, 91
   comtesse Riguidi, 91
snoek, braised, 137
solanine, 17, 110
solera method, 14
solticchi, 152
sorrel, 1, 4, 26, 28, 77, 81, 103, 110, 113, 117, 121, 162, 193
sorrel, mountain, 111
sorrel, wild, 77
sosaties, 23, 116, 155-157, 180
sosys, 152
soufflé, jakkalskos, 8, 10
soup
   American corn with mussels, 97
   bean and fat, 24
   beetroot, 161
   bortsch, 144, 161
   camp, 183
   cold, 161-162
   cold nut, 162
   curried crayfish, 23
   dried pea, 144, 145, 146
   gazpacho, 161
   green pea, 142, 143, 144, 145, 146
   mielie and green bean, 97
   oil, 161
   onion, 84, 144
   orange, 161, 162
   oyster, 127
   pea, dried, 144, 145, 146
   pea, green, 142, 143, 145
   Potage St Germain, 142, 143, 144
   tortoise, 170
South America, 16, 84, 92, 97
South Carolina, 41
south-easter, 131

South of France, 24, 105, 155
South of Spain, 11, 14, 24
Spain, 3, 11, 14
Spanish-reed chops, 155
spanspek, 93, 96
speckled rock pigeon, 60
speenvarkie, 34
spinach, 27, 28, 73, 77, 100, 102, 142, 144
spinach, types of, Portugese name for, 1
spit-braaivleis, 41
springbok, 50, 82
Springbokvlakte, 16, 120
squid, 137, 140
squid stew, 137
St Lucia Bay, 89
stamens, 95
starch, 120, 123, 124, 125
starling, red-winged, 61
steelkool, 26
steenbok, 50
Stellenbosch, 191
stew, see bredie
stewed prunes, 40, 43, 51, 64
Strand Street, 9, 23, 53, 99, 120, 127
strandkos, 136
Stromsoe, Mrs Aagot, 137
Stuart, Mrs, 68
strawberries, 33, 93
sucking pig, 34-36, 64, 171
suet, hard, 50
sugar
   bags, 147
   Demarara, 147
   samples, 150
sugarbush syrup liqueur, 21
sugar-stick, 20, 21
sundae, 93
supremes, 101
Suurveld, 122
swartstorm, 113, 116
Swedish oven, 108
sweet potatoes, 36, 55, 102, 108, 120, 121
Switzerland, 84

taaibos ash, 108
Table Bay, 111
tameletjies, 147-151
tameletjie, traditional pine nut, 151
tapioca pudding, 9
tarhonya, Hungarian, 3
tasajo, 84
tent-wagon, 180
Thames, 195
thorn trees, 60
Thunberg, 8, 73, 81
tigerfish, the Transvaal, 196
tisaans, 32

tomato bredie, 4, 23
tongue, 175-177
    camel's, 175
    cooked, 176
    lizard's, 175
    ox, 175, 176
    salted, 176, 177
    sheep's, 175
    zebra's, 175
Tonkin, 211
tortoise soup, 170
tournedos, 204
Transvaal, 25, 95, 122, 180, 181, 196
trigonephrus porphurostoma, 89
Tulbagh, 191
tulip, 81, 82
tulip stew, 81
Turkey, 3

uintjie
    bobbejaan, 81, 82
    bok, 82
    genuine, the, 81-83
    Hotnots-, 81
    ice cream, 83
    kaneel, 82
    klei, 82
    pudding, 83
    purée, 83
    purple, 82
    sand, 82
    slymblom, 82
    soufflé, 82
    soup, 83
    water-, 73
    witblom, 82
Ulm, 45

Vaerst, baron, 20
Van der Hum liqueur, 19, 20, 21, 23, 92, 151, 167
Van Oordt, Dr, 1
van Esveldt, Steven, 45
varkie, gespeende, 34
vegetable dishes, 4, 102-104
vegetable market, 9, 11, 61, 120, 127
vegetable purée, 16
vegetables, pod, 65
vegetables, root, 60, 104, 183
vegetarian 'meat dishes', 146
veldkool, 23, 26-28, 60
velouté, 188
veldpatats, 120
veld picnics, 183
veld sorrel, 4
Vera Cruz, 4, 8, 18
Vernon, Admiral, 31
Vienna sausage, 153
vine leaves, 90, 100, 152
Virginia, 41
vitamins, 4, 6, 27, 47, 99, 102, 111, 123, 124, 141
vlablom, 81

vodka, 11, 66
vol-au-vent, 130
volkspele, 25
volksraad, 2
Volmaakte Keukenmeid, 45
voorlaaier, 54
vrotpootjie, 108
vygies, 15

Wahl, Miss, 23
walnuts, ground, 64, 160
Walters, the, 14
warthog, 54
water birds, wild, 60
waterblommetjies, 4, 8, 24, 60, 73-77, 81, 110, 111
Waterberg, 54
Waterloo, 184
watermelon, 170
wateruintjies, 73
Wellington's army, 11
West Indies, 20
Westphalian cookbooks, old, 44
Westphalian pannas, 45
whale meat, 137
whitebait, 195
White House, the, 9, 23, 53, 99, 120, 127
white wine, 187-193
wild birds, 56-65
wild cauliflower, 26
wild fowl, 56
wild geese, 56
windy knowledge, 39
wine-cups, 33
wine spirit, 66, 67, 68, 70, 197
witblom-uintjie, 82
witkleisuiker, 147
Worcester, 45, 79, 120

Xerez de la Frontera, 11

yeast, 174

zebra meat, 175, 201-205